THE THIRD REICH AND THE HOLOCAUST IN GERMAN HISTORIOGRAPHY

TOWARD THE *HISTORIKERSTREIT* OF THE MID-1980S

BY ALFRED D. LOW

EAST EUROPEAN MONOGRAPHS, BOULDER
DISTRIBUTED BY COLUMBIA UNIVERSITY PRESS, NEW YORK
1994

EAST EUROPEAN MONOGRAPHS, NO. CCCLXXXIX

ISBN 0-88033-286-7
Library of Congress Catalog Card Number 94-61339

Printed in the United States of America

Books Previously Published by the Author

Lenin on the Question of Nationality, 1958
The Soviet Hungarian Republic and the Paris Peace Conference, 1963
The Anschluss Movement, 1918–1919, and the Paris Peace Conference, 1974
Die Anschlussbewegung in Österreich und Deutschland, 1918–19 und die Pariser Friedenskonferenz, 1975
The Sino-Soviet Dispute. An Analysis of the Polemics, 1976
Jews in the Eyes of the Germans. From the Enlightenment to Imperial Germany, 1979
The Anschluss Movement, 1918–1938. Background and Aftermath. An Annotated Bibliography in German and Austrian Nationalism, 1984
The Anschluss Movement 1931–1938, and The Great Powers, 1985
The Sino-Soviet Confrontation since Mao Zedong. Dispute, Detente, or Conflict?, 1987
Soviet Jewry and Soviet Policy, 1990

CONTENTS

Acknowledgments

I wish to express my thanks for the assistance rendered in my research to the National Archives, Washington, D.C., as well as to several university libraries, especially the library personnel of the University of Washington, Seattle, and its inter-library service, and the Library of Congress. I am also indebted to the German Historical Institute of Washington, D.C., where I worked both during the summer of 1990 and 1991 not only for the use of its resources but also for its support by sending me valuable materials relating to the "*Historikerstreit*." Mr. Klaus Schwabe of Hamburg deserves thanks for duplicating some materials from a few dailies and journals which were not accessible in the U.S. As usual, my wife Dr. Rose S. Low gave me valuable assistance in many respects. I appreciate that the Deutsche Verlagsanstalt, Stuttgart, gave permission to quote several lines from Gerhard Ritter's *Carl Goerdeler und die deutsche Widerstandsbewegung* (pp. 441–43) which I translated myself. I am also grateful for permission extended to quote from Joachim Fest's *The Face of the Third Reich*, Lenden.

"Forty years ago the overwhelming part of the [German] population who were children or not yet born could not acknowledge their own guilt for deeds which they did not commit. . . But their ancestors have left behind a heavy legacy. All of us, whether guilty or not, whether old or young, must accept the past. We all are affected by their consequences. . . He who does not recall inhumanity will be susceptible to new dangers of infection."

—Richard Weizsäcker, President of the Federal Republic
Frankfurter Algemeine Zeitung, May 6, 1987

PREFACE

There is a vast literature on the Holocaust exceeding perhaps the capacity of any individual scholar to master it completely. According to a 1987 source, a select bibliography has listed nearly two thousand studies in several languages and another one over 10,000 entries on Auschwitz alone. The very term "holocaust" has been widely used only since the 1960s. Of Greek origin, the word had a theological meaning signifying "burnt sacrificial offering dedicated exclusively to God," with a special focus on the martyred victims rather than its practitioners. Jews, therefore, had long rejected the term "holocaust," but the word has become commonplace referring to the mass killings of Jews by the Nazis during World War II, and is also used so in this study. The Hebrew word for holocaust is "Shoa." The Nazi term "final solution" for the mass murder of the Jews is a euphemism designed to conceal the atrocities and killings during the war. The Nuremberg trial proceedings did not remain silent about the crimes against the Jews, but in the view of the prosecution they were only a part, though a major and unique one, of all Nazi crimes perpetrated against many peoples.

The major purpose of this study does not lie in the exposition of significant writings about the Holocaust irrespective of the nationality of the authors, though the major writings form a yardstick by which the German judgment is assessed. The major thrust of this work is rather the description and analysis of the German studies of the Holocaust with special emphasis on the thought and sentiments expressed by major historians. This author saw his task in recording the reaction of German writers, the empathy of many for the Jews, and their revulsion about the persecution, dehumanization, and ultimately the mass murder of European Jewry. In other cases the major goal was to show the attempt to distance themselves from the horrid events in seeming objectivity or indifference, claiming scholarly detachment. It is the post-war German historical judgment, never far removed from prevailing German public opinion, which is the primary subject of this investigation.

In the early 1950s already the important works by Gerald Reitlinger in Great Britain and Léon Poliakov in France illuminated the special crimes against the Jews. But it was not until the Eichmann trial in Jerusalem in 1961 that the Holocaust assumed center stage. This trial focused upon the "War against the Jews," as later the American historian Lucy Dawidowicz called her book (1975) on the Nazi annihilation of European Jewry. In 1961 had appeared the American historian Raul Hilberg's magisterial work about *The Destruction of the European Jews*, which became a trailblazer for the study on the Holocaust. In the last decades German scholars have made notable contributions to the study of the Holocaust, which actually are the main focus in this study. Some German historians, however, and many publicists on the extreme Right have attempted to trivialize and minimize the atrocities and mass killings, attempts which were overwhelmingly rejected by international scholarship.

In the mid-1980s the dispute has burst forth anew and more acutely in the so-called "*Historikerstreit*" (feud of German historians). Several studies written in German and some in English focus primarily on the dispute of professional German historians. The present book differs from these treatises largely by a broader perspective and a larger time frame, and does not limit itself exclusively to the German scholarly and populist polemics of the 1980s. It considers also the earlier writings of the main discussants of 1986–87. In the case of some revisionists, these publications contradict or differ substantially from their later widely observed opinions, a circumstance rather neglected so far. While most treatises about the "Historikerstreit" have focused on major revisionist authors and their opponents in 1986–87, the present study elaborates on the many German historians who have already dealt with some of the same problems in earlier years. Actually, the "Historikerstreit" did not start in 1986, but much earlier. It had populist roots, which can be traced back to the era following World War II and even to the propaganda campaign of the Third Reich. The polemics of the mid-1980s, at times a bitter and angry dispute, is only a part of an extended intellectual and political encounter. Though German Jews have virtually disappeared as a significant factor and participants in German life, the past German-Jewish relationship continues to burden the conscience and the mind of many Germans, as well as to preoccupy the descendants of German

Jewry and the world at large because of the universal significance of the crimes committed.

The recent flare-up of the dispute is perhaps not surprising. With greater distance from the Nazi atrocities, with the growth of German democracy, the increasing role of the German economy, the German come-back and the greater assertiveness of democratic as well as neo-conservative and nationalist groups, including neo-Nazis and radical fringe elements, the stage was set for a clash between them.

Judgments about the Third Reich and the Holocaust made by revisionist historians of the 1980s, such as Ernst Nolte, Andreas Hillgruber, Klaus Hildebrand, Michael Stürmer, and their fellow travelers are often strikingly similar to views expressed after 1945 by unrepentant Nazis, extreme German nationalists, and neo-conservatives. Seen in this perspective, the so-called "Historikerstreit" of the mid-1980s cannot be properly judged in isolation by disregarding the long, partly repressed dispute about the Third Reich and the Holocaust going back to the destruction of Nazi Germany. The mass of new data revealed by Jewish, German, and international scholarship in the latter half of the twentieth century has not altered some basic disagreements and differences between critics on one hand and apologists and revisionists on the other.

The period focused upon in this study offers a bird's-eye view of German anti-Semitism since the late nineteenth century and an overview of German historiography, especially after 1945. An earlier work of mine, *Jews in the Eyes of the Germans. From the Enlightenment to Imperial Germany* (Philadelphia, 1979) dealt with the era of enlightened absolutism and the last stages of the Holy Roman Empire with its multiplicity of petty states, until the unification of Germany in 1870–71 and its outgrowth, the beginnings of German imperialism. As far as German Jewry was concerned, it comprised an era of tremendous changes, from the state of inequality of the eighteenth century to the French Revolution and its liberating impact on Germany, to the first emancipation of Prussia in 1812, the innovations of 1848–49, the complete legal emancipation of Austrian and German Jews in 1867 and 1869 respectively, to the threatening revival of anti-Semitism in the 1870s. It was then that the German-Jewish novelist Berthold Auerbach remarked, "Vergebens gelebt und gearbeitet" (I have lived and worked in vain). The rise of political anti-Semitism in Germany and Austria in the seventies and eighties of the nineteenth century foreshadowed the ultimate catastrophe of German Jewry and much of the rest of European Jewry.

The period dealt with in the nineteenth-century study was one of progressive changes for both Germans and Jews along several lines, toward liberalism, secularism, democracy, the national state, and emancipation. Still, progress in their mutual relationship up to 1870 and even more until 1890 was elusive. The cultural and social rapprochement between Germans and Jews did not solve the problem of their harmonious co-existence. In spite of genuine friendships and intimate connections between individual Germans and Jews, the German-Jewish co-existence was never idyllic or anything approaching it. The eye of friendship was perhaps never entirely closed, but the eye of hatred was always open. The student of the history of the German-Jewish relationship will see on almost all of its pages the harsh, intolerant features of hate. In the wild storm of time the waves of anti-Semitism often beat high, but even when calmer winds prevailed, those waves were always in threatening motion. The waters never stood still.

German anti-Semitism of the twentieth century was thus no historic accident, though its excesses and the ultimate Jewish tragedy, discriminatory exclusion, dehumanization, and physical annihilation, were perhaps historically not unavoidable. But Hitler and national-socialist extremism were helped along by the congruence of numerous factors, all favoring Armageddon. Among the most prominent factors was the traditional and persistent Jew-hatred harking back centuries to the late Middle Ages and the German Reformation.

Alfred D. Low

April 1993

I

GERMAN POLITICS AND HISTORIOGRAPHY: ABOUT THE THIRD REICH AND THE JEWS, FROM THE LATE NINETEENTH CENTURY TO THE EARLY POST-WORLD WAR II ERA

The Historic Legacy – The Late Nineteenth Century "Historikerstreit"

In the nineteenth century German Jews had been in the forefront of the struggle for the unification of Germany. Liberalism and nationalism had been closely linked to the struggle for a unified Germany and overcoming the feudal traditions. But soon after a united state had been created, integral nationalism gained the upper hand and liberalism receded into the background. In the new Reich, this nationalism grew by leaps and bounds intellectually, socially, and politically. While it is not the purpose of this study to render an account of the history of German political development, reference must be made to the expression of anti-Jewish thought by prominent and widely-read German writers, who were intricately involved in the rise of political anti-Semitism.

The noted historian and widely popular publicist Heinrich von Treitschke shed his early liberalism to fight aggressively for Germany's national unification under Prussian aegis. He became an admirer of Bismarck and a champion of intransigent German nationalism and expansionism, and also turned into a sharp opponent of the Jews. The professor, who had the ear of Germany's academic youth and shaped its political education, preached a pervading anti-Semitism, making Jew-hating once again fashionable in educated circles. At different times he feared that Germany's existence was threatened by

South German particularists, by Catholics, by socialists, by a vengeful France or a jealous Britain. Though Jews were not the only group singled out by Treitschke during his long career as a menace to a strong and unified Germany, he never failed to give them conspicuous mention. At the height of the anti-Semitic agitation in 1879–1880, he made them the primary target in a series of wide-ranging journalistic attacks.

Only some Jews, Treitschke claimed in the *Deutsche Geschichte des neunzehnten Jahrhunderts*, had manifested patriotic zeal during the War of Liberation; others had demonstrated a "readily comprehensible sympathy" for the emancipation by France. But Jews had not infrequently displayed an "astounding mendacity and presumption" about their numerical participation in the war. On the whole, Treitschke ignored or minimized past Christian outbursts against the Jews. The overall impressions he created were those of unwarranted Jewish aggressiveness, lack of patriotism, reluctance to assimilate—all of which explained and justified occasional outbursts of German impatience and wrath.

To Treitschke German national development was deflected by what he called "the intrusion" of Judaism. Unlike the Jews in the West, who were descendants of Spanish Jews, the German Jews were of Polish stock. In contrast to finer spirits among German Jews who pleaded for the abandonment of Jewish separatism and to such talents as F. Mendelssohn-Bartholdy, Veit, and the pious Neander, other Jewish writers "boldly insisted on the display of Jewish peculiarities." "These Jews without a country, vaunting themselves a nation within the nation" exercised a "harmful influence upon the still inchoate national self-esteem of the Germans." Treitschke castigated Heinrich Heine and Ludwig Börne, largely blaming them for the alleged decline of German literature, but praised Friedrich Julius Stahl, the Bavarian Jew who had become a convert to Lutheranism and champion of the Prussian monarchy and conservatism. In spite of his secular leanings, Treitschke supported the "Christian-German state" conception of Friedrich Wilhelm IV on the eve of the 1848 revolution and rejected Jewish demands for full equality in Prussia. Proud of his own descent from Czech Protestants who had found religious refuge in Saxony, Treitschke was not unsympathetic to religious toleration, but for him this idea, coupled with the notion of equality of all religious values, was confined to Christian denominations. As the historian Hans Liebeschütz has made clear, Treitschke in the last twenty-five years of his life, during which he was writing his *Deutsche Geschichte des neunzehnten Jahrhunderts*,[1] no longer believed in the equality of Judaism with Christianity. This absence of true religious tolerance was reinforced by his concept of the nation state, which aimed at national homogeneity and at the assimilation of religiously and nationally disparate elements such as the Jews.

Treitschke's vanishing liberalism partly preceded, partly coincided with the renewed attack against German Jews in the new Reich, spearheaded by the Christian Social Labor Party under the leadership of Adolf Stöcker. The financial crisis of the seventies, fear for the cohesion of the just-unified Reich, and anxiety over diversity and dissension spawned these attacks. Treitschke actually never met Stöcker personally, and in a strict sense of the word they were never truly political associates; but when returning to Berlin in 1879, Treitschke gave his blessing to the anti-Semitic movement without formally identifying himself with it. However, there could never be any doubt on whose side Treitschke stood; while Stöcker appealed to the lower social classes in the new Reich, Treitschke opened to anti-Semitism the aüditoria of the German universities. The *Vereine deutscher Studierender* [Leagues of German Students], which exerted considerable influence upon the German fraternities, became the vehicle of Treitschke's anti-Semitic program, adding racist overtones to it. Though Treitschke himself did not directly approve of racism, he was responsible for many ideological and political excesses. Students of his, including Hermann von Petersdorff, testified to his role in stirring up anti-Semitism among Germany's academic youth.

Of the deep changes which Treitschke observed after a long journey abroad and listed in his article in the *Preussische Jahrbücher* in November 1879 and January 1880, none was so "alienating" as the deeply emotional movement against the Jews.[2] But, he claimed, there existed in Germany a "reverse Hep Hep"; everybody could without fear say the harshest things about Germans and other peoples, but he "who dared talk in a just and moderate manner about an undeniable weakness of the Jewish character was stigmatized" almost by the entire press as "a barbarian and religious persecutor." The historian was aware that the English and French disdained "the German prejudice against the Jews." But in the West, the number of Jews were smaller; into Germany, on the other hand, there pushed from the East every year "a large number of ambitious youths who made their living by selling pants, youths whose children would one day dominate Germany's exchanges and the German press. The problem of amalgamation with this people grows."

"What we have to ask of our Israelite fellow-citizens is simple: they ought to become Germans . . . for we do not wish that after a millennium of Germanic customs there shouid follow a mixed Germanic-Jewish culture." It would be sinful to forget that many Jews, baptized and unbaptized ones, were German in the best sense of the word. But recently, Treitschke concluded, powerful groups of Jews did not want to become Germans; they displayed a "dangerous spirit of arrogance," and the impact of Jewry upon German national life had shown itself "again harmful in many respects." The loud anti-Semitic agitation was perhaps "a brutal and hateful, but a natural reaction of Germanic popular sentiment against an alien element." Even among the most educated elements of German society, "from among men who would scornfully reject every notion of clerical intolerance or national arrogance one hears today unanimously: 'The Jews are our misfortune'."

Among reasonable people there could be no talk about a withdrawal or even a mere diminution of the emancipation; this would be "an apparent injustice, a departure from the good tradition of our state, and would only sharpen rather than blunt national tension." Perhaps the task of amalgamation between Germans and Jews can never be fully resolved. But the contrast can be "alleviated" if the Jews who talk so much about tolerance will become really tolerant and display some reverence toward the faith, the customs and feelings of the German nation. Treitschke concluded with the pious hope that out of the ferment of these troubled years there might emerge a stronger national sentiment.

Among the replies to Treitschke's articles was one of Harry Bresslau, Treitschke's Jewish colleague at the University of Berlin, who in measured but unambiguous manner accused him of lending the authority of his name to the anti-Semitic agitation and of being unjust and offensive toward Jewish fellow citizens.[3] Another reply was written by the historian of Jewish history Heinrich Graetz, whom Treitschke had personally criticized. As Graetz counter-charged, Treitschke had directed a broadside against German Jewry in its entirety; Graetz aiso raised the question whether forty million Germans were actually in danger of being corrupted by a mere handful of Jews. He denied Treitschke's accusation that he was hostile to Christianity; he had merely depicted the thousand-fold sufferings of the Jews at Christian hands throughout the centuries. Treitschke himself had branded past persecution of the Jews as "Christian tyranny." As far as his own criticism of the great Germans was concerned, he had, after giving due recognition to the greatness of Luther, Goethe, and Fichte, condemned Luther for his anti-Jewish agitation and criticized others for their negative attitudes towards Jews.[4]

On November 12, 1880, the "Jew debate" had started with Treitschke's first article in the *Preussische Jahrbücher.* There appeared a statement in the Berlin press which was signed by seventy-five distinguished Germans. It lamented that "racial hatred and medieval fanaticism were now revived against our Jewish co-citizens in different localities, especially the largest cities of the Reich." "It had been forgotten how many of them, through diligence and talent in the crafts and trade, in arts and sciences, had brought benefit and honor to the fatherland.

> The command of the law as well as the demand of honor that all Germans are equal in rights and duties are thus violated . . . if now envy and jealousy are preached by the leaders of this movement only in abstract, the mass will not hesitate to draw from this talk practical consequences.

The legacy of Lessing was undermined by men who should announce from the pulpit and from the lecturer's pulpit that our culture has overcome the isolation of that tribe which once gave the adoration of one God.

There was still time to oppose the confusion and to avert national shame. The passion of the mob, artificially fanned, can through the resistance of prudent men still be defeated.

> Our call goes out to Christians of all parties to whom religion is the happy message of peace; our call extends to all Germans who treasure the ideal heritage of their great princes, thinkers, and poets. Defend in public declarations and calm enlightenment the foundation of our joint life: esteem for every faith, equal rights, equality in competition, equal acknowledgment of notable endeavors of Christians and Jews.

At the very moment the statement of the seventy-five notables appeared in the press, the distinguished historian Theodor Mommsen published the pamphlet *Auch ein Wort über unser Judentum* (1880).[5] He started out by lamenting the derision of Jews which had been heard in Germany to the astonishment of the entire civilized world.

Before the establishment of the new unitary state, religious and tribal differences had been ignored, but now there raged a war of everybody against everybody. After the *Kulturkampf* and the recent civil war over financial and monetary questions there had appeared "a new deformity of the national sentiment, the campaign of the anti-Semites." The anti-Semitic campaign, Mommsen charged, constituted a harmful retrogression, and no one had the right to look on in silence at this "suicidal agitation of national sentiment." An illusion had seized the masses "and their real prophet was Herr von Treitschke." What did he mean by demanding that "our Israelite fellow-citizens should become Germans? They are Germans just as he and I." He may be more virtuous, but does virtue make the Germans? The just-united German nation had "with the war against the Jews entered a dangerous road." Mommsen ridiculed the Germans' "fear of the Jews" as one "of the most silly perversions." Against any possible shortcomings of the Jews must be weighed capacities and excellences the possession of which has largely contributed to the anti-Semitic agitation. In the ancient Roman Empire, the Jews were an element of national decomposition; in Germany similarly by "decomposing numerous Germanic tribes the Jews worked toward the creation of a common German nationality.* That the Jews have been "working in this direction for generations, I do not consider a misfortune and I generally believe that Providence has understood far better than Herr Stöcker why for the development of the Germanic metal it was necessary to add a few percent Israel."

Mommsen finally expressed the hope that tolerance would return,

> not the one which is natural, the one toward the synagogue, but the more essential tolerance toward the Jewish characteristics for which they should not be blamed, since they were given them by fate. . . . The German nation of course was obligated to uphold the principle of equality as well as to battle open or covert violation of the law through administrative manipulation. This obligation of ours...does not depend at all on the good behavior of the Jews.

---

* In his polemics with Mommsen, Treitschke quoted this phrase from Mommsen's *Römische Geschichte* (III, 550, Treitschke, *Deutsche Kämpfe*, N.F. 125). In his rejoinder, Mommsen underlined its positive meaning. He had not intended to accuse; on the contrary, he had meant to compliment the Jews.

Treating them unfairly and making them feel alien carried a danger "both for them and for us." The civil war of a majority against a minority would be a "national calamity."

There followed, however, a more controversial part of Mommsen's remarks. Since it was "difficult and perilous" to remain outside Christianity, he recommended to those Jews whose conscience permitted renunciation of Judaism and adoption of Christianity that they consider this step: "The entry into a great nation costs a price." Baptism would break down all barriers between the Jews and the rest of their Germanic fellow citizens. Though Mommsen deserved full credit for his principled defense of the Jews and his spirited criticism of Treitschke's accusations, the recommendation relating to baptism revealed the weakness of German liberalism. It was out of tune with the concepts of secularism, the modem *Rechtsstaat* and in violation also of cultural and ethnic pluralism; the latter concept was not acknowledged by the modern nation state of the nineteenth century.

Literary Anti-Semitism

The different strains of German anti-Semitism in the last third of the nineteenth century are represented by personalities such as the historian Heinrich von Treitschke, the poiitical writer and civil servant Constantin Frantz, the philosopher Eduard Hartmann, the political economist and philosopher Eugen Dühring, the orientalist and theologian Paul de Lagarde, and the popularizer Julius Langbehn. Frantz's opposition to the Jews and Judaism was a revived Christian anti-Semitism, based upon the concept of the Christian state.[6] While some of the foregoing writers were still deeply rooted in the Christian heritage, others had moved far from Christianity, though traditional Christian thought and a kind of religious resentment of Jews as the brazen people, clinging obstinateiy to their faith, still appeared to stir them. Lagarde, preaching German Christianity, opposed traditional Christian faith, and rejected Jews on a variety of grounds, advancing religious, nationalistic, and partly racial reasons. Extreme nationalism, mingled with a varying dose of racism, dominated the thinking of Treitschke and even more of Dühring, Lagarde, and Langbehn. Racism was not entirely absent from the thought of any of these men, though they were not always conscious of it and often articulated their views in a far from consistent manner. Many of the writers, at least at some stage of their careers, had embraced a liberal political philosophy; and though they had long ago abandoned liberalism, a modicum of liberal thought survived in the heap of ultraconservative and nationalistic ideas.

All the foregoing writers rejected the concept of what they called a Jewish "state within a state," of a "Palestine" in Germany. Some asked for complete and earliest amalgamation and disappearance of the "Jews as Jews"; this demand was posed by friends of the Jews such as Theodor Mommsen and enemies such as Treitschke and Hartmann. Possessed of an anti-Semitism of fanatic intensity were men such as Frantz, Lagarde, Dühring, and Langbehn. The new anti-Semitism had unquestionably pathological traits, which the *Weltanschauung* of these authors clearly reflected.

Virtually all of the above writers also opposed the emancipation of the Jews and proposed reversion to an earlier state of inequality. Some like Frantz looked back to the Middle Ages as an inspiration for shutting the Jews once more into the ghetto; others like Treitschke disclaimed such intent, though with little conviction. Still others like Lagarde wanted to remove at least some Jews to Palestine or elsewhere, while fanatics like Dühring and Langbehn spoke of the destruction of Jewry and, raising the ante, made a distinction between the imposition of immediate restrictions and an ultimate solution, leaving the latter deliberately indeterminate.

All these writers ciaimed that Jews dominated Germany, that Germans needed to be "liberated" and that "dejudaization" was imperative. Most were resentful of the demonstrations of solidarity of German Jews for oppressed Jews abroad and claimed to be fearful of "Jewish world rule." The inability of apparently intelligent men, some rabble-rousers aside, to see the German-Jewish situation realistically and in perspective, not to mention with some detachment, is perhaps one of the most appalling lasting impressions made upon the student of German-Jewish history and of German anti-Semitism. While the fear of Jewish "world domination" was surely abused by some, who had quickly perceived its usefulness as propaganda, there can be little doubt that this fear was a symptom of a genuine and ravaging sickness to which many Germans had succumbed.

The paranoid fear of Jewish world rule and Jewish hegemony was only one of numerous anxieties of the "alien" Jew which gripped generations of Germans and served to rationalize a boundless hatred of the Jewish "infidel." That the Jews dominated their host peoples was merely one charge among many indictments flung at them in the course of history by many peoples, from the killing of Jesus, the *foetor Judaeorum* of antiquity, to the poisoning of medieval wells, the ritual murder of Christian children and the desecration of the host, to alleged responsibility for the spread of the plague, among others. Most, though not all, of these accusations had lost their credibility and therefore their usefulness in enlightened, rationalist, nineteenth century Europe, but the myth of Jewish world domination turned out to be an effective, if not perfect substitute for the earlier accusations.

Most of the authors mentioned above were politically of the Right, none of the Left. But socialism was by no means immune to anti-Semitism, and Jew-hating had also penetrated liberal and radical democratic circles earlier in the nineteenth century. In view of the absence of strong religious ties and the prevalence of free-thinking among many writers, one must add to the phenomenon of traditional Christian anti-Semitism a Jew-hating that was rooted in intolerance toward an alien nationality—national anti-Semitism—one based upon hatred of the Jewish "race"—racial anti-Semitism—and an "enlightened" anti-Semitism, which repudiated Jewish "superstitions," was critical of the alleged religious backwardness of the Jews (though sustaining itself through old-fashioned theological opposition to Judaism) and rejected especially the Old Testament and the Talmud. Whatever the past intellectual orientation of the aforementioned authors, their prevalent ideological and political philosophy was conservatism, which was closely tied up with an increasingly ultra-nationalist outlook.

Some of the writers cited reprimanded the Jews for their reluctance to embrace assimilation and German Kultur, while others rejected their Germanization and preached cultural and ethnic separation from them. Some favored mixed marriages and baptism to bridge the existing gulf; others spurned these means to a goal—complete amalgamation—of which they disapproved, hoping to keep the German people "pure."

The revulsion against the Jews to which such writings pointed hurt and disappointed the German partisans of preserving the status quo, the recently accomplished legal equalily of the Jews. It testified to the existence of deep roots of German anti-Semitism, which Bismarck's legislation had been unable to extirpate. The flourishing anti-Semitic literature cast a dark shadow upon the outgoing century. Deep pessimism marked the thought of many about the future of the Jews in Germany and in Europe in its entirety. The noted Swiss cultural historian Jakob Burckhardt foresaw a change of legislation in the Reich which would modify the full equality of the Jews. The philosopher Friedrich Nietzsche was even more fearful, both for the future of the Jews and for the future of Europe.

The Rise of Anti-Semitism in Imperial Germany and the Weimar Republic

The anti-Semitic flood before 1914 did not inundate Imperial Germany alone, but spread to much of Europe, including backward and autocratic Russia as well as the Third French Republic. Nor was it fed only by traditional centuries-old Jew-hatred. In nineteenth-century Germany there existed after the unification a traditional, largely Christian Jew-hatred. But there developed also a radical, uncompromising racist anti-Semitism. After World War I, the latter was growing more virulent in Germany and Austria.

In the last decades of the nineteenth century and in the early twentieth century political anti-Semitism did not attain its goals. But it was to produce long-range results prior to 1914 and thereafter. In Imperial Germany it took many forms. It found expression in the program and the activities of numerous student organizations, which explained its easy subsequent spread among civil servants, professional people, bankers, lawyers, professors, secondary school teachers, the medical profession, and others. A plethora of organizations of journeymen and skilled traders such as the *Deutschnationale Handlungsgehilfenverband*, which shared the anti-Jewish biases, comprised the German *Mittelstand.*

A major role in the anti-Semitic movement was played by the *Alldeutsche Verband* whose leadership in 1900 was taken over by *Justizrat* Heinrich Class. The organization engaged in a strongly nationalist and anti-Semitic propaganda based on racial criteria. While it championed German expansionism and world power, it claimed, like National Socialism later, that German and international Jewry was blocking the road of German imperial domination. Though the *Alldeutsche Verband* had a relatively small membership, its influence upon leaders of German society, politicians, and intellectuals was immense. Class's pamphlet *Wenn ich der Kaiser wär'* found widespread approval.

While in 1913, on the eve of World War I, Social Democracy defeated the rightist political parties, obtaining 35 percent of the popular vote, the election results proved deceptive in regard to the wide dissemination in German society of chauvinism, xenophobia, and anti-Semitism. The writings and ideas voiced in preceding decades by Paul de Lagarde in his *Deutsche Schriften* and German nationalists of foreign parentage or choice, such as Houston Stewart Chamberlain and Count Joseph Arthur Gobineau and their racist philosophy, added to the still vibrant religious and rising socioeconomic Jew-hatred. These conditions and, on the other hand, the relatively minor resistance to anti-Semitic propaganda even in leftist circles explain the rapidity of the success in spreading Jew-hatred in the Weimar Republic. Anti-Semitism became a unifying and integrating movement which penetrated even liberal groupings and the Social Democrats.

The spread of Jew-hatred in most other European countries, especially the Third French Republic, shaken by the Dreyfus affair, and autocratic Tsarist Russia in which millions of Jews lived deepened the impact upon Germany. The Russian pogroms against Jews, especially since 1881 when Tsar Alexander II was assassinated and prior to and after the 1905 Revolution and the support lent to it by Nicholas II and the Russian upper class, served further to encourage German Jew-haters. So did Austrian anti-Semitism since the election of *Oberbürgermeister* Karl Lueger in Vienna. The years 1914–18, despite the Jewish contribution to the war effort, did not diminish the strength of anti-Semitism, but rather enhanced it. In October 1916 a statistical study about the role of the Jews during the war—the so-called "Judenzählung"—was undertaken by the German military to face anti-Semitic complaints about Jews allegedly avoiding military services (*Drückebergerei*). There were other charges relating to supposed Jewish war speculators which were also hurled against Jews.

Immediately after the war, accusations leveled against the Jews related to the "stab in the back" legend, to their supposed responsibility for Germany's defeat and for the November Revolution, for being "Novemberverbrecher" (November criminals). This charge ignored the actual participation of Jews in the German war effort, the notable role of individual Jews in the war such as Albert Ballin, Walter Rathenau, and others.

In 1919, the *All-Deutschen* created an anti-Semitic fighting organization, the *Deutsch-Völkischer Schutz und Trutzbund*, which was able to gather 200,000 members and soon became known for its relentless hostile anti-Jewish propaganda. In the wake of Foreign Minister Walter Rathenau's assassination in 1922 by anti-Semitic rightists, the organization was prohibited.

According to Adolf Hitler's own account in *Mein Kampf*, the foundation for his pathological Jew-hatred was laid in Vienna. Though the earliest program of the NSDAP provided few clues to his murderous intent, the broad hate-filled attacks against alleged various international endeavors of the Jews—the domination of the world of finance, of international Marxism on the other side, of the world press being supposedly in Jewish hands, of Freemasonry and the Jewish invention of parliamentarianism—leave little doubt about the major thrust of Hitler's plans to "alienate" the Jews. When the Weimar Republic appeared on the way to recovery in the years 1924–28, anti-Semitism seemed to be receding. In truth, however, it remained a powerful integrating element in the total ideoloy of the NSDAP to hold members of different social strata together. The German public "adjusted" to the steady stream of anti-Semitic propaganda and lost the stamina to engage in combat against Jew-hatred which had sunk new and deep roots into German soil. Other parts of the Nazi program were all linked with the propaganda war against the German Jews. This was true of the fight against the "system," against Bolshevism, and of the Nazi hostility to the Weimar constitution, the "Bonzentum" [arrogant leadership] of the Social Democrats as well as the Nazi repudiation of "Zinsknechtschaft" (slavery of paying interests).

Hitler and Early Anti-Semitic Influence

Anti-Semitism was to become a cardinal element, the very core of Nazi ideology, and it was Adolf Hitler who made it so. Though in *Mein Kampf* he had pointed to Vienna as the source of his first decisive encounter with Jews, he had actually displayed racial Jew-hatred at an earlier age in Linz. August Kubizek, in *Adolf Hitler, Mein Jugendfreund* (1975), states that Hitler, about fifteen years old, had already displayed a fanatic anti-Semitism when he objected to the city's synagogue; more than three decades later, synagogues all over Germany and Austria went up in flames. It was in the Linzer *Realschule* that he was greatly influenced by some pan-German teachers.[6] According to Wemer Maser, a pamphlet of the *All-Deutscher Verband* [Pan-German League], published in 1904, made a lasting impression on him. *The Secret War-time Report*, written in 1943 for the 0SS by Walter C. Langer, held, however, that Hitler retained some Jewish contacts in Vienna (1907–13), including one with Dr. Eduard Bloch, the physician of his mother who later died of cancer. Nevertheless, his hatred of the Jews continued to grow. Other influences intensifying his obsession in the pre-World War I period were the

Austrian pan-German Georg von Schönerer and the Viennese Mayor Karl Lueger—to whom Hitler paid his respects as precursors of Jew-hatred in *Mein Kampf*—Richard Wagner whose musical accomplishments he revered and whose memory he cherished, himself author of *Das Judentum in der Musik* and fanatic Jew-hater, the anti-Semitic "Ostara" Pamphlets of Georg von Lanz-Liebenfels, a member of the Holy Cross until 1900, and Theodor Fritsch, author of the *Handbuch der Judenfrage*—a publication which by 1907 already had twenty-six printings. According to the American historian G. Fleming, Hitler saw his mission early in life in combining "traditional Christian anti-Semitism" with the Nazi brand of "biological anti-Semitism." In 1913 Hitler moved to Munich and when the war broke out he enlisted in the German army. After the war's end he became a member of the Army's "Enlightenment commando" in Munich, charged to provide information about the "Jewish peril" to his employer. According to Dietrich Eckart, *Der Bolschewismus von Moses bis Lenin. Zwiegespräch zwischen Adolf Hitler und Mir*, he contemplated the revival of propaganda of ritual murder. Medieval religious fanaticism, still alive in Eastern Europe, Russia, and even Austria, should be refurbished in Germany. Racial anti-Semitism did not disdain the weapon of medieval religious anti-Semitism to be hurled against the Jews.

Völkisch Jew-hatred: Erich Ludendorff. Other Views and Warning Voices in the Inter-War Era. Prince Hubertus Loewenstein and Hermann Rauschning

Anti-Semitism in the inter-war period was not limited to the Nazi movement but went far beyond it. Long before the emergence of National Socialism as a major power, all nationalist and *völkisch* segments of the German people had come to embrace it. Its wide dissemination explains the lack of resistance of the German population to the Nazis' paranoic Jew-hatred. The penetration of anti-Semitism even into centrist and left-oriented circles of the German people was responsible for the relative ease of the spread of an increasingly rabid Jew-hatred.

The Jew-hatred of the prominent military personality of Germany in the later part of World War I, General Erich Ludendorff, and his frenzied inter-war activity and, on the other hand, the criticism for instance of German Jews by a leading anti-Nazi activist, Prince Hubertus Loewenstein in the 1930s shed light on the prominence of Jew-hatred in the Reich and the absence of a fighting opposition in behalf of German Jewry and of a movement upholding the equality of all German citizens and their defense at a critical moment in German and Jewish history.

General Ludendorff, in the words of the historian Hajo Holborn, was a "narrowly professional soldier." "A military commander of real distinction, though without great originality," he became with Hindenburg a virtual dictator in the latter half of World War I. An authoritarian militarist and Pan-Germanist, he displayed in the post-war era an intense activity, but was early overshadowed by Hitler and the Nazi movement. He died in 1937. After the war, Ludendorff had trumpeted extreme nationalist ideas and anti-Semitic propaganda. In his *Lebenserinnerungen*, covering the period 1926–1933; he struck at Jews hardly less frequently than Hitler in *Mein Kampf* and proved to be a very fountainhead of Jew-bashing during the Weimar Republic.

His enemies, next to the Jews, were Freemasons and Jesuits, and, to a lesser but still considerable extent, the Pope, Rome, and the Socialists. He complained endlessly about the alleged "Judaization" of German *Kultur*. Though considering himself a "world revolutionary," he listed all truly "revolutionary parties, Jews and free-masons" and the "satanic lodges" which supposedly commandeered the communist movement, in turn dominated, he claimed, by the Jew. Unceasingly, he condemned in his memoirs "the Jew and his Helots, Rome and the Jesuits."[7] The Jews, the Freemasons, and the Jesuits were "one in their will and different only in their methods and ways." His fighting goals for the *Tannenbergbund*, in which he played a major role, were simple and clear: "Jews and other people of alien race can't be German citizens" and cannot be German officials or exercise the right of supervision over Germans. "Purity of race" was considered necessary for the "preservation of the soul." "Liberation from Jewish *Zinsknechtschift* would bring about well-being for all Germans and make an end to the terrible misery of German workers in all segments of the population." It would be difficult to distinguish the extent of racial and national slurs and animosity between the Nazis and Ludendorff. But the General did not preach annihilation or mass killing of the German Jews. On the other hand, Ludendorff's struggle against the Jews was not limited to the German realm, but, like Hitler's anti-Semitism, had also international implications. He held that French policy pursued "the high politics" of the Jews, which was also supported by the United States and Great Britain. Surely, Ludendorff's coterie and following among army officers made them not immune but rather receptive to Hitler's radical racist propaganda.

Prince Hubertus Loewenstein's resolute opposition to National Socialism was expressed in his book *The Tragedy of a Nation. Germany 1918–34* (1934)[8] and his vain struggle in 1935 against the Saar's annexation into the German Reich—an incorporation which constituted an early foreign policy success for the Third Reich. In a chapter on the Jews in this book he admited the penetration of anti-Semitism even into circles of the opposition to National Socialism. While he made some sound observations in this chapter, there can be little doubt that the age-old German anti-Semitism found an expression also in the work by Prince Hubertus Loewenstein.

According to the author, it was owing to the anti-Semitic propaganda of the Nazis that "millions and millions of German electors voted for Hitler," as many people hoped that anti-Semitism together with the pseudo-socialist program of the Nazis would produce better conditions under a Hitler regime. Nazi ideolgy made many Germans feel "superior" to the Jews. It was surprising that the leaders of the Weimar Republic did not combat Jew-hatred more vigorously. In truth, among many other people, including republican parties and even Socialists, there was according to the author "a certain amount of latent anti-Semitism" and many who publicly opposed the uncompromising anti-Semitism of Hitler, were probably prepared to admit agreement with the Nazi policy on the Jews. The Jews, the author held, were "not altogether without guilt," since they allegedly "provoked" anti-Semitism "by their own behavior." Prince Loewenstein admitted some Jewish ancestry, which largely explained his personal bias. Jewish self-hatred was, after all, a well-known phenomenon and many a half- or quarter-Jew by descent cursed the Jewish part in themselves.

Prince Loewenstein held that German Jews were "arrogant," as he believed to have observed as a fellow-student in Geneva of all places, and displayed other "undesirable qualities." Many German Jews were "snobs" and showed "too much of a sort of sham self-confidence." Yet anti-Semitism of many was only a mean form of agitation trumped-up and organized by irresponsible people. Intellectually capable German Jews, however, should have understood that it was in their own interest to avoid anything which might encourage anti-Semitism. Prince Loewenstein, though making such charges, asserted that he did not wish to excuse atrocities to the slightest degree. Jews, he held, should be proud of the misery they have had to endure "not as oppressed slaves of the ruling peoples, but as martyrs of justice." Prince Loewenstein's observations were a testimony to the Jewish alienation from most German parties and groups, republicans and, as he noticed, even people on the Left. German Jewry lacked indeed strong and reliable German friends and allies against Nazi Jew-hatred.

A former prominent Nazi Party leader who broke with Hitler, Hermann Rauschning, published *The Revolution of Nihilism. Warning to the West*, New York, in 1939, on the very eve of the outbreak of World War II, a book which caused a sensation.[9] Prior to the commencement of the Holocaust, he warned against the Nazi nihilist revolution which threatened to destroy the spirit also of Christianity. "One element of the destruction of Christianity must not be passed over," he wrote, "the disfranchising and destruction of German Jewry." He sharply denounced the conception of race and the forgeries with which national-socialist propaganda carried on its "demagogic" campaign of anti-Semitism. He foresaw that "it will be difficult to free the German body from this poison," though, despite his expressed pessimism in regard to the future of the German Jews, he apparently did not fully anticipate their real destiny. The "satisfaction of the instincts of envy and greed through the removal of Jewish competition in trade and industry, the expropriation of a part of the nation without compensation, and its brutal deprivation of all rights" has been accompanied by "the destruction of all right" and the training in revolutionary violence. "The appetite of the masses is in any case stimulated." Rauschning held that the anti-Semitic acts of the Third Reich are almost "a formal introduction" to a coming revolutionary upheaval. A general social upheaval will be the more inescapable, the longer it is delayed and it will be turned against the German social élite, though some of the latter in the past systematically made use of anti-Semitism. His analysis of the appeal of the anti-Jewish program to German masses turned out to be realistic and his pessimism regarding German-Jewish destiny amply warranted.

In a later book, *The Conservative Revolution* (1941),* Rauschning revealed that Edgar J. Jung, author of a "great book," *Die Herrschaft der Minderwertigen*, was his actual inspiration. A secre-

---

* Hugo von Hoffmansthal was probably the first who spoke of a "Conservative revolution"—the term being an inner contradiction—of a scale never known in the history of Europe

tary of Franz von Papen, Jung was assassinated by the Nazis at the time of the so-called Röhm Putsch on June 30, 1934; he had drafted Papen's widely noticed critical Marburg speech. In the new book Rauschning assured his readers that he did not wish to make excuses for Nazism. He rejected the notion that he was a German nationalist and expansionist simply because he regarded Germany as the natural leader of Central Europe. Like other Germans, he merely wanted, he asserted, "a new world equilibrium" and "to procure due rank for the German nation." Originally, he had had faith in his comrades of the NSDAP and voiced only "grief" that the nationalist movement which had great "opportunities" should have gone to ruin. But he had soon seen "the seamy side" in Nazism and began to realize that it would result in "the great tragedy of the German nation and the world." He thought that it was not the specific provisions of the treaty of Versailles that mattered to the German people, but rather the disappointment of those who fought in World War I and in its general outcome. He had entered the NSDAP in 1931 and did not meet Hitler until early 1932. Since Rauschning was then the only Nazi who had foreign affairs to cope with, the Führer had offered to him a candid revelation of his views on that subject.

Asked when he first realized the "error of anti-Semitism," Rauschning underlined that his own practical policy in Danzig showed that he was never an anti-Semite. The Jew, he developed, was "by nature critically minded."[10] "His clearness and boldness of judgment, his cool and logical thinking, are an indispensable complement of the German nature." The Jew was also "conservatively minded, a man of the law, an upholder of family, of tradition, of implicit obedience to the divine ordinance." In spite of long temptation to materialism, the Jew was always the most spiritual of all men. As long as the Jew clung to these two foregoing principles, he "is the greatest of enrichments within any nation." "But in Germany," Rauschning elaborated, a degenerate form of this Jewish spirit pushed its way into the foreground, frivolously juggling with anything and everything, taking pleasure in unmasking everything of moral worth and placing itself at the head of literature in which a sort of intellectual masochism prevailed, all the bounds were torn down which human civilization has set up to restrain its own dangerous and self-destroying lusts." In Rauschning's words, this was only one side of the picture—one side which in the Nazi view was the full truth. On the other hand, Rauschning recalled Julius Stahl, "the intellectual founder of our Prussian conservatism," and added:

> To describe the part played by the German Jews in German intellectual advance in the past 150 years would involve writing the whole history of that advance. This history was not a misappropriation of the German spirit.

He, Rauschning, had never embraced "racial anti-Semitism." The "Jewish strain" was "nothing more and nothing less than one of the German strains . . ." He compared the "Jewish Germans" with the Bavarian and Prussian Germans. He was in favor of "the complete assimilation of the Jews." Assimilation did not mean that every distinctive trait must entirely disappear.

Rauschning disclosed that he had various friends among Jewish Germans and "among no other Germans have I found more understanding than among the Jews." He held that his efforts to "counter the anti-Semitic enterprises of the Nazi party in Danzig were not wholly unsuccessful." He tried to answer the question why "the vulgar anti-Semitism of the Nazi party did not prevent him from joining the NSDAP." He and other comrades in Danzig regarded anti-Semitism as no more real a point "than any other in the very stupid Nazi program" which, he held, "was obviously not meant to be taken seriously." He had "so little belief in the anti-Semitic hullabaloo that I never broke off relations with Jewish acquaintances."

Looking back, he admitted having been mistaken on the question of the reality of Nazi anti-Semitism. When Jewish citizens of Danzig came to him to complain of persecution, he told them to have "patience," "that we are all in the midst of a revolution," that he aimed at "restoring legality and civic equality for our Jewish fellow-citizens as for the rest." Rauschning pointed finally to the desire of the Jews to preserve "the purity of the present-day Jewish race as the innermost essence of the faith." In the end Rauschning admitted that the Jew was everywhere on the side of freedom, criticism, and reason and that he must be on the side of every emancipation movement. He voiced the hope that the Jew will impress upon the peoples among whom he lives "his people's great qualities of order, traditionalism, and authority."

A moderate conservative and nationalist, Rauschning warned the Western world of the Nazi peril to Europe and perceived the threat of National Socialism and anti-Semitism to Jews and Germans. His attitude was characteristic for some segments of the German people, though few showed his kind of late courage and judgment.

Colonel-General Werner von Fritsch

The attitude of the German military élite during the 1930s was critical of Hitler, though for obvious reasons largely suppressed. His vast rearmament program and his success in foreign affairs, however, swept away their doubts and their courage. In regard to Jews, the military leadership was not inclined to look upon this question as a decisive one and was willing to acquiesce to Hitler's policy as expressed in the Nuremberg Laws.

In the conclave of November 5, 1937, when the Führer revealed to six participants his schemes against Austria and Czechoslovakia, as recorded by Colonel Hossbach, Field-Marshal Werner von Blomberg, and Colonel-General Freiherr Werner von Fritsch had shown reluctance to underestimate the strength of the French army and of the Czech defenses and had expressed anxiety over a possible conflict with Britain. Soon thereafter three of the participants were removed from their offices in connection with the Blomberg scandal. Von Blomberg had married, as was disclosed, a prostitute. Hitler who had attended the wedding, was furious, inveighed against Blomberg, Fritsch, and against the German military élite in general. He was determined to dismiss doubters of his political "intuition" and of his military genius. On February 4, 1938, on the eve of his Austrian adventure, the resignations of Blomberg and Fritsch were formally announced and many other generals either were relieved of their commands or assigned other duties.

The German military élite's attitude toward Hitler and the Nazi regime was ambiguous already in the 1930s. Like President Paul von Hindenburg, they could not forget the lowly social and military origins of "corporal" Hitler. On the other hand, they appreciated the support which the Führer gave to the strengthening of the German army and the crushing of the rival S. A. in the alleged *Putsch* of 1934.

Fritsch himself disclosed in a private letter dated September 4, 1938, to Baronin von Schutzbar the ideological closeness in essential points of the German military caste to parts of the Nazi program. As he wrote soon after World War I, he had come to "the conclusion that we would have to be victorious in three battles if Germany was again to be powerful," first "in the battle against the working class"—Hitler, already had won this—"secondly against the Catholic church, perhaps better expressed ultramontanism," and third, "against the

Jews."[10b] Anti-Semitism in the highest German military circles, even those which had not surrendered to Nazi ideology, was widespread, though it did not reach yet the extreme levels of the Nazi creed and of Hitler himself. In any case, genuine or alleged differences of the military élite with Hitler and skepticism and even hostility toward him were not likely to alleviate Nazi hostility and hatred of the Jews.

Historiography from the Third Reich to the Early Post-War Period

Long before the German Counterrevolution achieved success in overthrowing the Weimar Republic, nationalist and imperialist leanings, racism and anti-Semitism had sunk deep roots into German soil. When, after 1945, due to Allied prohibitions and the reversal of German attitudes and policy, National Socialism was uprooted, German historiography emerged blemished and discredited from the moral and scholarly abyss into which it had plunged. Compelled to shed some of its nationalist biases and imperialist ambitions, it faced special obstacles in coming to grips with the murderous racial anti-Semitism of the recent past as well as the earlier traditional Jew-hatred. Even respected elder German historians seemed unable to entirely shake off the prejudices so long rampant in their country. Among the latter were noted historians such as Friedrich Meinecke and Gerhard Ritter.

In the translator's preface to Friedrich Meinecke's *German Catastrophe: Reflections and Recollections* (Harvard University Press, 1950, published in Germany in 1946), the late Harvard historian Sidney B. Fay introduced Meinecke to the American public as "the most distinguished living German historian" and also as a "liberal" who was profoundly opposed to the Hitler regime. Praising his objectivity, Fay described Meinecke's early admiration and enthusiasm for what was "good and great in Prussian Germany" contrasted to his later days when the "flaws and weaknesses" of the Prussian regime became more evident.[11] These "weaknesses" of course had long been widely commented upon in the world at large. Many a reader must have had great difficulty fully agreeing with Fay's remarks on Meinecke, who only nonchalantly touched in the foregoing brochure on the worst Nazi crimes, those committed against the Jews.

Anti-Jewish vilification and outright slander had played a crucial role in German history, especially in the Nazis' success in coming to power and committing atrocities during World War II. These atrocities were unique and deserved special condemnation. Meinecke's critical remarks about Jew-hatred, however, were relatively few and far between and were partly balanced by rather unfavorable observations on German Jews. Meinecke's personal condemnation of Nazi murders, of their "horrible" nature and "degeneration" was never accompanied by express commiseration and empathy for the fate of the Jews. To the contrary, Meinecke praised the historian Heinrich von Treitschke as one of the "greatest" of German intellectual leaders of his time, totally ignoring that he was a prominent champion of Jew-hatred who had coined the slogan that the Jews were "Germany's misfortune."

In later years, Meinecke developed that there lived two souls in eighteenth-century Prussia, "one capable of culture, the other hostile to it." The negative side of Prussian discipline was the habit of conformity, often leading to "thoughtless subservience." Hitler's work, Meinecke held, must be reckoned as the eruption of the Satanic principle in world history. While the *Machtstaat* [state extolling power], the history of which began with Machiavellianism and Hegel, was not confined to Germany, Meinecke conceded that the "frankness and nakedness" of it was "specifically German." But he hardly condemned German anti-Semitism as such, but rather made it comprehensibie since the Jews allegedly displayed many character faults. Not the persecuting majority, but the persecuted minority was guilty! Meinecke held that the anti-Semitic movement "at the beginning of the 1880s" brought the first flash of lightning," ignoring thus centuries of consistently vicious Jew-hatred, inequality, and persecution. "Jews," he went on explaining, "who were inclined to enjoy indiscreetly the favorable economic situation now smiling upon them, had since their full emancipation [1869 under Bismarck] aroused resentment of various sorts."

"The Jews," he continued, "contributed much to that gradual depreciation and discrediting of the liberal world of ideas that set in after the end of the nineteenth century." The fact that besides their "negative and discrediting influence they also achieved a great deal that was positive in the cultural and economic life of Germany was forgotten by the mass of those who now attacked the damage done by the Jewish character." "Out of the anti-Semitic feeling, it was possible for an anti-liberal and anti-humanitarian feeling to develop easily—the first step toward National Socialism." The charges of Jewish "negativism" and "disintegrating influences" being rooted in the Jewish character, religion, or nationality, were age-old accusations. It is incomprehensible how a prominent historian could have repeated such accusations, all this after the Nazi horrors of the Holocaust!

In the Weimar period there were, according to Meinecke, many Jews who "drank too hastily and greedily of the cup of power!" This made them appear "in the eyes of persons with anti-Semitic feelings to be the beneficiaries of Germany's defeat and revolution?" Meinecke made no qualifying remark that the rise of anti-Semitism in the Weimar Republic on the grounds listed or any other ground had in reality no justification. The bulk of German Jews were not, as their enemies suggested, revolutionaries, but solid middle-class people and ardent German patriots. They had valiantly fought and died for the Fatherland; they were, of course, by no means responsible for Germany's military defeat. But the unceasing propaganda attacks on Jews, a mere 1 percent of the German population, played a major role in German public life, propelling Hitler and his cohorts to victory. Meinecke, however, trivialized anti-Semitism prior to 1880, during all the centuries of German hostility toward the Jews, asserting their allegedly adverse impact upon the life of the German people. Like many other Germans, Meinecke drew attention to Hitler's Austrian background and "the elemental passion in his racial dogma," which he had "formed in the overheated atmosphere of Austrian anti-Semitism," a convenient device of minimizing Jew-hatred in Germany and shifting it wholesale upon the shoulders of neighboring Austria.

In Meinecke's view, "the horrible expulsion of the German populations from territories that have had a German stamp since the Middle Ages unfortunately does not find us Germans blameless." This expulsion, he conceded, was only the answer to the fight for the conquest of the East which Hitler had undertaken and "into which he plunged us when he broke loose against Russia in 1941." The manner in which the fight was carried on became a "misfortune for us." Meinecke recalled in this context the Austrian playwright Franz Grillparzer's saying regarding the development from "humanity to nationality to bestiality." While not withholding criticism from the Germans and their mistakes, his heart went out to them. Yet in regard to the cruel and inhuman fate which befell the German Jews at the hand of the Germans, he expressed no comparable commiseration, although they too, like the Baltic Germans in their region, had resided in the Germanies for centuries, and though their lot was to be incomparably worse.

Admittedly, Meinecke showed no admiration for Hitler, the Führer's fanaticism, dedication to power for its own sake, his egocentrism, "boundless vanity," "the bad taste of his self-glorification" and "the senseless robber regime for which he exploited his people's last bit of strength as he clung to the remnants of his power." All this was utterly repulsive to Meinecke. Still, he devoted seven full pages to his elaboration of "the positive elements" of Hitlerism! As if these so-called "positive" elements were not harnessed to the evil drive toward subjugation and humiliation of all of Europe's non-German nationalities! Meinecke lamented amply the "German catastrophe" but remained silent about the greater and irremediable "catastrophe" of the Jews. His denunciation of Hitler and National Socialism was quite inadequate and deficient, as seen from the perspective of the Jews as well of that of general humanitarianism. The scope of the Jewish tragedy deserved unambiguous repudiation. Meinecke's "liberalism" and true dedication to German humanism was simply lacking in essentials.

In 1947, Meinecke, eighty-four years old, attempted in the foregoing booklet, an apologia for the Germans. Yet the late American historian Lucy Dawidowicz pointed out correctly: "No one reading this booklet would ever know about slave labor, concentration camps, mass shootings, death factories and the murder of six million Jews," although by the end of the war, these crimes had become well known through the International Military Tribunal at Nuremberg and other sources. As Dawidowicz had continued, "There is no record that Meinecke ever expressed any objection to anti-Semitism or ever defended the Jews from defamation during or after the Third Reich.[12]

Nor was the judgment of Gerhard Ritter about the German Jews qualitatively very different from that of Meinecke. Ritter had been active in the anti-Hitler Resistance. Following the failure of the anti-Hitler coup of July 20, 1944, Ritter was arrested and remained imprisoned until released by the Allied forces in April 1945. National-minded, he was a conservative and also an authoritarian. Like Meinecke, he rejected the notion that National Socialism originated in Germany, but rather held that the ground of European political tradition was shaken earlier, not in Germany, but by the French Revolution. Again like Meinecke, it was European mass democracy which constituted the "pernicious influence" that allegedly produced National Socialism. In his view, Hitler and Mussolini were not the first of their kind, but rather followed the "grand-style dictatorship of Napoleon," thus dismissing the progressivism of the latter. Racist and anti-Semitic ideas, according to Ritter, were "not indigenous to Germany proper,"[13] but originated in the southeastern part of Europe with its characteristic mixture of nationalities. He ignored thus Poland, Russia, and the unique development in Germany. Ritter devoted only two pages to anti-Semitism and the annihilation of European Jews, and this in a footnote, thus trivializing German Jew-hatred. When and wherever German anti-Semitism emerged, it was merely based on "economic resentments of the peasantry and the bourgeoisie"—rather populous segments of the German people. in any case, anti-Semitism was only related to the "heavy influx of Jews or to certain symptoms of corruption among them." Like Meinecke, Ritter held that the wild racist fanaticism of the Nazis originated in Austria and with Hitler, who superimposed it upon the German people, among whom it had never widely spread—a complete misreading of its depth and its duration. Yet he often contradicted this view, also when he rejected the notion that anti-Semitism was "an alien imposition on German traditions."

Following the German Revolution of 1918–19, German historians had not been enthused about the Weimar Republic and few had cared deeply about the new democratic constitution, the protection of minorities and especially of the civil rights of the German Jews. Though few full professors in the German universities were members of the NSDAP in the 1930s many joined the party later, among them Karl Alexander von Müller, professor of history at the University of Munich and in 1933, president of the Bavarian Academy of Sciences. Some, like Ludwig Dehio, became part of the so-called "inner emigration," withdrawing from active participation in professional associations and publications, while Nazis took the places made vacant by the dismissals and the emigration of Jewish professors and of leftists. Meinecke himself had lost the editorship of the *Historische Zeitschrift.* the most prestigious historical journal in Germany, after a service which spanned more than four decades.

Among several young historians who rapidly rose in the Nazi era was Walter Frank who became the editor of the *Historische Zeitschrift*. He also became president of the new *Reichsinstitut für Geschichte des neuen Deutschland*, which fell under control of the Reich Ministry for Education. An extreme nationalist and anti-Semite, he had written his dissertation at Munich on Adolf Stöcker, the founder of the anti-Semitic Christian Social Workers' Party in Berlin in 1878. In 1928, Meinecke himself had favorably reviewed Frank's dissertation in the *Historische Zeitschrift*. Frank continued working in the field of anti-Semitism when he wrote his second work on *Nationalismus und Demokratie in Frankreich's Dritter Republik*, comparing the France of Dreyfus with the Weimar Republic and picturing both as allegedly corrupted by Jewish influences. Frank's admiration of E. Drumont, the anti-Semitic author of *La France Juive*, of Maurice Barrès, the *völkisch* writer, and of Charles Maurras, the propagator of the dominance by an élite and of the *Camelots du roi*, was the more startling, since they were all prophets of revanche against Imperial Germany. An extremist on the Jewish question, Frank often acknowledged himself as a disciple of the pornographic Jew-hater Julius Streicher, and boasted to have been a loyal participant in the mass assemblies of the "Frankenführer." Judaism, he wrote, "is one of the great negative principles of world history," a parasite.[14] Walter Frank planned to turn the new *Reichsinstitut* into the very center of historiography in the Third Reich. He set up a six-man honorary council which included the historians Karl Alexander von Müller, Erich Marcks, and the Austrian Professor Heinrich von Srbik. Frank also appointed Wilhelm Grau, like himself a former student of Müller and also a "specialist" on anti-Semitism. Grau's dissertation had been on "Anti-Semitism in the Late Middle Ages." He became a contributor to the *Historische Zeitschrift* on the topic of the "Jewish Question." Frank and Grau quarreled later, an encounter which ultimately involved Nazi officials and even Hitler himself.

The anti-Jewish studies of the new Institute were published between 1937 and 1944 in the series *Forschungen zur Judenfrage* and comprised nine volumes. The first annual conference of the Institute was held in Munich in November 1936 with Rudolf Hess honoring it with his presence. Julius Streicher, editor of the pornographic anti-Semitic sheet *Der Stürmer*, considered a warm supporter of the Research Division on the Jewish Question, gave at the 1937 meeting a three-hour long address to the conference. Professors at leading German universities, among them historians, participated at the various conferences and became contributors to the *Forschungen zur Judenfrage*. The themes listed for these studies included typically anti-Semitic topics, as for instance, "Albert Einstein's Attempt to Subvert Physics." In the post-war period Gerhard Ritter, surveying German historiography of the twentieth century, described Walter Frank and his "host of fanatics as well as ambitious young National Socialists"[15] as wanting to constitute the élite and shock troops of the new national sociaiist historiography.

While Frank and Grau and their fellow Nazi historians focused attention on both German and European anti-Semitism as predecessors of Nazi Jew-haters, other German historians, especially after 1945, tended to look the other way, vigorously denying that anti-Semitism was a persistent phenomenon in German history. They wanted to lessen Germany's guilt for the Jewish massacres which had climaxed in the Holocaust, describing its occurrence to the devil himself. In their view, the mythology of deviltry was at fault, the German people its victim.

Great Germans and Anti-Semites. Claims in the Inter-War Era

The German Jew-haters have generally cared little for the great Germans, whose entire *Weltanschauung* contradicted their own crudity and vulgarity. Nevertheless, they made strenuous efforts to picture them as severe critics and bitter enemies of the Jews. "From Luther on," claimed the anti-Semitic historian Heinrich von Treitschke, "down to Goethe, Herder, Kant, and Fichte, almost all great Germanic thinkers were one in this feeling." Lessing, he claimed, "stood quite alone with his predilection for the Jews."[16] In the same vein as Treitschke, Houston Stewart Chamberlain, the English writer who became a German citizen and court philosopher in the imperial era under Wllhelm II, wrote later: "Almost all prominent men from Tiberius to Bismark have looked upon the presence of the Jews as a social and political menace"[17]—which was surely a distortion of Bismarck's thought and practical legislation, as were Treitschke's claims.

It was only fitting that most later anti-Semitic writers such as Adolf Bartels, the literary historian, Theodor Fritsch, the editor of countless *Anti-Semitic Catechisms*, Alfred Rosenberg, the "theoretician" of the Nazi movement, and Adolf Hitler himself in *Mein Kampf*, repeated these assertions. Hitler claimed Schopenhauer an anti-Semite and, in another context, laid the same claim on Fichte.[18] Culling quotes from the works of great or widely known German writers, the anti-Semites wished to demonstrate that the attitude of these literary men toward the Jews was always marked by dislike and repugnance. They were anxious to prove that they themselves were in the best company.

These assertions were denied by others, Jews and German Christians. Among the more noted replies may be mentioned some late nineteenty-century publications, the *Antisemitenspiegel* [Mirror], published under the auspicies of the League for the Defense Against Anti-Semitism, and the *Antisemitenhammer* [Hammer], a collection of testimonies gathered by the German Christian author Josef Schrattenholz. But these anthologies were far from comprehensive and were polemic rather than balanced and detached discussions. In the heat of the battle with a demagogic foe, truth could not easily emerge.

Some German literary historians, not to mention outright Nazi propagandists, were as hostile to Jews and Judaism as German intellectual and political historians. Josef Nadler, prominent professor of German Literature of the University of Vienna, claimed in the very introduction of his *Literaturgeschichte der deutschen Stämme und Landschaften* (Regensburg, 1932)[19] the continuing enmity of outstanding German writers to Jews and Judaism. He asserted that Johann Gottfried Herder was an enemy of the Jews—without offering any evidence. The same view was expressed by the anti-Semitic author O. Kernholt, *Vom Ghetto zur Macht, Leiping*, (1921). The latter had to admit that Herder's "hostility" to Jews was somewhat "peculiar," since he showed them a "certain benevolence." Another literary historian, Franz Koch, in a paper "Goethe und die Juden," read at the *Forschungsabteilung Judenfrage* of the *Reichsinstitut für Geschichte des neuen Deutschland*, on May 13, 1937, claimed Goethe as an illustrious forerunner of Jew-hatred.[20] Theodor Fritsch and Franz Koch quoted as proof of Goethe's alleged anti-Semitic convictions a few lines from his youthful farce *Das Jahrmarktsfest zu Plundersweilen* (1774). Actually one cannot read Goethe's Esther playlet without being struck by how closely it approximates a satire on Jew-hating.

Gotthold Ephraim Lessing, the playwright of "Nathan the Wise" and genuine friend of the Jews, could not be turned into an anti-Semite, though the widely read author Eugen Dühring promptly discovered Lessing's "Jew-related or rather half-Jewish pen," without offering the slightest proof of his wild assertions.

Opponents of the Jews have claimed Friedrich Schiller as one of their illustrious forerunners, again without furnishing the most spurious evidence. Julius Langbehn, *Rembrandt als Erzieher* (Leipzig, 1896), Nazis such as Gottfried Feder, *Die Juden* (Munich, 1933), and Count Reventlov, *Judas Kampf* (Berlin, 1937), though preferring the thought of German Romanticism about the Jews to that of the Enlightenment, placed the latter above that of the brothers Alexander and Wilhelm von Humboldt, but considered it, judged from the racist

Nazi point of view, still "unfortunate." Adolpf Bartels in 1933 claimed that the playwright Friedrich Hebbel in his political reports of 1848 to the *Augsburger Allemeine Zeitung* had shown "very sound German nationalist views," overlooking a pro-Jewish article of his in which he supported the emancipation of the Jews. Walter Frank's *Reichsinstitut für Geschichte des neuen Deutschland* made strenuous attempts to gather the works of anti-Semitic authors and to enlist them in their struggle against the Jews. This included the earlier pamphlet by K. R. Grunsky, *Wagner und die Juden* 1922.

Post-War Historiography about the German Opposition to Hitler: Hans Rothfels and Gerhard Ritter

In the early post-World War II period, historical science, scrutinized by the occupation authorities and slowly recovering at the German universities, kept its distance from rightist and nationalist extremism. Only the militant Right, somewhat masquerading, made attempts to minimize or whitewash institutions such as concentration camps and death camps and to deny the responsibility of the Third Reich for unleashing war in 1939. But immediately after 1945, German historiography was critical of revisionist writings, foreign and domestic ones. Since the 1960s populist, chauvinist, and revisionist trends became more pronounced and affected even serious conservative historians such as Gerhard Ritter. Despite the shock in the wake of World War II of the atrocities and of the German military debacle, Ritter retained some fundamentals of his philosophy, especially the emphasis on German nationalism and the concept of the *Machtstaat*.

Even after 1945, Gerhard Ritter was unable to find the roots of Jew-hatred in Germany's past. Despite overwhelming evidence to the contrary, he again tried to deflect the origins of anti-Semitism to other countries and regions in Europe. Hans Rothfels, a student of Meinecke, was similarly insensitive to the persistent and often shrill sounds of German Jew-hatred throughout the ages. Rothfels had lost his German professorship in 1934, but taught in the U.S. before returning to Germany in 1951. In his work on the *German Opposition to Hitler: An Assessment* (London, 1961) he tended to magnify the German opposition.[21] Like Meinecke and Ritter, he claimed that National Socialism was not a characteristically German phenomenon, but the product of European malaise. "In many respects," National Socialism could be considered the "final summit of an extreme consequence of the secularization movement of the nineteenth century"—

an attempt at rationalization and explaining away special German responsibility by placing anti-Semitism and "fascism" into the center of an all-European framework.

In September 1950, the German Federal Republic chartered the *Institut für Zeitgeschichte* in Munich, mandating that it focus on the study of National Socialism and the Third Reich. Among honorary members were Friedrich Meinecke, Theodor Heuss, historian and later President of the Federal Republic; among the advisory board members were Gerhard Ritter and Hans Rothfels, as well as some liberal historians. In 1953, the *Institut* began publishing the *Vierteljahrshefte für Zeitgeschichte* and some significant works about National Socialism, including studies about the murder of European Jews. While in his lead article of the first issue of the journal Rothfels laid down the ground rules of keeping "distance from all tendencies toward self-abasement and also against apologies," in Lucy Dawidowicz's judgment, many of the *Institut*'s publications had an "antiseptic quality," a style of "calculated objectivity" and avoidance of what the *Institut* researchers called "emotionalism," practicing a sort of moral "disengagement." The journal made a strong attempt to look at comparable phenomena beyond Germany, which were allegedly to explain the German experience. The result again was an attempt to trivialize German guilt by diverting attention from Germany to Europe, even the world.

Although Hans Rothfels' views on Jews and the German attitude on their persecution and annihilation emerge most clearly in his treatise *The German Opposition to Hitler* (London, 1961), anti-Semitism—a "primitive element" in the National Socialist movement required particular attention—he gave it the most cursory treatment, only two and one-half pages. Yet he was forced to admit that anti-Semitism had "a strong attraction for broad sections of the population and opened the door to the worst excesses as well as odious personal enrichment." A few sources listed center more on the prewar period, the *Kristallnacht* of 1938, rather than on the war and actual genocide. He focused on a handful of Germans, Quakers, Protestants, and Catholics, who were motivated by ethical and religious convictions—undoubtedly praiseworthy—but not necessarily by friendship for Jews. Rothfels believed that "such groups must have existed" not only in Berlin, but also in Munich and Augsburg. But he was compelled to admit that Jews who survived, being hidden by their German compatriots, represented "certainly a pathetically small number" compared with those who died. He pleaded that their names not be forgotten. There was no genuine attempt by the author to assess the responsibility of the many Germans who made the mass murder possible or those who silently stood by—later pretending that they were unaware of the Jews' terrible fate. Judging pre-war history after 1945, Gerhard Ritter held that the threats arising in Germany in the 1930s were increased by the extreme desire for peace in Great Britain due to the strong appeal of appeasement in all of Western Europe. Thus, the Entente powers failed to strike in time, namely when "Hitler dared to begin breaking international law."[22] In Ritter's view, the burden of guilt was obviously shifted from domestic German affairs to international politics involving non-German nations. Aside from the attempt to diminish German responsibility, Ritter's explanation did barely go beyond an exposition of the ancient Manichaean struggle between good and evil. When German troops occupied Prague in the Spring of 1939, the whole meaning of all history, in Ritter's view, had been falsified, "Satan had won."

Prior to it, in 1938, Germany, according to Ritter, missed the chance of a peaceful settlement due again to her "demonic obsession." Like Meinecke, Ritter abandoned a rational explanation of anti-Semitism, reducing it simply to the operations of the devil, thus avoiding scholarly historical analysis. The Munich agreement had nothing to do with statecraft or *Staatsraison*, "but with Hitler running amok."[23] With the Führer, "we stand face-to-face with criminality." While this study of Ritter properly assigned the main guilt for the outbreak of the war to national socialist Germany, on the other hand, it diminished it by introducing the devil theory. It also fell short of elucidating Nazi atrocities and, in particular, the brutal mass murder of the Jews.

Having himself participated in the Resistance movement, whose historian he became after the war, Gerhard Ritter did not pretend that he wrote his work *Carl Goerdeler und die deutsche Widerstandsbewegung* "without passion." Yet, though describing the sufferings of Jewry, he showed little genuine compassion for it. Clearly, the struggle against anti-Semitism played not a primary role in shaping the program of the Resistance. Their leaders were especially concerned with schemes of overthrowing the Führer, about isolating and perhaps killing him—though Goerdeler himself disavowed the latter objective—and of securing Allied pledges for the drawing of "just" post-war boundaries for the Reich. They focused on "autonomy" and "self-determination" and regard for German self-esteem and national sensibilities. In Ritter's view, Goerdeler and his co-fighters underestimated the demonic character of their opponents and probably also the "political blindness of the masses of the German people."

Gerhard Ritter considered Carl Friedrich Goerdeler the most active and intelluctually productive figure of the German Resistance against Hitler-Germany. Since 1930 *Oberbürgermeister* of Leipzig, he was a widely known local government politician, as well as a frequent writer in this field. Like many other German contemporaries, it took him a long time to comprehend the criminal character of national socialism, though he was early repelled by its noisy and violent propaganda. After Hitler's seizure of power he refused to raise the swastika above the Leipzig city hall and personally protected Jewish shopkeepers against plundering SS-men. As his biographer Gerhard Ritter pointed out, he first trustingly cooperated with the NSDAP and entertained a personal relationship with Hitler. While Goerdeler was abroad, the Party removed the Felix Mendelssohn-Bartholdy monument in Leipzig which had honored the Jewish composer. After his return, Goerdeler resigned in protest. Privately he accused Hitler of having falsified all great traditions of German history, of "having sullied the German name through horrible crimes," pointing especially to the brutal maltreatment of the Poles and the "deliberate beastly extermination of the Jews."[24] On February 2, 1945, Goerdeler was executed, since he was declared guilty of having known of the impending plot in July 1944 against the Führer.

According to Gerhard Ritter, it was only natural that Goerdeler had wanted to solve the Jewish problem in a "quite original manner."[25] He wanted to "compensate" the German Jews for their losses and maltreatments. Ritter kept silent about the killing of close to six million Jews, speaking in December 1944 of only one million Jewish victims. A "permanent solution" was to lift Jews out of the "undignified situation" of a "more or less undesirable" status as "a guest people" in European countries. He held it to be the task of a post-war conference of the Great Powers to create for them an independent state. He thought, among other projects of a Canadian or South American region, since Palestine, in his view, would be too small to accommodate all Jews. If the Jews could prove having rendered German military service, attained military accomplishments, or possessed old family traditions in Germany, they should not be refused German citizenship.

The same half-hearted stance Goerdeler developed in a meeting of the Freiburg Resistance Circle in 1942 on occasion of a proposal made by Gerhard Ritter himself. But these Freiburg suggestions were only partially utilized in the propaganda of the Resistance, and "in a very limited manner." Apparently, this Resistance group was hesitant to make even the slightest pro-Jewish propositions. Goerdeler's program fell pitifully short even of minimum standards.

True, at Christmastime 1944, Goerdeler, incarcerated following the abortive July 20, 1944 *Putsch* against Hitler, spoke of the "bestial assassination of a million [sic] Jews" and criticized the "cowardice of the German bourgeoisie which, partly unknowingly, partly in desperation," permitted such things to take place. In January 1945, one month before his execution, Goerdeler, in a memoir, despaired of the existence of God, who permitted millions of decent human beings—Jews were not mentioned as such and Goerdeler may have had non-Jews, including Germans, in mind—to die and suffer "without lifting a finger."[26] He raised in this context the question whether "we perhaps have sinned, because we were nationalists, meaning we claimed God for our nationality, for our people." Did all this misery occur "because I sacrificed politics to an ideal instead of doing justice to my immediate human obligations." He wondered whether the Lord punished now the entire German nation, even innocent German children, "because it allowed the annihilation of the Jews" without offering any resistance. Such were the thoughts of Carl Goerdeler, who considered himself a devout Christian, a German "patriot," willing to fight the "tyrant" for the sake of the Germans, for the oppressed nationalities of Europe, and, to a lesser extent, for the Jews.

It took some time after World War II before German historiography regained its balance, until it embraced unconditionally the values of Western civilization, of Western tolerance for and protection of minorities, and shed traditional, national, religious, and racial prejudices, including the long-festering Jew-hatred.

Accusations at Nuremberg, 1945–46

The formal accusations against the Third Reich and some of its surviving prominent leaders for their responsibility for crimes and atrocities were articulated before the international Military Tribunal in 1945–46 in Nuremberg. German popular and scholarly reactions were thereafter directed against its judgments, proceedings, and its sentences. The Nuremberg indictment cast light on Germany's aggressive wars, their preparation, and war crimes by reviewing German history after the First World War, by tracing the growth of the Nazi Party under Hitler's leadership and by analyzing its program. It reviewed especially the history of the unification of all Germans in Greater Germany, with emphasis on the claim for self-determination, underlining the demand for equal rights for the German people in respect to other nations, and the demand for "land and territory for the sustenance of our [the German] people and the colonization of our surplus population"[27] and race as the criterion for German citizenship, thus excluding Jews from the German community. It also quoted Hitler to the effect that the purpose of the Versailles treaty was the "death" for 20 million Germans! The indictment did not consider anti-Semitic propaganda as such a "crime." Its consequence, however, the mass murder of Jews, evidently was one.

Of the Nuremberg defendants five were glaringly absent from the trial and no longer alive: Adolf Hitler, Heinrich Himmler, Josef Goebbels, Martin Bormann, and the head of the Krupp combine, Gustav Krupp, the latter being declared mentally incompetent. A prime figure of the Nazi hierarchy accused was Hermann Göring who had held some authority until almost the end. After four years in British custody, Rudolf Hess had been taken back to Germany. Other defendants were the former Foreign Ministers, Joachim Ribbentrop and Konstantin von Neurath, the latter having served between 1933 and 1938, Franz von Papen, who had resigned as Vice-Chancellor in 1934 and had served subsequently as Ambassador in Vienna and, during the war, as envoy in Turkey, and Seyss-Inquart, who became Austria's Chancellor in March 1938 for a transition period. He served later in Poland and finally became Nazi commissioner in the Netherlands. Alfred Rosenberg, in the end the "philosopher" of the Nazi movement, was chosen to scorch Russia and prepare it for Nazi settlement. Hans Frank, Hitler's specialist for Nazi law, was later dispatched to Poland where he presided over mass murder. There were also the defendants Baldur von Schirach, long head of the Hitler Youth, and then *Gauleiter* in Vienna, Admiral Erich Raeder, chief of the German navy until 1943, when he was replaced by the commander of the German submarine fleet, Admiral Karl Dönitz. In the last days of the Hitler regime, Dönitz was chosen by the Führer to become his successor and head of the Nazi Party and State. Finally, there was Alfred Jodl, chief of operations in the Military High Command and Field Marshal Wilhelm Keitel, holding the top military post during World War II. In the dock also sat Julius Streicher, the notorious anti-Semitic propagandist and pornographer; Walter Funk who played a modest role in the German economy; Fritz Sauckel, an old Party member and head of the German labor program during the war; Hjalmar Schacht, financier and patrician who actually stopped playing a public role in 1938–39; and Albert Speer, Hitler's architect and young protégé who gained enormous economic power during the war. Finally, there was Ernst Kaltenbrunner, since 1942 Himmler's deputy and responsible for the atrocities committed by the SS; Robert Ley, chief of the German labor service; Hans Fritzsche, an official in the Propaganda Ministry. The Allied prosecutors asked the Tribunal to declare six Nazi organizations "criminal," including the brown-shirted SA and the black-shirted SS security service, Himmler's police apparatus, the Gestapo and the SD (originally the SS Security Service), and the Nazi "Leadership Corps." It also asked that the General Staff and High Command of the Armed Forces be declared "criminal."

Count One of the indictment charged the defendants "with conspiring or having a common plan to commit crimes against peace." The first acts of aggression were the seizure of Austria and Czechoslovakia and the first war of aggression was the war against Poland begun on September 1, 1939. In *Mein Kampf* Hitler had proclaimed Jew-hatred from the rooftops and to be propagated in schools and universities, among the SS and the SA, and among the German people generally. The indictment pointed to Chapter 2 of *Mein Kampf* which contained the "Master Race" theory and the doctrine of Aryan superiority over all other races and the right of Germans by virtue of this superiority to dominate and use other peoples for their own purposes. With the Nazis coming to power in 1933, the persecution of the Jews became official state policy which found expression in the Nuremberg laws of 1935.

Hitler had openly proclaimed that in the future soil will have to be won by the Germans "by the power of the triumphant sword." At the same time, however, the restoration of the German frontiers of 1914 was declared to be "wholly insufficient." The new German territory to be conquered lay "principally in Russia and the border states subject to her." Detailing Nazi plans of "aggression," the indictment made reference primarily to "meetings" on November 5, 1937 (the Colonel Hossbach Memorandum), May 23, 1939, August 22, 1939, and November 23, 1939, all obviously "carefully recorded" and preserved in the archives of the German government. The Tribunal was satisfied that Lieutenant Colonel Hossbach's account of the November 1937 meeting was substantially correct as were the specific plans that Austria and Czechoslovakia would be annexed by Germany "at the first possible opportunity,"

The Tribunal was also convinced that the German-Polish "negotiations" in August 1939 were "not entered into in good faith or with any desire to maintain face, but solely in the attempt to prevent Great Britain and France from honoring their obligations to Poland." The war therefore against Poland on September 1, 1939 was "most plainly an aggressive war," which was to develop into a war embracing almost the whole world and resulting in "the commission of countless crimes both against the laws and customs of war and against humanity."

Finally, great attention was placed on the "aggressive war" against the USSR. On December 18, 1940, Hitler issued Directive No. 21, initialed by Generals Keitel and Jodl, which called for the completion of all preparations and "to crush Soviet Russia in a quick campaign" before the end of the war against England and ordered that these preparations "will not be recognized abroad." Their purpose was the destruction of the Soviet Union as an independent state and its partition, the creation of the so-called Reich Commissariats and the transformation of some of the Baltic states, Byelorussia and other territories into "German colonies." Though it was contended for the defendants that the attack upon the USSR was "justified," because the Soviet Union was allegedly contemplating an attack upon Germany, it is "impossible to believe that this view was ever honestly entertained." Though Hitler and his collaborators originally did not consider that a war with the U.S. would be "beneficial" to their interest, apparently in the course of 1941 they revised their view and encouraged Japan to adopt a policy which would bring the U.S. into the war.

According to the Tribunal, certain of the defendants planned an aggressive war against twelve nations. They were therefore guilty of a series of crimes. These aggressive wars were also "wars in violation of international treaties, agreements or assurances." The Tribunal listed most of these specific treaties, though considering it "unnecessary" to discuss them in any detail in the Indictment. "It is clear," it held, "that planning and preparation had been carried out in the most systematic way" at every stage of history. According to Paul Schmidt, official interpreter of the German Foreign Office, the general objectives of the Nazi leadership were "apparent from the start, namely the domination of the European continent." When it is said that "common planning could not exist in a complete dictatorship," it is ignored that Hitler alone would not make an aggressive war by himself. The relationship between leader and follower did not preclude responsibility in foreign affairs just as little as in domestic policy by the German people.

Elaborating upon the Nazi conception of 'total war,' the Indictment asserted "that war crimes were committed on a vast scale," never before seen in the history of war. There followed a detailed account of murder and ill-treatment of prisoners of war and against Allied commando units, authorized by Hitler and approved by Keitel in several European countries, the mass killings of Soviet prisoners of war, the "murder and ill-treatment of civilian population," the so-called Night and Fog decree of December 7, 1941, by Hitler. The Indictment listed the practice of shooting hostages (Keitel decree, September 10, 1941) at the ratio of fifty or a hundred for one German life taken, the mass killings at Oradour-sur-Glane in France and Lidice in Czechoslovakia, and the means of terrorizing the people in occupied territories by means of concentration camps. Specially listed was the mass execution in the Jewish ghetto at Rowno and at Dubno.

The latter crimes in Poland and in the Soviet Union were part of a plan to get rid of whole native populations by expulsion and annihilation. In the words of Himmler in July 1942, it was not the Nazis' "task" to Germanize the East in the old sense, that is to teach people there the German language and the German law, but to see to it that only people of pure Germanic blood lived in the East. In regard to Czechoslovakia the defendant Konstantin von Neurath was accused of having planned in August 1940 to "expel" the Czechoslovak intelligentsia. But the "rest of the population was to be Germanized rather than expelled or exterminated, since there was a shortage of Germans to replace them." Under the heading "Pillage of public and private property" the Indictment charged the maltreatment of 5–7 millions of foreign workers who were not truly "volunteers." Himmler was quoted declaring himself unaffected if thousands of Russian females in Germany "fall down from exhaustion." Foreign workers were often lured with lying promises to be recruited as workers in Germany and dispatched from their country of origin "in trains without adequate heat, food, clothing, or sanitary facilities."

The "persecution of the Jews" was detailed in the Indictment. Ohlendorf, Chief of Amt III in RSHA from 1939 to 1943, in command of one of the *Einsatzgruppen* in the campaign against the Soviet

Union, testified regarding methods employed; firing squads to shoot the victims in order to lessen the sense of individual guilt on the part of his men. "The 90,000 men, women and children who were murdered in one year by his particular group were mostly Jews." The Indictment quoted the defendant Hans Frank in the Court: "A thousand years will pass and the guilt of Germany will still not be erased." By the autumn of 1938 pogroms were organized which included the burning and demolishing of synagogues, the looting of Jewish businesses, and the arrest of prominent Jewish businessmen. The seizure of Jewish assets had been authorized before the war. But the Nazi persecution of Jews in Germany, "severe and repressive as it was, cannot compare with the policy pursued during the war in the occupied territories." In the summer of 1941 plans were made for the "final solution" of the Jewish question in Europe, meaning extermination. There was "clear evidence that the leader of the *Einsatztruppen* obtained the cooperation of Army commanders," their relations described in one case as being "very close, almost cordial." Brigadier General Stroop, in charge of the destruction of the ghetto in Warsaw in 1943 sent reports to Germany in April and May 1943, notifying his superiors that he "decided to destroy and burn down the entire ghetto without regard to the armament factories," a decision which clearly revealed Nazi priorities. To Hitler and the Nazi fanatics the killing of Jews was more important than badly needed armament factories. Stroop's action at Warsaw eliminated, as he reported, "a proved total of 56,065 people."

In the death chambers it took between three and fifteen minutes to kill people. "After cremation the ashes were used for fertilizer and in some instances attempts were made to utilize the fat from the bodies of the victims." Special groups traveled through Europe to find Jews and subject them to the "final solution." German missions were sent to such satellite countries as Hungary and Bulgaria to arrange for the shipment of Jews to extermination camps. It is known that by the end of 1944 400,000 Jews from Hungary had been murdered at Auschwitz. Evidence has also been given of the evacuation of 110,000 Jews from part of Romania for "liquidation." Adolf Eichmann, who had been put in charge of this program by Hitler, has estimated that the policy pursued "resulted in the killings of six million Jews of which four million were killed in extermination institutions."

The International Military Tribunal at Nuremberg declared several organizations, including the SS and Waffen SS guilty of crimes, of having been "active participants" in steps leading to "aggressive war," and guilty of having participated in war crimes, and crimes against humanity. Only those who were drafted into SS membership by the state, having had no choice in the matter, and who had not committed crimes were excluded from this sentence. The Nuremberg judgment affected about 250,000 surviving German veterans of the combat SS. In May 1951 the first enabling legislation provided for pensions and other assistance to former professional soldiers, but specifically excluded all those who under the Nazis had violated fundamental principles of humanity and juridical legality. The combat SS men bitterly complained that they were made to share the heavy burden of guilt with the rest of the SS and that their honor was besmirshed. As one historian observed in regard to the relationship between combat SS and the rest of the SS, both were parts of the horror system of the Third Reich, linked with the *Wehrmacht*. He charged that the latter committed "horrible crimes." Hitler had always stipulated that troops had a dual function, one as soldiers and, in case of need, another one as police under Himmler. Among other functions, they had to accompany the transportation of Jews on their way to extermination camps. Besides, about one-third of the SD *Einsatztruppen*, the special mobile murder commandos, came from the Waffen SS.

The Holocaust historian Gerald Reitlinger has warned not to permit the SS to become "the alibi of a nation." The SS was not exclusively guilty for atrocities committed. "The crimes committed could not have been and were not executed by a single organization, however sprawling and powerful." "Without the minute interlocking of the Ministry of the Interior, the Ministry of Transport, Finance and Economics, the two High Command offices, Ministries of Labor and Armaments, and above all the Foreign Office," the "final solution" and all the rest would not have been carried out successfully.

The Western powers had no reason to abet German tendencies to make the SS the exclusive scapegoat, but many segments of German society had such an interest. Returning SS-men faced in postwar Germany renewed internment, forced labor, and other penalties. The Nuremberg judgment had engraved on their foreheads the mark of Cain. Several years after the war the former SS-men founded their own self-help organizations. In 1981, a former SS-General, Otto Kumm of Hamburg, founded a Mutual Aid Association (Hilfgemeinschaft auf Gegenseitigkeit, HIAG), refused to join the United Veterans Organization (VdS) and rejected a declaration of loyalty to the Federal Republic.

One of the accused in Nuremberg was the former Foreign Minister Joachim von Ribbentrop. In his self-serving *Memoirs* he attempted to acquit himself as well as Hitler, and to blame the Allies for misinterpreting the Führer who merely wished to protect Germany and Europe from Communism. Ribbentrop even claimed that it was not Hitler but others in his encourage who plotted to kill the Jews. But all of these assertions were widely refuted, including by the noted English historian and biographer of Hitler Alan Bullock in his introduction to Ribbentrop's *Memoirs*.[28] According to Bullock, Hitler's purpose was always aggressive, to secure a dominant position in Central Europe and from this base to launch a drive for *Lebensraum* in the East, which he had already proclaimed in *Mein Kampf* as the true great goal of German policy. Sire Nevile Henderson, British Ambassador to Berlin, saw only late in the day that good relations with England only meant for Hitler the "acquiescence of England" in his schemes for the redrawing of the Central European map.

According to Ribbentrop, Britain was mistaken in this view. Her true interests required her to strengthen Germany as the "bulwark of the West against Bolshevism." Bullock ridiculed the "glib claim" of the Nazis to have been the protectors of Europe against Communism. lt was well to remember, he continued, "the character of the protection which he offered, the racist doctrine, the concentration camps and extermination squads, as gross and sinister an outrage against humanity as anything for which the Communists can be held responsible." He recalled that Ribbentrop, who flew to Moscow in August 1939 to sign the Nazi-Soviet Pact and partition Eastern Europe with Stalin, was not fit to talk of the Allied "betrayal" of Europe to Bolshevism. It was not the Allies' policy first to launch an unprovoked attack on Russia and then senselessly persist in prolonging the war long after it had been lost which produced the 'Bolshevization' of half of Europe.

"From the moment I joined the NSDAP [1932]," Ribbentrop asserted talking about the "Jewish problem," I tried to bring about a revision of its anti-Semitic principles, or, at least, to have the Jewish problem solved by way of evolution through a numerus clauses." After the Nuremberg laws in September 1935, he, Ribbentrop, had a "long and detailed conversation" with the Führer about the Jewish question. When he in 1938 returned to Berlin as Foreign Minister, "I found an entirely new situation." After the assassination of Counselor von Rath in the Paris Embassy by a young Jew, Herschel Grünspan, and the following excesses of November 1938, Ribbentrop "always told Hitler that the enmity of world Jewry appeared unnecessary and that it was tantamount to having an additional great power as an enemy." Like Hitler, he magnifed the Jewish "power," but unlike the Führer he allegedly wanted him to desist finally from making the Jews the "paramount" foe. However, Hitler's conviction and obsession that world Jewry had systematically prepared the war against Germany was in the end responsible for its outbreak became more and more deeply rooted. In his view, the desired comprehensive settlement with Britain had been foiled by the Jews alone in that country and in America. Moreover, before and after the outbreak of the war with Russia, Hitler believed that International Jewry was also responsible for the communist threat in the East and that it had compelled Stalin to decide first to defeat Germany by an attack from the East and then to bolshevize her.

Ribbentrop asserted that he

> advanced my contrary opinion: I was convinced that the war had been caused by Britain's hostility to German aspirations. While Jewish influence may have contributed to it, it had not been the primary cause. . . . Hitler was immovable and always replied that I did not understand this issue. . . . American Jews who exercised almost complete domination over the American press, had systematically prepared for war and driven Roosevelt into his anti-German attitude. My proposals for a change in our Jewish policy were rejected.[29]

The Foreign Office, Ribbentrop disclosed, was told "that [Jewish] matters were matters of domestic administration and that it was therefore excluded from concerning itself with Jewish questions." When he again pleaded for a change in the "ecclesiastic and Jewish policies," Hitler replied "that he thoroughly disagreed with me on all matters." In another talk he asserted:

> You understand foreign policy, the Jewish question you do not understand. This is an ideological war between the Jewish bolshevist world and the world of Nations[:] . . . arms must decide.

Hitler personally gave a few instructions to the Foreign Office on the

Jewish question and those which he did send were generally concerned with representations to friendly governments asking that more attention be paid to the Jewish question and that Jews be removed from important posts. But this too led to unpleasantness with "our allies." Thus the Führer once sent Ribbentrop a message to the effect that a big Jewish espionage and sabotage organization had been discovered in Italian-occupied France and instructed him to make "serious representation to Mussolini."

In 1944 Hitler spoke "even more . . . of his conflict with Jewry and he became fanatically obstinate. But never, down to April 22, 1945, when I last saw him in the Reich Chancellery, did he ever mention the killng of Jews. That is why I even today cannot believe that the Führer ordered those killings." He believed that Himmler presented him with a *fait accompli.*

Though Ribbentrop's account in his *Memoirs* of Hitler and his relation with him must be taken with many grains of salt, his reference to the Führer's attitude and thought about the Jews deserves close attention. His attempt to acquit Hitler from the mass murder of the Jews merely because he allegedly never mentioned this matter to him and to shift exclusive responsibility to Himmler cannot be taken seriously, just as his assertion that the "true causes" of the Second World War should not be thought "in a lust for war or aggressive intentions of Germany's role or its leaders." While trying to protect himself, he refrained from accusing Hitler, still being under his spell, or claiming to be. In focusing on the Jewish question, it can also be doubted that Ribbentrop pleaded with Hitier strongly, if at all, for a revision of the anti-Semitic principles of the Party, trying to influence him toward "evolution" and a mere *numerus clausus.*

Like Joachim von Ribbentrop, Alfred Rosenberg, author of the *Mythos des Zwanzigsten Jahrhunderts,*[30] which sold more than a million copies, widely acknowledged "theoretician" of National Socialism and also executor of brutal Nazi wartime policies in the East, was sentenced to death at Nuremberg. He wrote *Lezte Aufzeichnunaen. Ideale und Idole der National-Socialistischen Revolution,* expecting that the Nuremberg judgment would soon lead to the loss of his life. It was posthumously published in 1955. He conceded that National Socialism was the "content" of his active life, emphasizing that he served the Third Reich loyally despite its errors and human shortcomings. He reaffirmed his "admiration" for Hitler, but admitted that in the course of time he had lost influence with him. In any case,

Hitler was a "demonic figure of formidable format" in the history of mankind and he still felt "compassion for his end" in the garden of the Chancellry—a fall which he found difficult to comprehend.

Rosenberg lambasted the Nuremberg trial. While conceding that events in the concentration camps were "inconceivable," he tried to trivialize "conspiracy" charges against himself and the other Nazi bosses. He claimed that Hitler's "humanity" had always been the object of his admiration and that "sharp" prewar utterances of the Führer against the Jews did not mean that he had actually planned their annihilation.

His own role in wartime Eastern Europe Alfred Rosenberg buried into complete silence. For years he had allegedly protested against some policies and measures, but admitted the accusation that in regard to the Jewish question not having acted similarly. He himself was convinced only that after 1933 a "separation" of German Jewry from the German people was in the interest of both. He had to concede, however, that at one time he had suggested to kill in retaliation for one German soldier not one hundred Frenchmen but only one hundred Jews.

His overwhelmingly apologetic attitude toward Hitler and sharp criticism of other prominent Nazis was merely to underline his increasing distance from Hitler. All this was written for the apparent purpose of exculpating himself and minimizing his own responsibility for his brutal regime in war-torn Eastern Europe. His writings, while incarcerated, were designed to justify his working in a leading fashion as ideologue and practitioner of National Socialism, to uphold Hitler's domestic and foreign policies, and, while accusing Hitler's coterie, to hold on to the vanished glory of Hitler's accomplishments, He also accused the Western Powers for their alliance with the Soviet Union, ignoring Hitler's own tie-up with Stalin between 1939–1941.

Albert Speer and the Nuremberg Trial

Another accused standing in the dock in Nuremberg was Albert Speer. According to Speer, *Inside the Third Reich (1970–71)*[31], Hitler before 1933 had announced

> that a few years later he would burn down Jewish synagogues, involve Germany in a war and kill Jews and political opponents, he would at one blow have lost me and probably most of the adherents he won after 1930.

Speer later blamed "the superficiality of his [own] attitude" and castigated his own "frivolity and thoughtlessness."

> By entering Hitler's party, I had already in essence assumed a responsibility that led directly to the brutalities of forced labor, to the destructions of war, and to the death of those millions of so-called undesirable stock—to the crushing of justice and the elevations of every evil.

To use his own words, Speer tried to "compartmentalize" his mind.

> On the one hand, there was the vulgar business of carrying out a policy proclaimed in the anti-Semitic slogan printed on streamers over the entrance to towns. On the other hand there was my idealized picture of Hitler. I wanted to keep those two apart.

As Speer revealed, he had been asked after his release from Spandau what he actually knew of the persecution, the deportation, and the annihilation of the Jews. For a long time he had tried to avoid these questions. But he no longer tried to do so; he averred that "in the final analysis, I myself determined the degree of my isolation, the extremity of my evasions, and the extent of my ignorance." In his *Memoirs* he admitted:

> Whether I knew or did not know, or how much or little I knew, is totally unimportant when I consider what horror I ought to have known about it and what conclusions would have been the natural ones to draw from the little I did know.

In the end he was convinced that no justification, "no apologies, are possible."

Speer tried to focus on distinction of "our tyranny" from all historical precedents focusing on "technocracy which had without compunction used all its knowledge in an assault on humanity." It enabled people to transmit commands to the lowest organs which the latter had "executed uncritically" and "shrouded in a degree of secrecy." Hitler, according to Speer, was the first to be able to employ the implements of technology to multiply crime.

In Speer's final view, as expressed in his *Memoirs*, he had participated in a war "which, as we of the intimate circle should never have doubted, was aimed at world domination." As Speer realized rather late, he was "part of [Hitler's] dream to subjugate the other nations." He had heard Hitler many times say that France was to be reduced to "a small nation," Belgium, Holland, even Burgundy to be incorporated into the Reich, Poles and Soviet Russians to be made into "helot peoples." "Nor, for one who wanted to listen, had Hitler ever concealed his intention to exterminate the Jewish people." Although Speer "never actually agreed" with Hitler on these questions, he had, nevertheless, designed the buildings and produced the weapons which served his ends.

According to Speer, the nine months of trials at Nuremberg had left their mark on "all the defendants." Even Göring who had entered the trial with an aggressive determination to justify himself, admitted in his final speech the terrible crimes that had been brought to light, condemned the ghastly mass murders, and declared that he could not comprehend them. Needless to say that all the defendants for obvious reasons hoped to sway the final judgment in their favor. Keitel asserted that he would rather choose death than be entangled again in such horrors. Frank spoke of the guilt that Hitler and the German people had laden upon themselves and warned the incorrigibles against "political folly" which "must lead to destruction and death." Even Julius Streicher in his final harangue condemned Hitler's "mass killings of Jews." Frank spoke of frightful crimes that filled him with profound shame. Schacht declared that he had stood "shaken" to the depth of his soul by the unspeakable misery which he had tried to prevent. Sauckel was "shocked in his utmost soul by the crimes that had been revealed in the course of the trial. Seyss-Inquart spoke of "fearful excesses." On the other hand, they all denied their own share or knowledge of the misdeeds and may simply have tried to escape the worst punishment.

There is little doubt that Speer at the time of his trial in Nuremberg and subsequently shrewdly presented himself as a mere technician, trying to distance himself from the others in the Nazi pantheon. In the book *Albert Speer, Das Ende eines Mythos*, Munich, 1982, which also appeared in English, the German historian Mathias Schmidt, has drawn attention to Speer's "ambivalence" and his endeavor to picture himself as the very honorableness among the Nazi leaders. In chapter 12 of this book, *Speer and the Final Solution*, (New York, 1981), M. Schmidt proves convincingly that—as the American historian Erich Goldhagen had indicated before—-Speer was guilty of more than mere approval of the persecution of the Jews and the murder of millions of them. He had been actively involved in the Jewish apartment evictions in the capital, though realizing the ultimate fate of the inhabitants. In a handwritten letter to Himmler he had expressed his "delight" that the inspection of concentration camps by two of his assistants had "resulted in a highly positive picture" He later heard Himmler's speech to SS leaders that the goal was to make "this [Jewish] nation vanish from the face of the earth." But for the sake of his own survival and that of the reputation of the German people, he was determined to manipulate the historic record.

While Ribbentrop and Speer escaped the hangman, Dr. Hans Frank, though avoiding condemnation on point one of the indictment by the International Military Tribunal in Nuremberg, conspiracy for planning World War II, was found guilty on points three and four, war crimes, and crimes against humanity, condemned to death by hanging, and executed on October 16, 1946.

Born in Karlsruhe, Baden, in 1900, participant in the abortive Hitler-Putsch on November 9, 1923, and fugitive from Germany, a member of the NSDAP since 1927, he became a *Reichstag* deputy in 1930, Bavarian Minister of Justice in 1933, and two years later Reich Minister without portfolio. In 1939 he served as chief of Civil Administration in Poland and later as *Generalgouverneur*, not to mention in many other capacities, as Commissar for *Reichsjustiz*, President of the Academy for German Law, and Reichsführer of the National Socialist League of Lawyers.

Facing the gallows, he wrote his confession *Im Angesicht des Galgens* (1953)[31b] in the Nuremberg *Justizgefängnis*, turned then to the Roman Catholic faith, and admitted his and Hitler's guilt for the terrifying crimes committed. He saw the root of the evil in Hitler's hostility to Christianity. But he frequently wavered between faulting the Führer and his continuing admiration for his "genius" and early accomplishments. Frank recalled that as a young man, "without knowledge of the world," he had fallen for Hitler and the Nazi propaganda. He never completely escaped the fatal attraction. To Frank, Hitler appeared as a "gigantic knight." But he turned energy into violence, power into brutality, dreams of hope into terrible, hate-filled nightly visions. Where love is missing, there is only the "realm of the devil." Hitler had "no conscience and no knowledge" (*wissenlos*). He was both a "superman" and an "*Untermensch*" [subhuman creature]. He was a "self-assured obsessed fanatic," "a demonic being"; a "satanic" figure. But Frank was still gripped by reverence and dedication to the Führer.

While he did not acquit Hitler and had contempt for his paladins, he occasionally blamed the Poles, Russians, Czechs, and the Allies. In spite of all the foregoing negative characteristics of the Führer, Frank hinted that there were other traits. Without such an assumption it remained "incomprehensible how a great, highly advanced people as the Germans could succumb to such a depravity." Frank was still not quite prepared to accept the image of the Führer as painted by his "deadly enemies."

Though admitting that he had been an anti-Semite, Frank denounced in his autobiography the perversity and inhumanity of the mass murder of the Jews. He also excoriated the maltreatment of other peoples, including the killing of many Germans. "An Austrian of some questionable descent," Frank compared Hitler with the Pied Piper of Hameln (Rattenfänger) who had promised to kill all the rats of the town, but made such wonderful music that he attracted all boys and girls, young men and women, leading them into death. For Hitler not only Jews, but occasionally all human beings were only "bacilli of the planet earth." Hitler was responsible for the destruction of the Reich and of Europe itself.[31c]

Frank referred to Hitler's testament in which he revealed that he had decided to kill the Jews because they allegedly had unleashed war—a revelation sweeping away all claims of "innocence" of the Führer by his apologists. Hitler's death sentence against the Jews, an entire people, was a "terrible deed." Frank acknowledged in Nuremberg Hitler's and also his own guilt for the murder of several million innocent human beings who were annihilated because of a "hideous collective judgment." This was a Nazi secret, Frank claimed, that was kept even from top leaders such as himself. Hitler thought that the knowledge of it could be limited to " a few people." As far as the Poles were concerned, Frank also claimed, again with little persuasion, that he had wished to treat them more rationally and humanely—a self-serving Judgment repudiated by the court. The latter recalled that on several occasions between October 3, 1939 to 1944 Frank had suggested that Poland be treated like a colony, that leading representatives of the Polish intelligentsia be annihilated because of potential resistance to German domination, and that he himself was responsible for the willful deportation of more than a million of Polish workers into the Reich and for the mass murder of three million Jews. Hitler himself, fear-ridden that he had "Jewish blood," had ordered Frank to investigate this matter confidentially and that Frank's own conclusion had been that it was "not completely impossible" that Hitler's father was perhaps a "half-Jew"—which would have made Hitler a "quarter-Jew."

Another codefendant at the Nuremberg International Military Tribunal, who wrote the book *Ich glaubte an Hitler* (Zürich, 1967) and spoke at length about the German and European Jews and their annihilation was Baldur von Schirach, of German and American ancestry, in his own words "three-quarters American." Since 1933 Youth Leader of the Reich NSDAP and since 1940 governor of the Vienna Gau, he showed at the Nuremberg trial remorse, but was actually responsible for the deportation and killing of Jews and others.

What did attract Schirach to Hitler? As he wrote, "He was the unknown soldier with the Iron Cross first class. This counted for us." In his own words Schirach was "anti-Semitic" and joined the party at the age of eighteen. Trying to excuse himself, he added that "no one had warned him" against the Nazi bible, Hitler's *Mein Kampf.* Glancing back, Schirach raised the question why he "hated" Jews. The seventeen-year old Baldur read the anti-Jewish pamphlet, *The International Jew* by Henry Ford, and thereafter the books by Arthur de Gobineau and H. St. Chamberlain, and Theodor Fritsch. The notorious Jew-hater and pornographer Julius Streicher, the "Frankenführer," also played a major role in winning him over to anti-Semitism.* But he denied any influence by his parents who actually had befriended individual Jews. Schirach claimed, however, that only a "few thinking human beings in Germany possessed sufficient phantasy to think through" the fighting slogan "Juda verrecke" [Judah perish]; this was the battle cry of the marching SA and SS. "We have not thought through much at that time."

In conversation with Hitler, Schirach had raised the question of the Jews and the party program, which did not spell out annihilation—whereupon Hitler told him not to worry about it. The program did not bind the party "one way or the other, once we have attained power." In his concluding defense at Nuremberg Schirach assumed full responsibility since he had "believed in Hitler." At the same time he wished to acquit German youth which had just grown up in

* In his biography, however, Schirach conceded that at Nuremberg even Streicher's co-defendants avoided talking with him, trying to distance themselves from him.

an "anti-Semitic state." But he expressed the hope that Auschwitz would signify "the end of anti-Semitism." Hitler's "racial policy was a crime"; this policy became "a disaster for over five million Jews and for all Germans"—of course in different degrees.

On important matters, especially Jews and Austria, Hitler did not tolerate contradiction. Schirach's wife, Henriette, the daughter of Hitler's photographer and friend Heinrich Hoffmann, whom the Führer had known since her childhood, was shaken by what she had observed in Amsterdam and, despite warnings by her husband, brought the matter up with Hitler. He bluntly told her in public to avoid "sentimental prattle." "Why do you worry about these Jewish women?"[31c]

In 1940 Schirach was assigned to Austria to become the governor of the Vienna Gau, one of the districts in which the country was divided after the *Anschluss* of 1938. Schirach, however, did not quite fulfill Hitler's expectations in Vienna, since he was allegedly too lenient and pursued a "pro-Austrian" policy. Hitler once burst out, regretting that he had taken the Viennese into the *Grossdeutsches Reich.* Schirach claimed that he was left at the Vienna post for tactical and "optical" reasons only. When he had started his assigment in Vienna, there were after a mass emigration of Jews only about 60,000 of them left in the city. Hitler allegedly told him that the Vienna Jews would be settled in the East in self-contained areas, and he trusted him and Dr. Hans Frank, *Generalgouverneur* in part of former Poland. That Schirach entertained some illusions and nurtured self-deception can be observed also in his speech to the International Youth Congress on September 14, 1942, when he called for the formation of a European Peoples Community in which the small nationalities would have equal rights with the great powers—a promise which ran counter to Nazi ideology and practice—but still excluded the removal of all Jews from Vienna.

Schirach witnessed at Nuremberg the testimony of Rudolf Höss, former commander of the concentration camp Auschwitz, disclosing terrible crimes. Schirach was finally compelled to "destroy the Hitler myth to make clear to the youth that I had educated them [to revere] a false idol." Thus he declared before the court on May 24, 1946.

> This is the greatest and most satanic murder in world history. Höss was only the henchman, Adolf Hitler commanded the murder. He and Himmler have jointly committed this crime which remains for ever a blot in our history.[31d]

This confession actually disregarded the complicity of the German power élites and of hundreds of thousands of Germans. Again Schirach concluded with the unconvincing excuse that German youth was "innocent," since it did not know anything of the annihilation of the Jews. In court he admitted: "We saw mountains of corpses, famished human beings, undernourished children, shorn women; horror and misery were shown to us, images which still stand before our eyes."

Schirach was pronounced guilty on count four of the indictment, crimes against humanity, and was sentenced to twenty years imprisonment.

Germans, Non-Germans, and Refugees on German Guilt

It was the accusation leveled at the Germans that they were guilty for the outbreak of wars twice in the twentieth century and of the atrocities and bore collective responsibility which was resented by the German public. Specific Allied policies of the first postwar years such as prohibition for many Germans of engaging in certain professions, suppression of rightist and nationalist and outright Nazi views, and trials of war criminals and imprisonments were sharply criticized by those affected and by other Germans. But in the first post-war months after the collapse of the Nazi regime the Allies unleashed a campaign showing the German population posters with the inscription: "This is your guilt." Field Marshal Montgomery proclaimed:

> This time the Allies were resolved to teach you a final lesson; not only that you are defeated—that you would have in the end recognized—but that you and your people are guilty of the outbreak of this war. Our soldiers have seen terrible things. You say you are not responsible. But these leaders have sprung from the German people. This people is responsible for the leaders.

Thus, the Germans were made accountable for the decisions and acts during the war, though the main American prosecuting attorney at Nuremberg, H. Jackson, had declared at the opening of the Nuremberg trial on November 21, 1945, that it was not the Allied contention to accuse the entire German people. The Germans and Allied opponents of the thesis of Germany's collective guilt asserted that "fascism" was not a German but rather an international phenomenon which had also emerged in the West. Still, in the first post-war years the Western world, including the countries neutral during the war, were shocked at the crimes of the national-socialist regime and its enormity and considered the deliberate planned killing of millions of innocent people as an unprecedented crime. They found it hard to believe that the people of the *Dichter und Denker* [poets and thinkers] had turned into the country of *Richter und Henker* [judges and executioners].

The question of the German people's guilt for the outbreak of World War II and for the atrocities committed during the war became a widely disputed topic in the German press as well as in international public opinion. It was also a much debated topic among German émigrés. The least importance it had for the Germans who had gone into exile in the Soviet Union. The *Internationale Literatur, Deutsche Blätter* in Moscow was since 1933 the main organ of official Soviet opinion which the German paper religiously espoused and from which it did not deviate. The by far greater portion of the emigration from the Third Reich had gone to the U.S. There, in New York, in the weekly *Aufbau*, since 1939 under the editorship of Manfred George, Emil Ludwig in the summer of 1942 stressed the necessity to deprive postwar Germany of power for the sake "of the protection of the world." The known evangelical theologian Paul Tillich, however, appealed to all "decent [*anständig*] Jews in America" to distance themselves from Emil Ludwig* Among Germans, however, Friedrich Wilhelm Foerster, known author, convinced European federalist and sharp opponent of German nationalism, turned against the former SPD deputy Gerhart Seger, asserting that militaristic Pangertnanism was a widespread sickness, a collective obsession which had affected even German Social Democracy.

The Archbishop of Canterbury and Hans Grimm

On November 29, 1945, the Archbishop of Canterbury had broadcast a message to the German people, reminding them that they were "not alone in suffering" at the present time: "In the evil days your armies brought destruction to your neighbors and they along with you suffer from the harsh process by which their liberation and yours was achieved." "For many years," he went on, "you have pinned your faith

---

* Hannah Arendt, a successor to Manfred George as editor of the *Aufbau*, warned in an article in the *Jewish Frontier* (January 1945), which was widely disseminated in Germany after the war, against the unwillingness to distinguish between "good" and "bad" Germans.

on one man, to one doctrine, and they have led you into the abyss." In his rejoinder the nationalist author Hans Grimm recalled that the Archbishop previously had publicly declared that for five years no peace should be concluded with Germany. Now, Grimm, turning the table, claimed that Germans were "compulsively silenced," had experienced expulsion from Silesia, Pomerania, East Prussia and the Mark Brandenburg as well as from North-Bohemia, where Austrian Germans were "persecuted and robbed."[32]

In his own defense, Grimm claimed that his book *People without Room* which had been immensely popular in the 1920s and had been hailed by Nazis and Rightists, had been misunderstood. He himself had not been a member of the NSDAP, though the had defended the "biological view of foreign policy." He asserted, furthermore, that most historians were "definitely the victims of bias." Past British fears of Germany were plainly "superstitious." In the inter-war period Grimm had spent some time in England. He had always admired the British people but had finally concluded that "the growing aversion of the British to the Germans bore a strong resemblance to the developing aversion felt by Germans for the Jews"!

As a matter of fact, Grimm repeatedly defended National Socialism as it existed in its "early days." "It was then a moral [!], one might even say, a religious rather than a political movement." It was "trying, even unconsciously, to consummate the imperfect German Reformation begun by Luther." National Socialism did not lose its distinct religious character until the war was well advanced.

At the time of his writing, the knowledge of the mass murder of German and East European Jews and of Nazi atrocities was widespread and virtually indisputable. Thus Grimm wrote,

> The aversion against the Jews requires an explanation because of its atrocious consequences. For it seems that the inhuman atrocities committed against the Jews under the later [!] Hitlerism excuse and justify every sin which has been and is being committed against Germany, and that they substantiate *a priori* every false [!] abominable charge raised against the German people.

Having made again a sharp distinction between the allegedly noble early National Socialism and its later stages, Grimm totally ignored the indissoluble ties between both, the rabid Jew-hatred practiced already in 1933–34 and the anti-Jewish Nuremberg legislation in 1935 which decreed the pariah status of German Jewry. Superstition, Grimm continued, played a part in this antipathy to the Jews, a superstition allegedly similar to that which England cherished against the Germans in the middle of the 1890s! Grimm disregarded that this English antipathy had not materialized in any anti-German legislation in the United Kingdom.

Prior and during World War I Jews had flocked in increasing numbers into the Reich. These immigrant Jews, Grimm claimed, "elbowed out the middle class and yet remained foreigners." Some of the Eastern Jews brought with them "sharp business practices" and sowed the "seeds of political corruption" in Germany. "In its arrogance the Jewish fungus adulterated, disturbed and contaminated the mind and the behavior of the Germans." All this, rather reminiscent of Heinrich von Treitschke's utterances half a century earlier, was in Grimm's view apparently a fitting epitaph to the Holocaust.

After 1933 Grimm himself had gotten into trouble with the Nazi regime. From the start he allegedly rebelled against the chosen Führer, "the superficiality of his Austrian [!] character, his voracious and rambling mind," and was shocked by "horrifying events such as the suppression of the Röhm revolt" in 1934 and the "spontaneous [?] popular uprising against the Jews" on the night of November 10, 1938, the so-called *Kristallnacht*, when Jewish temples were burned to the ground. But on the basis of his own personal experience Grimm could not discern anything positively evil in National Socialism "between pre-war 1933 and the start of the war in 1939." He also went so far as to justify the peacetime foreign policy of Hitler, including the *Anschluss* of Austria and the establishment of a "protectorate" over Bohemia and Moravia.

In the 1930s independent Czechoslovakia, Grimm continued, was in view of its dealings with Russia, a potential threat to Germany. Though "the appalling fate of the Jews and the crimes perpetrated against them weighed on my soul like lead," he decried Pastor Niemoeller who used the "propaganda figure" of six million Jews having been killed by the Nazis. While Germans invaded the Netherlands, Belgium, Denmark and Norway, the Reich government merely tried "to force England" more quickly. Grimm bitterly complained about the destruction of German cities by aerial bombardment without ever raising the question of the earlier bombing of British cities such as Coventry and London and of the mass bombing in the East. He never ceased lamenting the fate of Germany and the Germans! While he occasionally recoiled from the "gruesome mass slaughter of the Jews" which had "allegedly" happened, he tried to balance this by quotations from the Old Testament when Jews acted in accordance with Jehovah's harsh commandments against gentiles. When he referred to the supposedly decent behavior of Germans in occupied France—no mention of Oradour, the killings by the Gestapo and the forcible transport of French workers to Germany—he relied on the questionable testimony of his own son! Quite similar in character were numerous little stories told of some villages and little towns in wartime Germany which were supposed to belie the thesis of widespread venomous anti-Semitism in the Reich.

The harsh treatment of Germany after 1945 was reduced by Grimm to pure Allied vengefulness and retaliation and "terrible willful misunderstanding." He particularly resented the "lack of respect for German feelings as a nation." He did not blame the German masses, but rather masses everywhere! He recalled that for more than a thousand years the German Reich had been the rampart of Europe against the East. During all this time Germans had clung to the Christian faith, "never mind about Hitler." "Germany in the past had not only thought about her own security, but about that of Europe in its entirety."

Grimm was not unaware that Germany "must accept the fact that for decades we shall be barred from the intellectual world as pariahs," but he recalled the great Germans of the past and the debt the world owed to them. He also expressed his appreciation of a remark by the English historian E. H. Carr, but omited to quote the following German couplet, in the latter's view so "characteristic of the Nazi spirit":

> Und möchst Du nicht mein Bruder sein
> So schlag ich Dir den Schädel ein.*[33]

Grimm warned England that a maltreatment of Germany and the Germans would only "proletarianize" the German nation and ruin Germany as well as damage British interests, indeed the interests

*And if you don't want to be my brother, I'll beat your brains out.

of all of Europe. Having justified Hitler's policy of conquering all of Europe, Grimm claimed to be a "good European" and interested in the genuine unification of Europe. Victorious Allies demanded the "indiscriminate condemnation of everything that can be brought under the heading of 'wicked German nationalism' and 'wicked militarism'." While Hitlerism was criticized, the Führer, himself "untutored" as he was, was credited with having "rightly divined the political forces in every country of Europe." His "curse" was only that "Great Britain and the British politicians misunderstood him and Germany."[34]

Thus, "in the fight against the mass, the Führer himself succumbed to it and to a personal demagogic insanity." But despite shifting blame onto England and English politicians, Grimm occasionally voiced his alleged admiration for England—following thus Hitler's example!

German Defense and Responsibility

Nazi imperialistic domination of non-German countries and their excesses found a good number of Germans trying to defend them. One of the earliest shrill and chauvinist German reactions to the West and its policies in the wake of the catastrophic Nazi debacle came from Heinrich Hauser's *The German Talks Back.*[35] A non-Nazi, but stridently nationalistic German who had spent the war years in the U.S., he returned after the war to his native country. The political scientist Hans J. Morgenthau in the introduction to the "angry" book warned that it would be "infuriating reading for Americans."

The author, a firm believer in Prussian values, so much denounced by Germany's enemies prior and during two world wars, endorsed the philosophy of Prussianism, the essence of which, according to Morgenthau, was "militarism, imperialism, autocracy" and "more than this."

According to Morgenthau, Hauser may not have spoken for the German people as a whole, but he spoke for the politically active intellectual élite who have tried to express what millions of Nazis and non-Nazi Germans have felt and thought at least since the beginning of the 1930s. In Morgenthau's words, their "barbarism," signifying a primitive level of the human mind, did not fit at all the Germans, "a highly gifted nation, second to none in sciences and technology." Hauser held that if a great nation turned away from God and dedicated itself to evil things, there applied only one term, "Satanism." It is of some interest that German scholars such as F. Meinecke and G. Ritter and H. Morgenthau, a German-Jewish refugee scholar in the U.S., despairing of finding a valid rational explanation for the rise of Nazism, under the impact of unprecedented atrocious happenings hit upon the same "explanation," "the devil theory."

Another book about the German question appeared soon after the end of the war and was also originated abroad, beyond Germany's linguistic boundaries, in Mexico. Alexander Abusch, a communist, published there *Der Irrweg einer Nation* in 1945.[36] In their books, Adolf Hitler and Alfred Rosenberg had, according to Abusch, elaborated a theory of "dehumanization" and a plan of staging a surprise attack against the world, aiming at its "domination." National Socialism far exceeded the reactionary character of traditional Prussianism, sweeping away its definite conception of honor and guarantees for at least a limited security and legality. It reached back into the Middle Ages. "Then in times of famine, pestilence and other diseases the rulers of Germany let some witches burn" or organized pogroms against the Jews for having caused misfortune. Hitler's "witch" was the "international Jew" who in his mind was guilty of every crime and misdeed under the sun.

Of Hitler's "realm of Hell" remained only the corpses of famished victims, depots full of their clothing and shoes and among them quite small shoes of children. Maidanek, Oswiecim, Mauthausen, Buchenwald, Belsen-Bergen, Dachau and other camps of annihilation merged into "a picture inextinguishable in German history." The Germans themselves lacked the strength to overthrow "the Reich of bestiality" which had "grown from the dreams of criminal brains to reality on German soil."

During the years 1933–39 the German people was transformed into an instrument of threatening the world. Just because the opponents of Hitlerism were strong before 1933, their co-responsibility for the following terrible events was very great. The entire bungled history of the German nation had become an object of German criticism and self-examination and needed a thorough purification. Germans must now "repair" the crimes that German hands committed. Though Marxist-Stalinist views dominated Abusch's account, there is a greater degree of shame and self-accusation here than was customary in contemporary or subsequent communist accounts of the Nazi era in German history. Communist propaganda, not yet fully coordinated, had not yet had time to make a full impact, shifting most of the guilt on the ruling classes.

In 1946 the philosopher Karl Jaspers offered in *Die Schuldfrage* [The Question of Guilt] the most comprehensive analysis of the guilt problem.[37] The booklet was widely applauded in Germany and abroad by people of different ideological persuasions. Jaspers differentiated between four different concepts of guilt. There was first the criminal guilt consisting in violation of law to be punished in court. Second, there was political guilt by statesmen the consequences of which citizens must bear. It is punished by the victor who takes account of natural law and international law, decrees of reparation (*Wiedergutmachung*) as far as possible, and imposed limitations of political power and political rights. Third, there is moral guilt; every human being bears moral responsibility for acts committed. That "command is command" is no valid excuse for executing immoral orders. Repentance and renewal are in order. Fourth, there exists finally a metaphysical guilt. There is or should be solidarity between individuals which makes everyone responsible for every injustice in the world. Jaspers acknowledged only "a political guilt of the entire German people." He rejected the concept of collective guilt, since "a people as such does not exist."

One of the most gripping factual and autobiographical accounts of *The SS State* (Stockholm) was published in 1947 by Eugen Kogon, himself an inmate of Nazi concentration camps. There was, according to Kogon, hardly a German in the Third Reich who did not know that the jails were overcrowded and that people were relentlessly executed. Thousands of judges and police employees, lawyers, and pastors knew that the dimensions of the misdeeds were horrendous. Many business people who were making deliveries to SS camps, industrialists who demanded from the Main Economics and Administration Office and concentration camps slaves for the plants, employers of labor offices, knew what was going on.

> Not a few civilians, who were active on the margins of concentration camps, extraordinarily uneasy German soldiers and Field Gendarmes were aware of the terrible atrocities in the camps, ghettos, cities and villages of the East.

Gerd Tellenbach, Professor of History at the University of Heidelberg, authored the booklet *Die deutsche Not als Schuld und Schicksal* (1947).[38] As he wrote,

> As a German one would have preferred to be silent, since

> after everything that has happened, our people stands in deepest mistrust and has little chance to be heard. Germans have lived with the same disgust as people everywhere else, and with even greater horror,

since one felt responsible for the crimes of a leadership against which one was perhaps helpless, which, however, still large segments of the people, giving their consent to it, have helped to power. Also the inhuman cruelties against the Jews have been condemned by Germans as well as all decent human beings.

Not as deeply entangled as Albert Speer, Eugen Kogon, and Gerd Tellenbach, and partly on opposing sides, was the Swiss historian Walther Hofer.[39] His attempt to distinguish between the German national character and Nazi legacy were evident, but his rejection of National Socialism, including its Jew-hatred, was total (*Nationalsozialismus und die deutsche Geschichte*, 1957, also 1972). The question of the relationship between the two phenomena was by no means only of historical interest. Both the Nazis and the victorious powers agreed that National Socialism was the logical outgrowth of everything which was genuinely German. National Socialism had proclaimed to be the heritage of all Germans, starting with Luther, Frederick the Great, the Freiherr vom Stein, Scharnhorst, Gneisenau, Clausewitz, Bismarck, and Friedrich Nietzsche and Richard Wagner. Only Goethe with his cosmopolitanism and humanitarian ideal was rejected by the Nazis. The spirit of the Prussian state and the Prussian army were glorified by Nazism. Thomas Mann had rejected the thesis of a bad and good German. There was only one German who through the devil's cunning became the worst. Similarly, Benedetto Croce called the history of the German spirit demonic and tragic.

Walther Hofer believed that the key of German development lay in the essence of Romanticism. He pointed out that the antidemocratic movement in the wake of World War I had a generally European character, though specifically strong German traits in it were undeniable. Regarding the history of totalitarianism, Frenchmen, Russians, and others have greatly contributed to its growth. Nationalism, militarism, and imperialism were by no means a peculiarly German phenomenon, though they have spilled over the shores of German national history. The historical balance of twelve years of national-socialist domination has been "terrible." The soldiers of the USSR stand at the Elbe and Europe was exposed to the greatest threat in its history. "The German name is burdened with the greatest crimes of human history and has been sullied in a formidable manner." Twelve years have sufficed to squander a hundred years of historic labor.

Erich Kordt, the author among other books of *Wahn und Wirklichkeit* (1948),[40] served in the German Foreign Office and held several diplomatic posts abroad. In the years 1943–44, while in Shanghai, he started writing a comprehensive study of Hitler's foreign policy and after his return to Germany in the autumn of 1946 he decided on the publication of his book. Dr. Karl Heinz Abshagen, foreign correspondent in several West European capitals and in the Far East, made several contributions to the study. In the second edition of the work Kordt voiced his views that a critical treatment, free from glossing over the "aberrations of the immediate past," should contribute to the regaining of the "valuable German intellectual forces," help to overcome "hatred and bitterness," and lead Germans to "a positive collaboration at the future of our continent and of a more peaceful world."

While following the First World War the thesis of the Germans' sole guilt for its outbreak was soon challenged, a similar result for the study of the history and pre-history of the Second World War was not to be expected. After that war the representatives of the Allies have not stopped proclaiming the guilt of Hitler and his coterie. But going beyond it, they have made the entire German people responsible for past events. Kordt referred to the American Secretary Henry Morgenthau and Lord Vansittart, the influential official at the British Foreign Office, and to Foreign Minister Anthony Eden. Focusing on the growing role during the war of Himmler and of Reinhardt Heydrich—the latter charged by Hitler with the murder of the Jewry of Germany and of much of Europe—the author condemned Hitler for the "mechanical, passionless, and thereafter only more terrible insanity."

While Kordt's account of the Nazi atrocities and crimes reflects their impact upon a professionally sensitive German diplomat, an assessment by a British historian, Ian Kershaw, writing in the Bonn Republic about the same misdeeds more than two decades later, mirrors the ambivalent if not indifferent reaction of the German public to the annihilation of German and European Jews.

In Volume II of *Bayern in der NS-Zeit*, edited by Martin Broszat and Elke Fröhlich, Ian Kershaw, writing on "Antisemitismus und Volksmeinung. Reaktionen auf die Judenverfolgung."[41] pointed to the central role of anti-Semitism in the national-socialist *Weltanschauung*. He held that despite a burgeoning literature on Hitler, the fundamental philosophical views of national-socialist Jewish policy and the events of persecution some basic questions had been neglected by the scholars. Distinguishing between "latent and dynamic anti-Semitism," the author concluded the dynamic "Jew-haters were probably only a small percentage of the population," but "the number of real friends of the Jews was probably even smaller." Anti-Semitism was not decisively combatted by any German social group, special interest or philosophically engaged circle.

The churches had considerable influence upon the population but used their influence "most only in purely church affairs." The protest in regard to the Jewish question in 1933 followed strictly theological points of view. Ambivalent in its own position and uncertain about the possible resonance in the population, the "official" church restricted itself in its commentary about the persecution of the Jews. That the regime treated the "Endlösung" of the Jewish question in a strictly secret manner proves that the national-socialist leadership could not count on popular support of mass murder. Still, the latter cannot be ascribed only to the criminal ideological insanity of Hitler, Himmler, Heydrich, and other leaders of the Third Reich. The "final solution" could not have been possible without the preceding steps of the elimination of the Jews from German society, which had taken place in the full light of public life and in form of the anti-Jewish legislation and had been approved by large segments of the German population.

II

THE POST-WAR GERMANIES AND THE REBIRTH OF EXTREMIST NATIONALISM.

ALLIED OCCUPATION AND THE REVIVAL OF GERMAN NATIONALIST PROPAGANDA

In the post-World War I era, the Weimar period and following the military collapse after World War II, traditionally conservative groups, monarchists, National Liberals, many members of which were strongly nationalistic and imperialist-minded, looked upon Germany's defeat as the consequence of a "total stab in the back," the result of alleged treachery. They hoped to repeat the successes scored after World War I with this propaganda. The most radical foes of Imperial Germany were Conservative Revolutionaries who saw the deeper roots of the debacle in the alleged lack of authoritarianism and lack in consistent nationalist-imperialist strivings and achievements. After World War I they had been supported by freebooter armies, the Free Corps and the many fighting leagues (*Kampfbünde*)—the members of which battled Slav border raiders—and volunteers fighting Communist insurrections. Many of these groups in turn had been inspired by the potentially rebellious prewar German youth.

After World War I some German territories were ceded to the enemy, others were temporarily occupied. But Germany retained her sovereign status. A major goal of the total Allied occupation of Germany after 1945, however, was her demilitarization and denazification. In view of the totalitarian character of the Nazi regime, it had left a lasting imprint on the German psyche. Ten percent of the German population had been members of the NSDAP and millions were members of various auxiliary or associated organizations. Thus, denazification posed formidable problems for the occupying powers. It led in March 1946 to the turning over of the entire denazification process to the Germans themselves. In October 1946 the law for the liberation from National Socialism and Militarism acknowledged fundamental gradations of German culpability for the outbreak of the war and the atrocities committed. It distinguished between five categories of the population: major offenders, offenders, lesser offenders, followers, and exonerated.

The first reactivation of German nationalist policies occurred while Germany was still divided into different zones of Allied occupation. In January 1946 in the British zone the journalist Heinrich Wulle, a monarchist, folkish-minded and anti-Semitic, had been linked with General Erich von Ludendorff and Gregor Strasser. A former *Reichstag* deputy from Pomerania, he had been imprisoned in 1938 and remained incarcerated for two years. In the postwar era he and Joachim von Ostarii founded the *Deutsche Aufbau Partei.*[1] A stronger element of Christian beliefs appeared then in Wulle's writings, but racism remained an important ingredient of his thought. While in the Nazi era his preoccupation with Teutons and Prussians was pronounced, after 1945 the notion of the *Abendland*, of Western civilization, marked his thought.

In the American zone of occupation Heinrich Leuchtgens, who had been a member of the Hessian diet in the Weimar period, was dismissed from his post in Friedberg. In the post-war period he founded a new party, the National Democratic Party (NDP). Though inveighing against National Socialism, he did not succeed in gaining the favor of American officials who denied him a publishing license, but in 1948 he published the *Nationaldemokrat.* The NDP turned finally from a conservative, nationalist and monarchist party into a radical nationalist party which gathered within its ranks incorrigible Nazis. When the British and the Americans were ready to turn the government over to the Germans, radical nationalists were prepared to wrest influence and power from the more moderate conservative German nationalists.

In 1949 the offices of Military Governors in the Germanies were closed. New German states emerged in the West, the German Federal Republic, and in the East, the German Democratic Republic. German Nationalism raised its head, though, in both states the Germans still remained under the strong influence and supervision of the Western powers and of the USSR respectively. But the growing self-assertion of the Germans, the rebirth of German nationalism in combination with the lingering among Germans of the ideological legacy of the Wilhelmian Reich and of the Third Reich produced a plethora of nationalist thought and rightist mini-parties and political groups as well as of cultural organizations.[2] About seventy-five political and interest groups were founded during the years 1949–1953. The Allied restrictions on German political life were abandoned, denazification practically ceased, and all licensing requirements by the Allies regarding publications were virtually abolished. This gave rise to the revival and the dissemination of extreme nationalist and also ill-disguised anti-Semitic propaganda.

American Spokesmen: General Lucius D. Clay and John J. McCloy, and German Political Leaders: Konrad Adenauer and Kurt Schumacher

In 1947 William L. Shirer reported in *The Washington Post* that the Germans were awaiting a new Führer, and the *New York Herald Tribune* and Delbert Clark informed the readers that "Neo-Nazism" was rising. Many Jewish organizations warned Jews to drop any thoughts of returning to Germany. General Lucius D. Clay, U.S. Military Governor of Germany, on the other hand, did not favor the emigration of Jews from Germany, considering it a "great mistake" for Jewish leaders to advocate such an "evacuation." But only a small minority of Jews shared this view. Close to 70,000 foreign Jews brought to Germany from Eastern Europe as slave laborers had survived, but these "displaced persons" (DPs) had no wish to remain in Germany. Nor did Jews wish to return to the Baltic region or the Ukraine, now again under Soviet rule. John J. McCloy, U.S. High Commissioner for Germany, recommended to the Germans that the real measure of a rejection of the past was the development of the old, allegedly tolerant attitude of the Germans towards the Jews. This was easier to talk about than to bring about.

Not all Germans had resumed the malicious Nazi propaganda against the Jews, but the great majority was not inclined to radically better their attitude toward them. Admittedly, the material and spiritual chaos in Germany at the end of the war, German homelessness and hunger, their being ill-clothed and ill-fed and their decline in productivity focused the Germans' immediate attention on their current misery rather than on the past misery at German hands of conquered and suppressed non-German peoples and of Jews in particular; this despite the urgings of the Allies to the Germans to try to make amends to the Jews and the realization of German guilt by many of the leaders and spokesmen of the post-war Germans, Kurt Schumacher and Konrad Adenauer.

Kurt Schumacher, leader of the Social Democratic Party in the post-war era, who himself had greatly suffered in concentration camps, said in 1947 in a conversation with fellow Germans he found that they had "never expected the degree to which Jews were persecuted in Germany." They declared "complete disapproval of persecutions."[3] These exchanges took place before the extent of the "great crimes against humanity" became known. At the same time Schumacher pledged that "the politically and racially persecuted [people] can count on the support of my party for equitable reparations." Having been long subjected to lying Nazi propaganda, post-war Germans were doubtful of any, including "Allied" propaganda and "reeducation" efforts. Disbelief of course, denying or minimizing Nazi crimes was a natural reaction, obviously dictated by self-interest.

Chancellor Konrad Adenauer, seventy-years years old, prewar mayor of Cologne, recalled that he had always been on "the best of terms with my Jewish fellow citizens." A Catholic and an enlightened man, he thus addressed the newly elected German parliament:

> Let me say a word about certain anti-Semitic tendencies once again discernible among us. We condemn these tendencies in the strongest possible terms. We consider it outrageous and incredible that after all that has happened under Nazism there should still be people in Germany to persecute or despise Jews for no other reason than that they are Jews.

Adenauer often recalled that Danny Heinemann, his former Jewish schoolmate, had offered him after his removal from office under Hitler financial assistance. As early as 1947 the first attempts by Adenauer to meet Chaim Weizmann, President of the new Israeli Republic, about reparations were rejected; the Jewish President did not wish to meet any German. The wounds inflicted upon his people had struck too deep and were not yet healed.

The Tortuous Road to "Wiedergutmachung"

Only in April 1951 two Israelis met Adenauer and accompanying diplomats in Paris.[4] It was not before September 27 of the same year that the German Chancellor appeared before the Bundestag suggesting that the relationship between the Jews and the German people be placed on a new and sound basis, taking into account "the terrible crimes of a past epoch." He promised that his government would undertake to educate the German people "in the spirit of human and religious tolerance" and would combat anti-Semitic groups with "rigorous and relentless punishment." The Federal Government was prepared to work out "a solution to the problem of material restitution and thus clear the way for a spiritual healing of this immense suffering."[5] Adenauer received much applause. With the exception of extreme Rightists and Communists, many deputies, even of the Bavarian party, welcomed and supported the statement of the Chancellor. Following a meeting in London between Konrad Adenauer and Nahum Goldmann, a Zionist, an American citizen, born in Poland and educated in Germany, an agreement was reached emphasizing that the settlement was primarily a "moral problem." In addition to Arab opposition to the agreement, there was also a German opposition, especially by businessmen who set high hopes upon the Arab trade. The cash payment for every murdered Jew, as Nahum Goldmann expressed it, amounted to a mere one thousand German marks! After overcoming the opposition in the Israeli parliament, consisting of the Herut party, the Communists, and other small groups, the Knesset decided to accept reparations from Germany. But details remained to be settled. After a meeting between the Foreign Minister Moshe Sharett and Konrad Adenauer in neutral Luxembourg, the Chancellor presented the treaty to the German parliament for ratification, which occurred on March 4, 1953. While the Christian Democrats and the Social Democrats voted for the agreement without reservations, the Free Democrats, closely allied with big business,[6] allowed its members to vote according to each delegate's 'conscience.' The only people opposed to it remained the extreme Right, two members of the neo-Nazi Socialist Reich Party, and the extreme Leftists and Communists. The latter followed the rigid Soviet line, repudiating any debt to the Jewish people and claiming that Soviet Communism had wiped out "fascism," the guilty party. The agreement was ratified by a vote of 238 of the 358 members of parliament. Thirty-four members opposed it and as many as 86 abstained! The foregoing settlement did not take note of individual claims of Jews in Germany. As one German official close to Adenauer told the author Norbert Mühlen in 1950:

> Whatever we do, it can never be enough. . . . We cannot make amends for the loss of someone's parents gassed at Auschwitz. . . . We cannot pay damages for the mental

> anguish, the emotional embitterment, the indignities and scare which the Nazis inflicted on our Jewish fellow citizens. Of course, we must try . . .

In his *Memoirs* (1953–55) Adenauer had spoken of normalizing relations with the Jews expressing the need for showing "German good will" through material help, but tried to avoid giving the impression that the "injustice" which had occurred could be "atoned" thereby.

Rightist Propaganda

Despite momentous changes in the post-war German political and intellectual life, extremist nationalist propaganda never fully disappeared from the German scene. Most of the nationalist activists after 1945 were either unrepentant Nazis or extreme chauvinists. Politically ambitious, they were seeking licensing from the occupation authorities and later from the German authorities. Among them were men like Joachim von Ostarii who led a splinter organization out of the DKP and wished to found the National Unity Party of Germany. Later he tried to create a League for German Renewal (*Bund für deutsche Erneuerung*). The British authorities, however, found the nascent organization "militaristic and chauvinistic," and denied him a license.[7]

Another activist in the British zone was Adolf von Thadden.[8] He planned to find followers among old traditionalist and nationalistic segments of the population, expellees and refugee groups and among the GUD (*Gemeinschaft unabhängiger Deutscher*). Major Otto E. Remer who on July 20, 1944, had played a role in foiling the plans of the anti-Hitler insurrectionists, proclaimed in the post-war period that National Socialism could not be crushed: "The idea marched on, Christendom did not end with the death of Christ either."

In the American zone extreme nationalists appealed primarily to Germans who were economically disaffected and resentful. Many among them had been prominent in the NSDAP or in ultraconservative politics and hoped for a political revival of extreme nationalism. This appeal was directed to the mass of declassés who were disgruntled, disfranchised and discredited individuals who had lost their employment. While the occupying powers in 1948–49 receded from the German arena, new opportunities arose thus for radical nationalist elements to appeal to the German electorate. Foremost among the new activists were the old German nationals who would claim some anti-Hitler activity in the Third Reich and younger Nazis who had been cleared under various amnesties such as individuals of the *Black Front*.[9]

One of the most unexpected developments of the post-war era was what one author called the "international of nationalism." As another observer remarked: "Out of the crisis of the nation state some nationalists in post-war Germany have developed the concept of a *Nation Europa*."[10] To some extent this ideology has not completely vanished from the contemporary German stage. After 1945, Germany, humiliated, divided first into four zones, then into two states, was pitted against the colossus of the East and of the West, the Soviet Union and the U.S. Even after having gained sovereignty in the West and within the limits in the East, Germany, squeezed in between these giants and overshadowed by them, groped toward strengthening their states through reunification. Though the victors had pledged it to them after the war, they were in no hurry to bring it to fruition.

German Nationalism and "European Universalism"

The striving for European unity, for overcoming the traditional divisive nationalism of the nineteenth and twentieth centuries, became after World War II a widespread general phenomenon of European politics. Europeanism became fashionable also among Germans. European universalism promised to suppress or at least to minimize individual European nationalism which was felt to have been a major cause in two world wars. German Catholic and Protestant religious ties with their co-religionists in Europe as well as German socialist links with fellow Social Democrats on the continent, and German liberal, democratic and conservative ties with ideological brother parties in the West created religious and political ideological connections in Europe which transcended divisive national boundaries. Economics too created new links with European countries and held out brighter prospects for the future, though they frequently accentuated their national diversity.

Even among ultraconservative and rightist groups the ideology of Europeanism made startling progress, pushing nationalistic thought seemingly into the background. Actually, the repression of German nationalism by supra-national European thought and ideology was quite misleading. Many ultra-conservative nationalist circles preferred to hide behind a universalism which overarched nationalist thought. They did not actually shed their chauvinism and racism, but merely modified their language to make their ideology fashionable and more widely acceptable. They did not relinquish their extreme German nationalism, their folkish outlook, their romanticism and even their racism and the geopolitical philosophy in the inter-war period. Like the Conservative Revolutionaries of the 1920s and the members of the youth movement, German rightists and ultra-nationalists stressed again the concept of Germany as a major power for stability (*Ordnungsmacht*) in Europe, a notion which had an anti-Bolshevik point and opened the way for a re-entry of a strengthened Germany into the European family of nations. German Rightists recalled the non-German elements of the SS—volunteers from many European countries who during World War II had served the Third Reich, but allegedly also joint European interests.

What many of the German Rightists aimed at was a rebirth, a renovation of Pan-Europe under German auspices. It was this league of different national groups with a rightist if not fascist orientation, which characterized the "international of nationalists." Germany alone could not dream to stand up as an equal to either the Soviet Union or the U.S. But Germany as the prospective leading economic power of continental Europe could perhaps make a claim of equality with either of the two superpowers. But such an emerging German power had to camouflage its ambitions and expansionist plans beneath innocent-sounding phrases. Such a Germany had to talk of a supra-national Europe rather than of a Europe dominated once again by German bayonets.

One of the first moves toward an international "fascist front" occurred in Rome in 1950. In the post-war period Italy, which was not occupied by foreign powers, a Fascist Party, *Movimento Sociale Italiano* (MSI), attempted to establish ties with sister-parties in other parts of Europe. It started publishing its own journal, *Europa Unita.* Fascist delegates from many European countries converged in Rome in October 1950. The Austrian delegate Karl-Heinz Priester spoke of the fight for 'Nation Europa" on a "folkish nationalist basis," but distanced himself and his fellow travelers especially in regard to the Council of Europe, organized in Strasbourg. The concept of "Nation Europa" was actually directed against the European movement and the democratically oriented Council of Europe in Strasbourg. Another congress of the embryonic Fascist International took place in Malmö, Sweden. The following year the organization called itself *Eu-*

ropäische Soziale Bewegung. A branch of it was the *Deutsche Soziale Bewegung* founded by Priester in 1951. He rejected the new political situation in West Germany, extolling instead the "idea of the Reich."

An Alsatian folk movement was founded in 1951 by a professor of the Strasbourg College of Agriculture, Frederic G. Becker. He came out for an *Europäische Volksbewegung (EVB, Mouvement Populaire Européen)* which aimed at the political unification of Europe on a federal basis. The EVB was intertwined with the *Deutsche Soziale Union* under the leadership of Dr. Otto Strasser and the Zeppelin pioneer Hugo Eckener.[11] The EVB also had branches in France, Austria, and other European countries. Thus, a supra-national concept was used by some ultraconservative-nationalistic circles in various European countries to further their selfish chauvinistic purposes. Quite active along these lines was also the Austrian Theodor Soucek, the author of *Wir rufen Europa* which harbored Nazi ideas, and the movement *Sorbe*, founded in Graz in 1957.

For many Germans and other European Rightists the program "Europe in Africa" proved of great appeal.[12] It signified the penetration and exploitation of Africa not by a single country, but by several European nations. This meant that the doors of Africa would be opened up once again to Germany which prior to World War I had possessed several African colonies. It promised to further German political ambitions. At the same time the propaganda for "Europe in Africa" was also based upon exclusion and dislike of America which was pictured as an enemy of European imperial strivings. In the wake of the Suez crisis of 1956 there was a flurry of propaganda suggesting Germany to go it alone in Africa. Numerous German-Arab associations were founded, but its prospects turned out to be inflated.

One of the means of strengthening Germany's potential power was collaboration with rightist and semi-fascist organizations abroad. The impulse for a British-German Nazi organization of the post-war era was the National Information Bureau or *Natinform.* In 1950 radically racist English veterans had split from Sir Oswaid Mosley's fascist union movement and tried to establish contact with Germany. Prominent was a fascist group comprising *F. Baron and Friends.*[13] A leading German involved in this group was Wolfgang Sarg, editor of the *Socialist Reich Party (SRP)* and its youth journal. Sarg had been a fanatic Hitler Youth member who propagated "Nation Europa" against Jewish world imperialism and communism and propounded the view that Germany was the "natural leader nation of

Europe." He organized a congress which met in Oldenburg on May 2–3, 1953. The German organization subsequently broke with the English branch and with Sarg himself. The latter was arrested by German authorities in July 1953 and again in 1956, when he was convicted of having formed an unconstitutional neo-Nazi organization.

With the development of the Cold War the West German situation changed substantially. The growing Soviet domination of Eastern Europe, including of the DDR, and the apparent Soviet threat to Central Europe altered the outlook both of the Western Powers as well as of the German Federal Republic. The Western Powers were increasingly in need of the cooperation of the West German state. The military of the German Federal Republic experienced a rebirth under democratic emblems. The DDR opposed German rearmament, as did also the extreme Right in the Federal Republic. In the immediate post-war period the prestige of traditional military circles had declined. Recalling now their past degradation and what they considered defamation and post-war humiliation, they were not willing to let by-gones be by-gones. They accused the Western Powers of having committed grievous errors of policy. The Allies, they charged, had during World War II fought the wrong enemy. Despite resentments many rightists were resolved, nevertheless, not to overlook any chances for the rebuilding of German military strength.

Emergence of German Militarism. *Deutscher Soldatenbund*

In 1945 German militarism had suffered a body blow. German armed forces had been disbanded and the German General staff dispersed. The property of veteran organizations was confiscated and new activities of theirs were prohibited. Professional officers and soldiers had lost their social status and traditional prestige. Many were even deprived of their pension rights and other privileges. The German response to the radical change in the international situation, in Bonn's policies and desire for rearmament against the Bolshevik threat to Europe, and to the communist domination of Eastern Europe caused some satisfaction in German rightist circles. After 1945 they had soon accused the Western Powers of having picked the wrong foe—Hitier instead of Stalin.

Goebbels' strident wartime propaganda that Hitler had fought for "Western civilization" again made headway in German rightist circles. When this propaganda suffered abysmal failure, the Nazis invented another legend to prepare a comeback. They repeated that

Hitler's mission had been to organize Europe into an anti-Communist bulwark against the Asiatic peril. But National Socialism had been stabbed in the back by Western plutocracy. Thus with the growth of the East-West split many Germans felt vindicated and no group more so than the extreme Right.

According to the Nazis, the anti-Hitler plot of July 20, 1944 was the work of traitors. The plot furnished the Nazis with a convenient alibi that the insurgents debilitated the Reich and ultimately contributed to Germany losing the war. It became in their minds a touchstone separating the "loyalists" from the "Reich enemies." The "loyalists" rejected the claim that the anti-Nazis had a loyalty concept to the German nation which they placed above that to the Führer. Even for most "non-poiitical" German officers' armed resistance against Hitler was inexcusable. It amounted to naked treason.

During the Cold War the response of the former leading German military officers to new Allied demands for German rearmament differed. There were the so-called "neutralists" who clung to the slogan *ohne mich* [count me out]. Other officers, however, saw in German rearmament a great opportunity both for Germany and for themselves. They swallowed their resentment of past wrongs done to them and supported the Bonn regime, the Americans, and the West. They were anxious to rebuild Germany's military-nationalist traditions. They were prepared to support the Bonn government under certain conditions, but they asked for the re-establishment of the "honor" of German soldiers, the prompt release of all "war criminals," an end to "re-education" and an end to the government of Germany by the "forty-fivers," those who had gained a voice after the catastrophe of 1945. There were finally recalcitrant Nazis who rejected any cooperation with the Bonn government.

In the various veteran organizations former officers outnumbered enlisted men at times seven to one. Prominent among them were *Heimkehrverbände* (Returning Prisoners of War Associations). Others sought to cultivate the "ideals of soldierly comradeship." The former Chancellor Heinrich Brüning warned that the Bonn government would suffer a "shipwreck," just as Weimar had done, unless it succeeded in making the war generation "convinced bearers of the state." As also Chancellor Adenauer fully understood, Bonn needed the support of veteran organizations.

In August 1946 the Allies had declared all military and quasi-military organizations illegal, depriving all former soldiers and officers of all of their personal rights, sickness benefits, and disability and retirement emoluments. But in the winter of 1949–1950 the U.S. government practically reversed itself. The *Deutscher Soldatenbund*, an organization which adopted this name in 1951, asked not only for adequate pensions and disability payments, but acknowledged also the "ideal" of a national revival. One of the most active veteran groups was the *Schutzbund ehemaliger deutscher Soldaten* (Protective League of Former Soldiers). Soon after its founding the *Deutscher Soldatenbund* counted 10,000 members. It published the *Deutsche Soldaten-Zeitung.*[14] During the summer of 1951 thousands of ex-soldiers attended gatherings of veteran associations and wildly applauded their former commanders, many of them still dedicated to National Socialism. Many nationalists and Nazis criticized the political structure imposed in the post-war era.

One nationalist activist, the former Nazi Colonel Ludwig Gümbel demanded publicly the exclusion from the future armed forces of all those who had given proof of their anti-Hitler sentiments. The Bonn government, stung by criticism in the West, unleashed in the end a press campaign against Gümbel and associates.

The New Stahlhelm. The International Tribunal at Nuremberg and the S.S.

In the years prior to Hitler's seizure of power, the *Stahlhelm* played an important poiitical role in Weimar Germany, constituting also a military force. It had split between Duesterberg—who, the Nazis discovered, had been the grandson of a baptized Jew—and Franz Seldte who became Labor minister in Hitler's cabinet.[15] Only about one-third of the former *Stahlhelm* men had followed Seldte's lead. Duesterberg himself survived the fall of the Third Reich.

In the post-war period the *Stahlhelm* was in no great hurry to re-establish its organization, but in 1951 it was founded anew. Now Thomas Girgensohn, a former SA official, was chosen chief of staff of the organization. But the new *Stahlhelm* stressed loyalty to the Bonn constitution and underlined its desire for peace. It came out for the unification of Germany, the freeing of all prisoners of war, and the return of ail expellees to the soil of their fathers.

The German Party (DP), Chancellor Adenauers loyal "coalition" partner, approved the new 12-point program of the *Stahlhelm*,[16] which was widely accepted by rightist elements. While the old *Stahlhelm* had displayed the imperial flag with the German eagle and the imperial colors black-white-red, the new leaders of the *Stahlhelm* insisted that the republican flag was to be carried on all public occasions. Though emphasizing their dedication to the new Bonn constitution, the new *Stahlhelm* leaders confidentially maintained connections with extremist nationalist groups such as *Natinform* and the Hungarian national-socialist movement ("Hungarist"). Compared to the one million fighting corps of the Weimar period, the new *Stahlhelm* remained a pitiful "movement." Its ideology, which had extolled military rearmament, was bound to lose its attraction after the disastrous outcome of the war. The federal law which prohibited the wearing of uniforms deprived the *Stahlhelm* of one of its most effective propagandistic and psychological weapons.

Postwar Youth, the Universities, and Nationalist and Rightist Organizations

Between 40,000 and 70,000 boys and girls in the Federal Republic were organized in the early post-war period in radical, nationalist, Nazi or folkish and anti-democratic youth groups.[17] There was a jungle of groups, leagues, associations, clubs, communities, fellowships, and orders, most of which were ideologically anti-liberal and anti-democratic. Many of them cuitivated a *bündisch* romanticism reminiscent of earlier decades. Some, like the Thule organization, extolled folkish sagas and Nordic poetry and engaged in readings before the campfire, cultivating romantic fashions. They extolled Nazi writers and former nationalist authors, such as Hans Grimm who had created the concept of the German "people without living space," E. G. Kolbenheyer, Will Vespers and similarly oriented authors, and acclaimed the writings of H. F. Blunck, the former President of the Nazi Reich Chamber of Literature. The folkish and *bündisch* leagues after World War II relinquished the imperialist notions of Grimm's pan-Germanism, but did resume their traditional national agitation (*Volksarbeit*) along Germany's ethnic frontiers. Their members made propaganda forays into the northern regions of Schleswig-Holstein, of the "threatened" Alsace-Lorraine and especially of South-Tyrol to preserve folk identity after resorting to terrorist measures, using bombs and bullets. Not only non-Germans but a great many Germans have tried to account for the persistence, long after the destruction of National Socialism, of radically nationalist sentiments and of anti-Semitic prejudices among German youth. This seemed startling because of the absence of state-supported nationalist and anti-Jewish propaganda and the absence of any personal recollection of German Jews by most of the younger generation. But they were unable to shed the anti-Semitic poison injected by the government and their elders during the Nazi era.

In view of the Nazi past the family unit could hardly be considered an obstacle to the dissemination of the Nazi philosophy and of anti-Semitism—rather the opposite. Yet an inadequate history curriculum, the disregard of twentieth century contemporary history, as distinct from earlier periods, the absence especially in the early post-war period of an unbiased and democratically-minded teaching staff may well have contributed to the persistence of many a prejudice, including Jew-hatred. Recent history was usually reserved for the ninth school year—often the last year of formal schooling for the great majority of students.

Conservative nationalism in the West German universities went hand-in-hand with anti-liberal and anti-democratic reaction after 1945.[18] It found representation especially in the post-war movement reestablishing conservative nationalistic "corporations," the typically German form of academic fraternities. Though the Allied Control Council in 1945 had outlawed student corporations, the latter resumed organized activities in 1949. By 1960 the number of "corporated" students had risen to 49,000 among a male German student body of about 150,000. One of the oldest traditions among the various types of student organizations in German universities was the so-called "Corps." Though generally not concerned with contemporay politics, they were on the whole conservative and economically reactionary. They wore "colors" in public, a narrow varicolored sash across the chest and a small visored cap with an identical color scheme. They were required to engage in saber duels for real or pretended slights for the sake of "honor." In the nineteenth century and thereafter they professed "Christian ideas" in which they found justification for a vulgar kind of anti-Semitism. Originally the *Burschenschaften* had combined a sort of liberalism and radicalism, but in the period 1860–1870 they vigorously competed with the aristocratic corps students. Usually, after graduation, fraternity students entered the free professions, obtained secondary school teaching positions and also found employment in administration, commerce, and industry.

The New Burschenschaften and the League of National Students (1956)

In the 1920s, the German Student Union had been granted official recognition. It began to merge with the violently anti-Semitic Austrian and Sudeten German student associations, emphasizing their old pan-German and racist ambitions. In many respects German student associations paved the way for National Socialism, but in 1935 the NSDAP, anxious to marshal all student forces and bring them under its own strict control, obliterated by decree the entire traditions of student societies. Totalitarianism was to destroy any organizational structures which had traditional sources of its own. But this did not prevent the post-World War II journals of rightist students to strike a strong national pose, to continue *Deutschtumsarbeit* and *Grenzlandsarbeit* (work for German *Kultur* and in border regions), to voice preferences for undemocratic forms of government and to criticize the demon (*Ungeist*) of 1945. The *Burschenschaften* rejected the notion that German history had taken a wrong turn (*Irrweg*). They identified the interests of Germany and of Europe by claiming that those who fought against Hitler's Germany had committed treason against Europe as well.[19]

The League of National Students (BNS) founded in June 1956 at Heidelberg was a radically nationalist association which soon established branches at many other German universities. Its program was clearly German reunification, support of ethnic Germans in foreign countries including Austria, and making claims in regard to the *Sudetenland*. Though their applications for licenses were rejected by many universities, they engaged in some activities which led to clashes with opponents. In their publication *Student im Volke* they strongly supported the "Reich" concept and asserted that National Socialism had made historic contributions to the greatness of the Germanic race. They were sharply critical of German "self-flagellants" whom they also accused of "soiling their own nests." In December 1958 their student paper raised the question of the magnitude of the Nazi crimes against German Jewry, asserting that an accurate statistical assessment was not possible. They tended to minimize these crimes and, at worst, held them to be crimes of individuals only, the pathological excrescence of an otherwise healthy system. They attacked the Nuremberg trials and the denazification policies of the first post-war years and objected to the "generous" compensation payments to Israel. No breast-beating was needed to reconstruct a sound and strong

German nation. All in all, the BNS rejected the new Bonn Republic and saw in it a mere dependency of an extra-European power. It made an apparent "historiographical" effort, trying to revive a slightly purged national-socialist *Weltanschauung*. In January 1960, following the display of swastikas on the Cologne synagogue, the Berlin BNS toned well-known Nazi songs which triggered a rash of anti-Semitic demonstrations throughout Germany. The latter in turn produced a vigorous democratic backlash. The Berlin city government declared the Berlin chapter of the BNS a subversive organization and promptly banned it. Their publication *Student im Volke* suffered demise. Its place was taken by the *Deutscher Studentenanzeiger* (DSA) in Munich which claimed to be an "independent form" of German University student activity.

Among German rightists of the post-war era the devoutly Christian Conservatives withstood the attraction of the refurbished Nazi movement, steadfastly rejected all totalitarian pretensions and spurned Hitler's biological materialism. They came out in support of the Bonn Republic. Bonn's moral legitimacy rested largely on the claim to be the legatees of the martyrs of July 20, 1944, many of whom were Christian conservatives.

Populist Nationalist Literature and Nazi Memoirs

After World War II German journalists published numerous essays on Nazi persecution, on the war-guilt question, and on the role of the Resistance. Books, brochures, periodicals, and newspapers were distributed through a variety of channels. Bookclubs or reading clubs provided such outlets. In this way a far larger number people were exposed to nationalist ideas and myths than actively participated in radical groups and parties, and a far larger number of Germans were reached than attended political rallies, listened to "national" speakers or voted for splinter parties of the Nationalist Opposition. Manfred Jenke's *Conspiracy of the Right* has stressed the central importance which nationalist publishing firms had assumed propagandizing nationalist, folkish, and conservative authors. Their renewed acceptance was evidence of the continuing appeal of this type of literature which attempted to renovate National Socialism through partial justification of the Third Reich and through simultaneous attacks against those who had destroyed it.

In this literature, memoirs of soldiers played a primary role; foremost among them were those by Hans Friessner, Heinz Guderian,

Erich Raeder, Paul Hausser, Albert Kesselring, Erich von Manstein, Siegfried Westphal, and others. Friessner blamed the "treason" of the Romanians and Hungarians for Germany's defeat, the material superiority of the Russians as well as Hitler's amateurism, stubbornness and the "lunacy of his strategic insights."[20] Friessner did not utter a word about political problems and his own political abstinence, like that von Manstein's, in regard to the "final solution." To the contrary, according to Friessner, every soldier must understand "the necessity of harsh retribution" against Jewry, the spiritual bearer of the Bolshevik terror. In his second autobiographical volume leading up to 1939, von Manstein claimed that the *Reichswehr* had "not meddled in politics," this silence and passivity allegedly being a "badge of honor."

In *Remembrance of a Soldier*, Guderian willfully closed his eyes to everything but military problems and castigated the conspirators of July 20, 1944. He himself sat on the Court of Honor and surrendered to the People's Courts all officers of the July conspiracy. He justified Germany's historic mission of serving as Europe's bastion against the Eastern menace. About concentration camps he claimed to have "become aware of the inhumanity perpetrated" only "after the collapse." Helmut Sündermann, an 'old fighter,' post-war publisher of Nazi and other extremist and nationalist literature, tried to appropriate Nazi legends. His books which had also licensed editions appeared in several printings. The author praised Hitler, staunchly maintaining that he had had peaceful intentions.

Hitler's legend was largely upheld in numerous memoirs of Party dignitaries, by Rudolf Hess, Konstantin Hierl, chief of the Nazi labor service, Wilfred von Oven, Goebbel's personal press officer, Alfred Rosenberg, the "theoretician" of National Socialism, Friedrich Christian von Schaumburg-Lippe, one of Goebbel's aides and one of many aristocrats who became enthusiastic Nazi partisans, and Friedrich Grimm, radical nationalist publicist, attorney, and Professor of Law. In the Third Reich he had been a member of the Nazi *Reichstag* and became later defense councilor for a number of prominent former Hitler officials.

The popularity of nationalist and Nazi literature was due to the still widespread attraction of war and its apparently glorious moments for many members of Germany's armed forces. A German plebiscite in 1948 disclosed that 65 percent of the former members of the national-socialist party and 49 percent of the nonmembers considered National Socialism "a good cause."[21] This judgment rested not so much on dedication to national-socialist ideology but on its claimed social achievements, on German order and the security of the German wage policy. The later deterioration under National Socialism was, according to Hans Grimm, due only to the doings of a bourgeois "Zwischenschichte," a middle layer of the German population.[22]

While Hitler himself was criticized both prior and after his seizure of power and rejected by rightist circles around Otto Strasser, Mathil de Ludendorff and some former *Stahlhelm* leaders, others such as Alfred Rosenberg in his *Last Observations.* despite all admiration for Hitler, blamed him because he killed Captain Röhm for tactical reasons, because of his Eastern policy, and because of other views and attitudes.[23] Ribbentrop, Hans Grimm, and others also made other critical observations about the Führer.

One way to rehabilitate Hitler in the post-war era was to claim that "the Führer did not know" of all outrages committed and to insist that it was only men in his immediate retinue who were guilty of some crimes. Alfred Rosenberg and Peter Kleist reassigned responsibility for the book-burning and for the *Kristallnacht* of 1938 to Himmler who, they charged, had thus blackened the reputation of National Socialism.[24] The attempt to lighten Hitlers burden by increasing that of the other members of his entourage was, considering the flood of contrary evidence, plainly ludicrous. Göring himself and others at the Nuremberg Trial have tried to follow a different course. By shifting all responsibility onto Hitler's shoulders, they tried to absolve themselves.

The German term for reparation payments for the persecution of the Jews is "Wiedergutmachung." There was of course no possibility of "making good" irreversible atrocities which had resulted in the gruesome killings of millions of non-Germans, Jews and gentiles. The foregoing German word itself was totally inadequate, and a plain euphemism. But no post-war German institutions such as the *Woche der Brüderlichkeit* [week of Brotherhood], youth journeys to the memorial in Bergen-Belsen or similar endeavors, church activities, left-organized demonstrations or "reparation" payments were sufficient to restore normal relations between Germans and Jews.

The Extreme Right and the Image of National Socialism

Among the plethora of rightist politicai splinter groups which emerged in the wake of Germany's political and military catastrophe in 1945 was also a large number of national-socialist underground organizations. Though the totalitarian political and economic structure of National Socialism was shattered, Nazi fanaticism and its ideology were by no means completely uprooted. Yet because of the partition of Germany into four zones of occupation, a union of these disparate political groups and of the special region for Berlin immediately after 1945 was not in sight.

Some of the political groups took part in the electoral campaign for the *Bundestag* in West Germany in 1949. The following year there emerged from these groupings the *Nationale Rechte* and the *Deutsche Reichspartei.*[25] While these parties gathered under its wings former German Nationals (*Deutschnationale*) and *Völkische*, they claimed to be opposed to National Socialism, merely emphasizing conservative and monarchist views. Though they were able to send some representatives into the communal assemblies, they did not succeed in gaining representatives in the various *Landtage*. The emergence of these groups aroused a certain uneasiness in the Germanies as well as abroad, showing that Germany had not entirely shed its dark past. Of greater importance than extremist rightist political parties were, however, so-called *Verbände* [associations] which had quasi-political goals, nationalist youth organizations, journals, and publishing companies. In the decades after 1949 the *Verbände* had a total membership of about 112,000 individuals. Yet as far as German public opinion was concerned, they were a negligible force.

What was the image of National Socialism in the post-war writings of the radical Rightists? The latter dealt largely in apologetics, though many of its spokesmen tried to distance themselves from National Socialism as such. They attempted to justify some organizations such as the Waffen-SS, its ideolgy and its practices. In their view, going farther back, the dictate of Versailles played a key role in the rise of National Socialism. They thus fastened blame on the Great Powers. According to Peter Kleist, the Allies' "harsh stance" in 1919 was a major cause of the Nazis' ultimate success, radicalizing the German masses. In the extremist rightists' views, the nationalist post-World War I reaction offered a defense against the threat of the seizure of power by the communists (KPD). Without Hitler, the rightists claimed, Ernst Thälmann, communist leader, would have taken over control in the Reich. Hitler was credited by Kleist with having saved not only Germany from Communism but Europe in its entirety, a view shared by many other rightists. That the German communists, following the Stalinist line, denounced the SPD as "social fascists" had prevented the formation of a united anti-fascist front. That they cooperated to a significant degree with the NSDAP in the years before Hitler's seizure of power and thus played into Nazi hands was ignored by the post-war anti-communist agitation as well as by communists. Furthermore, in the view of rightist publicists, the elimination of the Weimar democracy was primarily due to the failure of the Weimar democratic parties. Rightists also pointed to the "legality" of the Nazi seizure of power, especially to the enabling act of 1933, while keeping silent about the illegal measures taken by the Nazi regime to suppress constitutional liberties in Germany. Hardly any of the rightist extremists took note of the scholarly literature which had been published after World War II and had offered an objective analysis of the causes of the eclipse of the Weimar republic.

As mentioned, Hans Grimm extolled the "young National Socialism," allegedly a noble, moral and religious rather than a political movement, opposing it to the later "insane Hitlerism" which produced the catastrophe. Alfred Rosenberg, Nazi ideologue, had emphasized in his *Letzte Aufzeichnungen* that the synthesis of German nationalism and socialism was desirable, but that it had never materialized.[26] It was "trampled to death" by the Nazis. The failure of the synthesis between the two ideologies was allegedly the deeper cause of Germany's breakdown in 1945. To the contrary, the historian Friedrich Meinecke claimed that the synthesis of the two ideological currents explained the strong appeal of National Socialism over the long stretch.

National Socialism, according to some post-war revisionists, had its "good sides," such as disciplining the youth. In the view of some Nazi apologists, the "good and positive" elements of National Socialism should be appreciated and preserved. Ultraconservatives frequently praised the creation of the true *Volksgemeinschaft* [people's community], the *Arbeitsdienst* [labor service], the overcoming of "degenerate art," protection of the peasantry, strengthening of the white race against colored races. Hitler furthermore was frequently credited for the building of the *Autobahn*, the creation of *Grossdeutschland* and the defense of Europe against Bolshevism. Most of the post-war apologists of National Socialism did not claim that it had been faultless. But the spiritual foundations and the totality of its conception of ruling the German people by the Party, respectively the Führer, were not only widely accepted by its defenders, but extolled, while only its alleged exaggerations were critically looked upon. The Radical Rightists, if not outright denying that Germans had committed major atrocities, tried at least to minimize or even to justify their outrages. Ultra-rightists openly asserted the right to slander alien ethnic and religious groups and to discriminate against them, all in the name of freedom of speech which they had made a point to deny to others.

Some post-war neo-conservatives have tried to trivialize the actual significance of concentration camps, of the Gestapo, the SS and the SD. Since the evidence relating to the horrors was indisputable, other rightist publicists have tried to distance themselves from these organizations. As far as the concentration camps were concerned, they have claimed that they were an English invention and that the German models had been not so bad as their foreign critics have pictured. They have gone further, claiming that primarily criminals, asocial individuals, or simply disturbing elements (*Störenfriede*) had been incarcerated in these camps.

They have also denounced the trials against former concentrations camp overseers and employees. As the *Deutsche Gemeinschaft* wrote: "The gallows of Nuremberg are symbols of the 'justice of vengeance'."[27] Radical rightists have attempted to minimize especially the vast scope of the annihilation of the Jews. While the accusations at the Nuremberg trial listed the number of Jewish victims as 5.7 million, the German scholar H. Krausnick spoke of six million Jewish victims, including not only Jews by religion, but all those of Jewish ancestry.[28] Next to their desire to trivialize the mass annihilation was the consideration to reduce the demands of *Wiedergutmachung*. Some rightist authors such as A. von Thadden, Soucek, and Sundermann have completely ignored the facts. According to them, the gas chambers were utilized for disinfection but not for killing. The enforced assistance of Jewish helpers assigned in any case responsibility for the mass murder to Jews themselves. Some have pointed to the Zionist leader Chaim Weizmann and his alleged declaration of war against the Third Reich in September 1939. Other ultra-rightists attempted to picture "world Judaism" and Nazi Germany as comparable belligerent powers! One even asserted that Adolf Eichmann had been "Volljude"[29] who had carried the anti-Semitic germs into the SS. Fiction was elevated to bizarre heights!

The ultra-rightists were preoccupied not only with denying and lessening Germany's guilt, but they also hurled accusations against the Allies. One Wilhelm Sluyse in *Nation Europa* pointed to the existence of a Dutch concentration camp in 1945,[30] to post-war murders of renegades in France, Italy, and Czechoslovakia. Others even referred to collective persecutions in past centuries such as the burning of witches, excesses during the religious wars and those in the French Revolution, not to mention the more recent atrocities such as the Soviet murder of Poles at Katyn and brutal French colonial repression in North Africa. All this and more was part of a balance sheet (*Gegenrechnung*) which allegedly showed that both sides, the Germans and the Allies, had "sinned" at times. Thus they were really "even" (*quitt*). German rightist publicists have pointed especially to the relentless war-time air bombardments of German cities. They ignored the origins of all of it, the national-socialist policy of aggression and brutal methods of warfare. Actually, Nazi torture and annihilation could in no way be attributed to war as such, to mere belligerency, but to long-range Hitlerite and Nazi planning of destruction and annihilation.

While in the wake of World War I the question of war guilt had played a major role in Germany, the end of World War II first produced no similar reaction. The Nuremberg trial had established for the great majority of people everywhere the full responsibility of Hitler-Germany and National Socialism for unleashing the war with all its horrors. But following some revisionist publications abroad which seemed to acquit Germany of sole responsibility for the war, former Nazis and German chauvinists felt encouraged and began to raise their voices to express revisionist views of their own. Some came to the defense of a polemical treatise by one Wieland, *Wieviel Welt (Geld-) Kriege müssen die Völken noch verlieren*, (Hamburg, 1957), pointing to the alleged real culprits for World War II, Jews, bankers, and Freemasons. Thus was revived the pernicious legend of the *Protocols of the Elders of Zion*, which had played a role in Russia and had spread to post-World War I Germany. Even the attempt to blame "international finance capital" for the outbreak of the war was only a poorly disguised policy to blame the Jews. The hostility of Winston Churchill was easily explained; he had always considered himself a "Zionist"! Real or alleged Jewish advisors to President Woodrow Wilson and FDR had formed the "clique" who turned out to be the true "war criminals."[31] While Hitler's policies were admitted as being rooted in violence against other nations, his actions were considered justified attempts of the suppressed Germans to obtain freedom from the chains of Versailles. To other rightist extremists communism seemed the sole guilty party. But in either case the Jews were a main target.

In a number of German writings between 1933 and 1949 it was ciaimed that even Hitler was financed by American-Jewish bankers, especially James Warburg, to prepare for and wage war against France. Erich Ludendorff partisans blamed not only Hitler but also the Jews, a view repeated by anti-Semitic scribblers such as Reinhard (René Sonderegger).

Neo-conservatives admitted that Hitler's policies were being root ed in violence against other nations, but his actions were considered justified attempts of the suppressed Germans to shake off the chains of Versailles. German post-war Rightists approved Hitler's foreign policy of the 1930s the major purpose of which was to secure only "equality" for Germany. They thus ignored that the Führer actually desired and strove for the subjugation of Germany's neighbors and of all other European peoples, openly admitted in *Mein Kampf.* Hitler's successes in the interwar period were contrasted with the alleged failures of Weimar Germany's foreign policy. The later opposition of England and France to Hitler's expansionisrn was explained on the basis of their hostility to Germany and their illicit "intervening" in the affairs of Central and Eastern Europe. Intervention in these regions was justified for Germany. But such a policy by the West was castigated.

The Munich agreement, as could be expected, was cheerfully greeted by German nationalists of the post-war era. Yet thereafter British and French policy of resistance to further expansion of the Third Reich in Eastern Europe was rejected outright. England and France aside, the U.S. especially under FDR's leadership was seen as having been the main culprit in blocking Germany's expansion of her *Lebensraum* in Europe, American writers such as the Roosevelt-hater Charles C. Tansill and the sociologist Harry Elmer Barnes were eagerly embraced by German revisionists. Poland's foreign policy on the eve of the war was sharply criticized, as it had also been by the Nazis in 1939. Post-war German pubiicists found it somewhat awkward to have to defend the Hitler-Stalin pact which had permitted the Soviet leader to expand westward. All in all, writers of the ultra-rightist persuasion turned to the question of guilt for the outbreak of World War II with the same fanatic intensity as German historiography had dealt with the question of war guilt after World War I. But this did not hold true for German post-World War II historiography, since

Hitler's foreign policy left little doubt about the Nazi responsibility for the start of World War II.

German ultra-conservatives have accused the German Resistance during World War II of responsibility for the defeat of the Reich rather than giving them credit for the struggle against tyranny and slavery. The Resistance movement had aimed at Hitler's overthrow and at the *Reich*'s losing the war. These charges had actually been raised earlier by Nazi propaganda during the war. It was a new "stab in the back" legend and recalled the similar widely disseminated legend after World War I which became a dogma in the Third Reich. An important feature of the extreme Right's outlook was the belief in the surviving Jews' conspiracy in world affairs and the castigation of those who discredited these baseless charges.

Ultra-rightists frequently extolled the Prussian character, its simplicity and other alleged moral qualities, all in contradistinction to the frequent acute charges against Prussianism. The radical Right considered itself the preserver of Prussian virtues. Many of its accusations were aimed against alien denigration of the Prussian and German character. In the opinion of Knütter, no new rightist organization, including the *Deutsche Partei*, could in the early post-war era gain a large following. National Socialism was largely discredited. The total defeat, the general destruction of cities and factories, the numberless German victims, dead or crippled, the widespread misery, the scarcity of food and of most goods was more than most Germans could endure.

Still, there was a steady stream of individuals into the camp of former Nazis. Despite assurances to the contrary, many extremists remained influenced by the national-socialist model. Even Otto Strasser, though hostile to Hitler, could after the return to Germany not escape the powerful attraction. All the different newly founded Right-extremist groups succumbed to the lasting and persistent influence of National Socialism, though most of them for obvious reasons disavowed it publicly.

The Ludendorff Movement

General Erich Ludendorff's pre-World War II activities, among which anti-Semitism figured prominently, have aiready been discussed. But the Ludendorff movement, thanks partly to the endeavors of his widow Mathilde Ludendorff, did in the post-war world not entirely vanish from the German intellectual and political scene. The Ludendorff Movement, like that of Otto Strasser, attracted after 1945 considerable interest in West Germany not only because it continued the anti-democratic and anti-liberal outlook,[32] but also because of its decidedly anti-Hitler orientation. Even for many German rightists and ultra-nationalists it was impossible to ignore that the Hitler-era, though it had raised spirits and expectations, had produced bitter delusions because of its ultimate debacle.

Ludendorff's official program, containing his "Kampfziele," embraced Greater Germany, deprivation of German citizenship for Jews, glorification of racism, emphasis on autocratic leadership and on militarism, and hostility toward parliamentarianism and the Christian churches. Ludendorff's political philosophy, despite its apparent ideological similarity to Hitlerism, made its break with it. The reasons for the break between Hitler and Ludendorff go back to 1923, the year of Hitler's failed *Putsch*, and to 1925, the year of the Presidential election in the Weimar republic when Luddendorff, urged on by Hitler, ran for office but suffered a humiliating debacle. Hitler thereupon lost interest in Ludendorffs following; after all they were former political enemies, sectarians, and religious fanatics led by a paranoid personality and his wife Mathilde, in Hitler's words "that hysterical woman" (*hysterisches Frauenzimmer*). The clash between "two such pathological maniacs as Hitler and Ludendorff," men of monumental ambitions and pretensions, became thus inevitable. In their press the Ludendorffs had castigated Hitler's foreign policy, having joined forces with such "hirelings of the Roman Curia" as Mussolini and Franco.

Persuaded that Hitler had become the terror instrument of Jews, Freemasons, and Jesuits—actually the main enemies and propagandistic targets of National Socialism—the Ludendorffs had found, nevertheless, many positive elements in National Socialism; among others, they praised the Nuremberg Laws and the anti-Jewish pogrom. In 1937, weeks before the general's death, Hitler had called on him, effecting a sort of reconciliation, and recognized in a manner Mathilde Ludendorff's German God Cognition (*Deutsche Gotteserkenntnis*), giving it a status of equality with other Christian confessions.

After the war, Mathilde Ludendorff claimed that her husband had entertained closest relations with most prominent German generals who had later been dismissed by the Führer, Werner von Fritsch, Werner von Blomberg, and General Ludwig Beck who had warned against Hitlers war plans. She even insisted that Ludendorff had been the driving force of the *Putsch*. But the post-war denazification tribunal, little impressed by these claims, concluded that the Ludendorffs had promoted the interests of the Third Reich and Hitlers doctrine "in the most exaggerated form."[33]

The political scientist Bernard Willms, author of *Die deutsche Nation* (1952) , had risen to be a leading theoretician of West German ultra-nationalism. The so-called "anti-fascism" was for Willms only "collective self-hatred." The condemnation of the crimes of Nationai Socialism was for him a weapon in the continued struggle to hold down the Germans as a nation, "the continuation of war against Germany with other means." The demand to close the "wound Hitler" for the sake of the 'national identity' was made by Willms more effectively as well as more radically then by other Germans. He voiced these views in numerous right-extremist journals, including the *NPD-Studenten Zeitschrift* and the *Franfurter Allgemeine*. The line of separation between conservative and right-extremist simply evaporated. The German Right made a strong appearance in publication, the book market and in war literature.

Foreign Support for German Rightists and Nationalists

Extreme German Rightists and nationalists had in the postwar period found aid and comfort among former Nazis as well as their non-German fellow-travelers, some of them political stooges or intellectual captives. Among them was the fanatically anti-Bolshevik Maurice Bardèche, an activist in the post-war *European Social Movement*, former professor of literature at Lille and after the war jailed for several months. *Nuremberg ou la terre promise*,[34] translated into English, criticized the Allies for their allegedly discriminatory treatment of Germany at the Nuremberg trial. A similar goal of discrediting the Western Powers was *The Secret Causes of the Second World War*, a translation of the work of seven authors brought out by Karl-Heinz Priester, a rightist activist, in which the authors placed the guilt for the outbreak of war in 1939 on the conspiracy of Allied warmongers supported, as they were, by Jews, communists, and Freemasons—all allies in the eyes of the Nazis. There were finally the books by the British fascist leader Sir Oswald Mosley, among them *The European Revolution*, and a counter-indictment of the Allies for alleged brutalities by the former Romanian ambassador to Germany, General Jon Georghi's *Automatic Arrest* (1956). To it must be added

René Sonderegger's *Spanish Summer*, the author being a Swiss anti-Semitic propagandist who in an earlier pamphlet, in 1935, had praised the notorious *Protocols of the Wise Men of Zion* for their keen discernment of Jewish religion. Hermann Lutz, a German-American author, who had emigrated to the U.S. in 1946, denied in his book *Nation of Criminals in the Heart of Europe?*, not only this question, but considered the Germans the victims of Allied criminals, vehemently criticizing the Versaiiles treaty. In 1961 the revisionist David L. Hoggan targeted in *The Enforced War* Franklin Delano Roosevelt as responsible for the outbreak of the European War. The German historian Helmut Krausnick rejected Hoggan, who ignored documentary sources, and even charged him with forgery. Other books widely quoted by German nationalist and fevisionist authors were finally the noted British diplomatic historian A. J. P. Taylor's bizarre treatment of *The Origins of the Second World War*, the American sociologist Harry Elmer Barnes' *Hypocrisy Unmasked*, the American Charles C. Tansill's *The Backdoor to War*, and Charles Bewley, *Eire's Ambassador to Berlin between 1933–39*, an old defense counsel for the Irish Republican Army who published an admiring biography of Hermann Göring, all defenders of lost causes. Former Nazis and other nationalists welcomed the work of the Frenchman Paul Rassinier, a Resistance fighter, former socialist deputy who described his concentration camp experience in *The Life of Ulysses* (1959), a book which had been banned in France. He became a widely sought speaker in rightist and anti-Semitic circles in Germany, asserting that the maximum number of murdered Jews was only half a million and that it had been imperative to destroy Russian Bolshevism.

Of the numerous nationalist and semi-fascist periodicals which flooded European countries in the post-war period was *Nation Europa* judged to be extremely nationalistic, but camouflaging it behind the deceptive banner of internationalism. In 1959 the Institute for Contemporary History in Munich listed the journal in its bibliography under the category "Neo-Nazism." In the May 1955 issue of the journal Hitler's name appeared at the head of the first page, above the date of his suicide. Knut Hamsun, well-known Norwegian writer, proclaimed Hitler "a fighter for humanity and a proclaimer of the message of the right for all nations" and considered himself "his close follower," "bowing his head at his death." The editor-in-chief of *Nation Europa*, Arthur Erhardt, expressed his appreciation of Hitler's passing. While holding his measures vis-à-vis the Jews and Eastern peoples "not only unworthy but also unwise," he, nevertheless, praised Hitler, "whom many of the best Europeans followed confidently."

The rise of extreme nationalism and ultra-conservatism in the wake of the end of the World War II was a residuum of most intense Nazi propaganda which still gripped the German mind and some non-German extremists. The military debacle and the widespread destruction in Germany had not extinguished all vestiges of Nazi thought and Nazi political ideology. Though democracy under Allied control made some progress in the German zones and later in the Bonn Republic, the process of mental and psychological recovery was far from smooth.

Authoritarian leanings of the German populace remained strong and nationalism was always ready to spring into action. Anti-Semitism and xenophobic sentiments were still widespread. Old legends relating to the harsh peace treaty of Versailles, the belief of the maltreatment of Germany in the interwar period and of the heavy reparation payments imposed, the justification of Germany's "peaceful" expansion before 1939 and the notion of the "encirclement" of the *Reich*, still constituted the ideological mind-set of many Germans. So did the legend of the narrowness of Germany's *Lebensraum*, of the hostility of the Jews to Germany and of their ambition to dominate Germany and Europe in its totality. Germans accused Jews and others of their exaggerated accounts of German misdeeds during the war. These and other myths made their reappearance soon after 1945. They were first repressed in the Allied zones and by the German govemments in the West and partly also in the emerging DDR, but never vanished completely from the discussion among Germans. Even a superficial comparison of these distortions with those voiced decades later by "revisionists" in the *Historikerstreit* of 1986–87, if not earlier, reveals clearly the precedents of the historians' dispute.

III

THE RISE OF HISTORICAL AND POLITICAL REVISIONISM, 1965 TO THE EARLY 1980s, AND DEMOCRATIC AND LIBERAL RESPONSES

By 1965 the early and intermediate post-war era seemed to reach its end. Neither the young Germans and young university historians, who were sympathetic to their endeavors, were inclined to blame Hitler alone for the atrocities, but rather reprehended the autocratic institutions of Germany. This was the climate for the student rebellion of 1968. More or less simultaneously, the Social Democrats, led first by Willy Brandt and then by Helmut Schmidt, replaced the ruling conservative regime in 1966, a conservative government which had formed a coalition with the liberal Free Democratic Party. Historians, teachers, and writers in general turned to the past, trying to master it by disclosing the shortcomings of Imperial Germany and focusing on the militarism of Prussia, Bismarck's authoritarian leanings, the weakness of the regime of William II, of German democracy and parliamentarianism. In this past German anti-Semitism had also made major strides. The groundwork for the new criticism had been laid earlier by the trial of Adolf Eichmann in Israel in 1960 and the subsequent Auschwitz trials in Germany in 1964. This criticism was enhanced by the publication of scholarly studies relating to Nazi foreign and domestic policy and the death camps.

The social-liberal era in post-war Germany came to a conclusion in 1982. The Free Democratic Party abandoned the coalition with the Social Democrats, switching back to join with the Christian Democrats. This political change was accompanied by the "Wende," reversing the progressive developments of the 1970s. The sharp deterioration of East-West relations following the Soviet invasion of Afghanistan was bound to further affect American-West German rapprochement as well. The U.S. Ambassador to the Federal Republic,

Richard Burt, virtually supporting the German neo-conservatives, thought it timely for the Germans to "free themselves from the tragedy of the period 1933–1945." It was not surprising that such comments encouraged Germans to revise their outlook on the past and future.

Many popular German magazines embraced revisionism, which often was little distinct from rightist tendencies. Revisionism often attempted to trivialize and legitimize the misdeeds of National Socialism, making them appear "normal." Revisionism even tried to exculpate Germans from many crimes and to place ultimate responsibility for Germany's excesses upon her neighbors. Examples of the "Verharmlosung" (minimizing) practiced can be found in their choice of language. The Nazis and their apologists talked publicly less of the murder of the victims than euphemistically of *Sonderbehandlung* (special treatment) of the Jews and of the *Endlösung* (final solution) of the Jewish problem rather than of Jewish annihilation. The terror machine had been set up in 1933 only to "save" the German people and state. The war was carried on, the Nazis claimed and many post-war revisionists repeated, not only "for the salvation of Germany" but also for saving Europe from Bolshevism. Terrorist mass murder and war were not caused by Germany but by its enemies! Communists were accused of setting the *Reichstag* afire and Jews were declared responsible for the outbreak of the war, which was to establish their domination. Such accusations were to justify the persecution and annihilation of German and all other European Jews. The war against Poland was explained as a legitimate war, designed to liberate the allegedly suppressed German minority in that state, and the war against the Soviet Union was proclaimed as an unavoidable defensive war. While German government circles as well as most post-war German history professors kept their distance from fascist publications, the latter tried to disavow or trivialize Nazi crimes and to rehabilitate its practitioners.

The growing Cold War led in Germany to the rise of a neo-fascist party, the NFD.[1] In the election to the *Landtage* in 1966 to 1968 the NFD obtained between 5 to 10 percent of all votes. Yet the simultaneous victory of leftist forces resulted in pushing neo-fascism back and removed its threat for the next years. Democratic reforms at the universities strengthened anti-fascist trends among West Germany's youth.

On May 10, 1975, a mass demonstration occurred in Frankfurt by the Left on occasion of the fortieth anniversary of the liberation from fascism. On April 22, 1978, an international anti-fascist demonstration took place with representations from seventeen European countries. In November of the same year a mass demonstration was organized on occasion of the fortieth anniversary of the pogrom night in November 1938 (*Kristallnacht*).

In the 1970s, on the other hand, a neo-conservative offensive had begun. A Hitler-wave commenced to sweep the country. A flood of brochures, articles, movies, and TV programs had inundated West Germany. Their emphasis lay on the claim that Hitler and the Nazi system had their positive side, especially in regard to full employment and the enthusiasm it aroused in the entire German community. Two special publications entered the arena with scientific claim. The journalist Joachim Fest authored a Hitler biography which became a best seller and was also recommended as a text for schools. The same welcome reception was given to another book by the journalist Sebastian Haffner. Known historians and political scientists applauded these new publications. According to Fest, Hitler's mistake was not to have mobilized all forces of Europe for the war against the Soviet Union.[2] He had also erred in fighting against the West. Haffner pointed out that Hitler had done extraordinarily well when he abolished unemployment and performed an "economic miracle." Fest and others thus ignored that it was only the preparation for war that wiped out German unemployment. During the war "good citizens and fathers" had simply become "used to killing." Such books were favorably received by some historians, among them Andreas Hillgruber and Klaus Hildebrand, and rightist publicists.

The offensive from the Right had started before Chancellor Helmut Kohl and the new government had assumed power. His reign coincided with an intellectual and moral turnabout, the *Wende*. For a long time there had been talk about the need for a new national consciousness to which Germans, like all other nations, were entitled. Germans pointed out that many Europeans expected that the *Bundesrepublik* assume a strong leading role in international politics. It was therefore imperative that she did not limit herself to playing merely the role of a growing economic power but also that she grew politically. Germany should overcome being split into two parts and unify. This was propagated by several authors in the book edited by Kühnl. *Nationalismus, die nationale Frage* (Cologne, 1986).[3]

Glorification of the Distant Past. "Sinnstiftung" by Conservative Politicians and Magazines

Germans complained that the full development of the economic and military power potential of the Bonn Republic was hampered by the memory of National Socialism and of its crimes. The conservative politician Franz Joseph Strauss demanded that Germany finally "step out from the shadow of Hitler" or, as the historian Michael Stürmer put it, Germany "free herself from the curse of the years 1933–1945."[4] Other historians, turning to Germany's past, paid special attention to distant periods of German history, to illuminate eras in which positive German qualities had emerged. Thus the Staufer era exhibit highlighted a time far removed from National Socialism. This was a period marked by the splendor of the Holy Roman Empire which had enjoyed hegemony on the continent. There followed the exhibit of the Wittelsbach dynasty in Munich which raised Bavarian state consciousness. Then followed a Prussian wave. It was a revised conservatism which propagated these new ideals: service for the whole community was praised as was readiness for sacrifice and sufferings. Fatherland, family, and military strength had then been extolled. Plans were developed for a museum of German history and also for a national memorial in Bonn. Michael Stürmer, advisor to Chancellor Helmut Kohl, Erlangen historian and editorialist for the *FAZ* formulated it thus: History promised to be a great guide toward identity. It was important "to find patriotism again." "He will win the future who fills the memory, coins the concepts, and meaningfully interprets the past." The Federal Republic needed a higher purpose (*Sinnstiftung*) which so far only religion and patriotism had been able to offer. Thus, the historian had allegedly a political, even quasi-military task. That history was to serve political interests emerged also in the guidelines which the CDU-CSU adopted for the "house of history" of the *Bundesrepublik* Germany.

In a major address on April 28, 1986, the conservative Bavarian politician Franz J. Strauss, quoting a reader's letter in a Bavarian journal, asserted that it was time that Europe did not look upon the year 1945 as a defeat for Germany, but saw in it rather a defeat for Europe. In addition, the guilt for the outbreak of World War I, the greatest crime against European civilization, should be distributed "equally."[5] The responsibility for many wars lay simply in the "Mittellage" of Germany in Europe. The basic ideas underlying these "conceptions" were the rejection of Germany's major guilt for the outbreak of two world wars and a repudiation of the assertion that Germany and National Socialism were the main culprits. The West should acknowledge that even national-socialist Germany had fought the right enemy, the Soviet Union. In fighting the latter, the Third Reich had represented the interests of all of Europe. It was the U.S. and its allies that had erred in fighting the Third Reich!

On February 2 and March 30, 1985, the *Bayern-Kurier* pointed to what it considered Allied guilt in conducting World War II, for the bombardment of German cities, the barbarities of the Red Army, and the post-war crime of the expulsion of Germans.[6] The Bavarian Minister of Justice Lang accused the German opposition of harming Bonn's reputation. His fellow Bavarian J. F. Strauss insisted that silence about Auschwitz was imperative since "no people can in the long run live with a criminalized history." The eyes should be directed toward the future rather than the past. This was equivalent to saying that the Germans should bury the past by simply ignoring it. What was necessary was to overcome the partitioning of Germany so that Europe, politically united, "could speak with one voice" and that Germany in the "orchestra of world powers" no longer stood in the second row.[7] Some of these themes were echoed and elaborated by neo-conservative historians.

On the 8th of May 1985, President Richard von Weizsäcker in a notable address declared that this day was the anniversary of the liberation of the German people. The orator, a moderate conservative, clearly repudiated the thesis of the German right wing, the so-called "Aufrechnungsideologie." This was the ideology of attributing guilt to the Allies for their alleged misdeeds during World War II, which followed and actually paled compared to Nazi atrocities.

Weizsäcker rejected, however, the comparison of Nazi crimes and Allied responses.

> We must not see in the end of the war the cause of the flight of the Germans, of their expulsion, and lack of freedom. Its cause lies rather in its beginning. . . . We must not separate May 8, 1945 from January 30, 1933,

the end of the war from its inception, the Nazi assumption of power. In this context Weizsäcker listed German and non-German victims who had dared offering resistance. He referred to the numerous citizens of the Soviet Union and of Poland and the "hostages" of other nations who had been murdered. Among the German victims of the Resistance he specifically singled out workers, trade unionists, and communists "as well as the Resistance in all states occupied by us [Germans]." He denounced the German-Soviet non-aggression pact as the immediate cause of the war. He then elicited in his own party sharp opposition because of its unwillingness to fully discuss Germany's responsibilities for her past.

Other German politicians, however, pursued a different course. A conservative non-apologetic line was increasingly endorsed by many leading German dailies such as *Der Spiegel*, *Die Welt*, *Der Bayern-Kurier*, and also the *FAZ*, though the latter still claimed to follow a "liberal" course. Similarly the politician Alfred Dregger asserted that the lack of a sense of historical consciousness (*Geschichtslosigkeit*) and the "ruthlessness against one's own nation" were "most regrettable." "Our people will not be able to survive without a basic patriotism which is quite natural for other nations.[8] He who abused the principle of "overcoming the past" must be contradicted, since he made "our people incapable of facing the future."

Such strident demands for a revision of the German image and of German historiography most often included an urgent appeal to tone down, if not completely revise, the assessment of German policy toward the Jews, to illuminate alleged Jewish weaknesses of character and erroneous attitudes which had supposedly contributed to the outbreak of Jew-hatred. The latter, revisionists pointed out, had occurred in many other countries and over many centuries. Views like these furnished the background for the eruption of the German historians' feud in 1986.

The New Generation of German Historians and German-Jewish History

Differences of opinions and interpretations had marked German historiography for a long time, though German nationalism, the conviction that the German people was superior and more advanced than most of its neighbors and the drive to extend German power and influence over other parts of Europe had been widespread and were widely approved. The intoxication had also affected German historical writing for a long time. Following the debacle of World War II, however, the earlier virtual unanimity of German historical scholarship on the following topics of German and European history had suffered a body blow. The post-war period saw first a far-reaching unanimity of German scholarly opinion concerning Germany's imperialist drive for domination, errors committed in World War II, and major responsibility for the excesses against the Jews and the maltreatment of other European nations. But recently the pendulum had swung in the opposite direction. The economic and political recovery of West Germany was bound to alter the critical self-image of the Germans.

The period roughly between 1965 and the early 1980s had produced a new generation of historians, a majority of whom had shed the nationalist prejudices of their predecessors and shared most of the critical approaches of non-German scholars. They combined a scholarly outlook with a critical eye on the German past, including Germany's treatment of the Jews, especially the Nazi atrocities and mass murders during the Holocaust.

These historians included Herman Mau and Helmut Krausnick, Eberhard Jäckel, Gerhard Ritter (author also of a later relevant work in 1965), Joachim Fest, Karl D. Bracher, D-A. Uwe, J. Thiess, and Martin Broszat.[9] They all repudiated the ideology of National Socialism and the brutal reality of the Third Reich, its claims against non-Germans and its denunciation of the German opposition, and the mass murders of the Jews. J. Fest tried to downplay the latter. Some attempts were made even by M. Broszat and G. Ritter to look for mitigating circumstances such as the "revolt of the masses" to partly excuse the Germans. But most historians, including the foregoing, seemed shocked and did not hide their disgust and shame. German historiography had finally taken note of the ugly specter and the inhumanity of the Third Reich. In this era German historians did not deny the complicity of the German army, of the prominent German élites and did not unconditionally acquit the average German. The new generation of historians denounced the myths which had captivated the thoughts and feelings of the German masses and did not disavow the Holocaust. While not minimizing the role of Hitler in the destruction of German Jewry, the historians here analyzed did not intend to exculpate the German people in its entirety. Even many so-called functionalist historians did not aim at exculpating the average German. These historians adhered to the view that unforeseen opportunities of the war rather than persistent evil Nazi intentions led to the mass murder of the Jews.

J. Thiess and A. D. Uwe pointed to Hitler's and the Nazis' attempts to blame the Jews for allegedly striving toward world domination—in reality a cardinal goal of ill-disguised Nazi ambitions. M. Broszat's criticism of Germany extended not only to Nazi élites, but also to the old élites of Imperial Wilhelmian Germany and their drive for *Lebensraum*. On the other hand, M. Broszat spoke of Jewish "myths" regarding the Holocaust rather than of German "myths" which ultimately led to mass killings. M. Broszat and Detlev Peukert disagreed about the importance of the *Alltag* in the Third Reich and the relative innocence of the average German.

In *German History 1933–45. An Assessment by German Historians* (London, 1964) the authors and editors Hermann Mau and Helmut Krausnick focused on persecution in the Third Reich and that of the Jews in particular. In their view, the Nazi regime "looked forward to the complete subjugation of Europe after the war." As early as January 30, 1939, Hitler had prophesied that one result of the new war would be the "extermination of the Jewish race in Europe."[10] With his plan to attack Russia Hitler combined the idea of exterminating its Jewish population as being allegedly the foremost enemy of German rule. During the first months of his annihilation project in Russia, he must also have decided to exterminate all other Jews within the German sphere of power. It was the "final solution of the Jewish problem." Once the Russian campaign had started, four "action groups" under the Security Service (SD), Gestapo, and the Criminal Police were given the task of rounding up Jewish men, women and children by telling them that they were to be resettled and then shooting them. There is no doubt, the editors and contributors to this study continued, that the *Wehrmacht* was fully informed. In a number of instances the field commanders made protests or intervened. "But in general the army, preoccupied with its own problems and being constantly threatened with the dictator's displeasure, turned a blind eye." A number of soldiers even endorsed the "stem but merited punishment of Jewish sub-humanity." in spite of the highly developed jargon with which the regime "camouflaged" the planned mass murder of Jews, it was obvious enough what the so-called Wannsee Protocol of January 1942 actually meant. The great pains which Nazis took disguising the Jewish extermination program showed how conscious they were that "they had long exceeded what they dared admit even to their own people."

Eberhard Jäckel. "Intentionalists" and "Functionalists."

In a special chapter of his work *Hitler's Herrschaft-Vollzug einer*

Weltanschauung entitled "Der Weg zum Mord an den Juden," Eberhard Jäckel dealt with the preparation for the mass murder of the Jews. Removal of the Jews was Hitler's oldest goal which he had voiced already in a letter of September 16, 1919.[11] After 1929 the concept of "removal" included often the meaning of killing. In the second volume of *Mein Kampf* (1928) he wrote clearly that the separation of Jews was possible only "through the sword" and that such a procedure would be a "bloody" one. He also developed that the Jewish question had a significance for the entire world and regretted that at the start of the First World War 12,000 or 15,000 Jews had not been eliminated through poison gas. He made clear that the murder of a part of the Jewish population in Germany should take place during the war and that it was a means to win the war. To Admiral Horthy, the Hungarian regent, Hitler declared on April 17, 1943, that the Jews were comparable to tuberculosis germs and should be killed.[12]

According to Jäckel, and differently from Mau-Krausnick, Hitler encountered in his pursuit of killing the Jews less resistance than to his war plans. Some military leaders, however, opposed first the murders in Poland. Hitler was surprised that the killing of Jews occurred without German resistance. Until the end "he never lacked willing helpers." The mass murder shocked, temporarily at least, even Goebbels and men around Göring, and made Himmler once lament that also Jewish women and children had become targets of the annihilation. In this context Himmler assured Gauleiters and generals that he was not "blood-thirsty." Hitler, however, looked with satisfaction upon his anti-Jewish crusade and achievements. So did finally his paladins and the fanaticized cohorts in the SS.

In the dispute between the so-called "intentionalists" and "functionalist" school of interpretation of the Holocaust Jäckel took a clear-cut stand in behalf of the former. The terms had been coined by Tim Mason in 1981. The intentionalists placed all responsibility for the mass murder of Jews on Hitler, his ideology and policies. The functionalists maintained that there was no direct relationship between the ideological dogmas of National Socialism and its policies and that "decisions were functionally linked to one another and did not follow a preestablished plan." The two schools differed in their contrary interpretations of the origin and the implementation of Nazi policies toward the Jews. Most non-German historians of Nazi Jew-hatred are intentionalists, excepting Karl Schleunes' *Twisted Road to Auschwitz*

(1970). Many German historians, including revisionists such as E. Nolte, A. Hillgruber, K. Hildebrand, were also intentionalists. The intentionalists have shown a straight line leading from Hitler's expression of anti-Semitism in the early 1920s and voiced also in *Mein Kampf* (1924) to later testimonies. Jäckel spoke of the indefensible allegation of some historians that Hitler did not know what happened to the Jews.

In a later book *Hitler in History* (1984) Jäckel stressed that it was Hitler who ordered the Holocaust.[13] The extermination of European Jews in the Second World War or more precisely the German attempt to kill as many of them as possible was "an undertaking unique in modern history." The "operation was ultra-secret." Much was transacted orally, particularly on the highest level. Of the few relevant documents many were destroyed before the war ended. And of those that survive many contain code names and terms that further "hamper" the task of clearly establishing their contents. Many participants in the atrocities died before they could be interrogated. Most survivors were evasive to save their skins.

Eberhard Jäckel also questioned whether Hitler did give a direct order of mass killing, which had been denied by M. Broszat and other so-called functionalists. Jäckel did not accept functionalist interpretations that the killing programs evolved gradually from series of separate killing operations in 1941 and 1942 and from the impossibility of further evacuation and settlement of Jews in Europe. Hitler, according to Jäckel, was the only anti-Semite who had "ever expressly advocated systematic killing by the state as a means of resolving the Jewish question."[14] He had set himself two goals, a war of conquest and the elimination of the Jews, and regarded all other aspects of politics "simply as means to achieve these goals." In his second book, not published until 1961, Hitler had explained in detail why he wanted the Jews to be eliminated.

Hitler's hatred was certainly irrational but specific as well. In his view, the German Jews had to be eliminated since they undermined Germany's capacity for the struggle for living space. But he also wished other countries to eliminate their Jews as well. In 1941 he declared to a foreign statesman that he would confront each state with demands to kill the Jews. On January 30, 1939, Hitler publicly declared—as Jäckel put it, prophesied—that the result of another world war would be the destruction of the Jewish race in Europe. In several proclamations he projected a relationship between war and the solution of the Jewish question.

Functionalist historians have suggested that the whole anti-Jewish operation may not have been ordered or premeditated at all. Jäckel's view was that all officials in charge of the Jewish question, from Göring and Himmler to Heydrich and Eichmann, were fully involved in Jewish emigration, evacuation, deportation, and later outright murder. At least some of them were "shocked or even appalled when the final solution went into effect." To be "sure, they did not disagree with it." Still, Hitler was the "prime and only instigator of the Holocaust."[15] He was convinced that the destruction of the Jews was "his gift to the world." But years of persistent effort were required by Hitler to bring even his collaborators around to his plan to mass-murder the Jews.

> He may have made various vague suggestions here and there, both in public and within his inner circle to various collaborators who were competing against each other for his favor. He may have held out prospects of promotion. He may have flattered or threatened, appealing to loyalty, playing one supporter against the other, according to the acquired art of ruling by his system of government.

E. Jäckel concluded his essay with the assertion that while an understanding of Hitler's racial program of annihilation was "probably beyond our reach, it is necessary to clarify these matters" not merely for historical scholarship "but above all for the sake of the victims."

The assessment by Gerhard Ritter of Hitler and the Third Reich twenty years after the end of the war was a scholarly account of the horrendous events which had occurred in Germany and on the entire continent. In *The German Problem* (1965) G. Ritter wrote:

> We Germans and the world in general will long continue to be haunted by the question: how was it possible that a civilized nation like Germany fell prey to an adventurer of Hitler's quality and stained its name by the millions of ghastly crimes that were committed under his orders.[16]

Hitler's rule "appears to present-day Germans too incredible to be acknowledged in its full enormity, as a part of German history. Some of us close our eyes to it, call for an 'emancipation from history'," and "dilate the horror by calling attention to the multitude of monstrous acts done elsewhere, today as in the past."

None of the numerous explanations "rid our nation of the charge that at least for a time it gave its loyalty and frenetic applause to a monster of a man." Even before 1933 more than a third of the electorate voted for Hitler, and at the time of his overwhelming successes, he was certainly admired by a substantial majority as a national hero.

> His speeches, bragging charged with hate and contempt for internal and external opponents, full of malicious slanders, delivered with shrieking rage that today makes us shudder—did not produce moral disgust in his audiences, but deafening applause. The very questionable 'leaders' with whom he surrounded himself, did not arouse suspicion but, on the contrary, awakened readiness for unremitting service for the Party.

True, in all this was a great deal of "misguided patriotism."

> But the tragic evidence remains how dismally lacking vast numbers of Germans [even among the educated] were in political judgment. No less distressing and shameful is the cowardice and hypocrisy of countless men who adapted themselves to the totalitarian regime—among them many . . . who had been entrusted with maintaining the great tradition of German culture. The things that were common knowledge, beginning with the mass murders of June 30, 1934 [the killing of Captain Ernst Röhm, SA leaders and some of their following] were amply sufficient to prove to every thoughtful person that Germany was being run by a band of criminals.[17]

All this needs to be frankly admitted, but beyond it is the duty of the historian to make comprehensible what at first glance seems "incomprehensible." Germany's recent history had destroyed "once and for all the nineteenth century's naively uncritical faith in man's natural benevolence and in the ennobling effects of modern civilization." It has become clear not only in Germany but in many other places, especially in Lenin's and Stalin's Russia, that modern civilization is "morally no more than a thin coat spread over a fearful potential for human bestiality." Still, Germans must try to "move beyond self-accusation to a historical understanding of what happened." Gerhard Ritter has written here an honest and perceptive analysis of National Socialism during the Holocaust.

Yet the following pages of his reveal apologetic tendencies especially when drawing attention to "a series of similar or comparable developments in other European countries, which also showed "a radical transformation of authoritarian constitutions" and to his placing special emphasis on a "revolt of the masses" which was directed against guidance by established, traditional political élites. Gerhard Ritter stressed the highly developed propaganda techniques of the Nazis and the appearance of the "mass man" concerned with material well-being rather than with individual liberty of mind and action. It was a mistake to claim that Hitler's rise to power was "inevitable."[18] Certain features of German political thinking did favor Hitler's propaganda and many circumstances in Weimar Germany facilitated his rise to power. Yet the one-party state developed also in Russia and in Italy. The sharp opposition to the Versailles treaty was shared, Ritter recalled, even by the parties of the Left. What launched the Germans was not only national ambition, need for self-assertion, but "our impatience." The Germans overlooked that they were on the road to being accepted again into the European community and that France was growing less interested in maintaining her continental hegemony. Under a half-way rational leadership Germany would have played a role as the Free World's barrier against Bolshevism and in maintaining peace in Europe.

The support which during the height of the "Historikerstreit" of the 1980s Ernst Nolte, Professor in Berlin, received from some conservatives and "neoconservatives" was the more disturbing, as many of them were noted historians or responsible and respected journalists.[19] A case in point was Joachim C. Fest. His Hitler biography (1970) had been widely acclaimed. However, the book contained no special chapter, not even a sub-chapter on the Holocaust and the special role of the Jewish question in Hitler's rise to power; the latter was rather subdued. The same holds true of Fest's publication *The Faces of the Third Reich* (1970).[20] But due to their omissions, these critical works left the reader still puzzled that their author would later, in 1986, have rushed to the defense of the hostile writings of E. Nolte.

In the Hitler biography Joachim Fest pilloried the Führer's "insanely mounting anti-Semitism," offering only the "excuse" that the Jews, in the Führer's delusion, were the natural allies of Bolshevism. Hitler's decision for mass extermination was made, according to Fest, during the period of active preparation for the Russian campaign. In *The Faces of the Third Reich*, Fest painted a frightful picture of practitioners, technicians, and functionaries of the totalitarian rule, the Nazi bigwigs around Hitler, a clique which "was unique in its mental sickness, ruthlessness, inhumanity, and criminality." In 1939 Hitler might have been able to secure most of his foreign policy goals by way of legality. But out of arrogance and impatience, corrupted by success and "deceived by his own foolish and trite platitudes," he reverted in international affairs to the "putschist solution" that had failed once in domestic affairs. He started a war which, he anticipated, would result in German cities becoming heaps of ruin and in which "our sacred soil will not be spared." But as he assured his cohorts, he was "not afraid of this."

The prominent German political scientist and historian Karl Dietrich Bracher has dealt with Jewish history prior to 1933 in a subchapter, "The Role of Anti-Semitism" and during World War II in another one, "The Murder of the Jews" in *The German Dictatorship* (1970), in a brief but penetrating manner. Differently from some who have claimed that the years before 1914 witnessed a decline of anti-Semitism, Bracher offered a survey of anti-Jewish hatred in both Germany and the Austrian Empire in the decades before World War I. National Socialism, like its Führer Hitler, was the product of this war, but it was given its shape and form by

> those basic problems of modern German history which marked the painful road of the democratic movement. Among these were the fragility of the democratic tradition and the powerful remnants of authoritarian institutions before and after 1848; the susceptibility to nationalistic and imperialistic ideas, a product of the belated and never fully realized creation of a German national state; the problems arising out of the unexpected defeat and the resultant stab-in-the-back legend, and the widespread disgruntlement over the Versailles peace.
>
> The permanent crisis of a republic which never won the full support of the majority of the people, the explosive consequences of the Depression on this highly industrialized, socially and religiously divided state with the feudalistic, traditionalistic remnants, and, finally, the middle class fear of proletarization and Communism and the added resentment and panic of a rural population threatened by the spread of modern technology.

To it came the near-religious veneration of a Führer.

In terms of social psychology, Hitler, according to Bracher, represented the disfranchised little man eager to "compensate for his feelings of inferiority through militancy and political radicalism." The Third Reich came into existence as a result also of effective deceptive maneuvers as well as of a series of avoidable errors.

In the end the democratic forces were in the minority *vis-à-vis* the totalitarian, dictatorial parties of the National Socialists and Communists. In this situation "a large portion of Germany's top echelon went over to Hitler after 1933." The forces of a dark underground of German and European social and national conditions played a part in Hitler's coming to power. Bracher concluded with a quotation from Friedrich Meinecke about the power-state and Macchiavellism which, though not confined to Germany, were decisive factors in Germany's development. "The history of the power-state began with Hegel and was to find in Hitler its worst and most fatal application and extension."[21] Though not excluding general European factors in the rise of National Socialism, it did not occur to Bracher to dispute the primary German factors generating its growth. His judgment of National Socialism was unambiguously critical and totally negative.

The SS-ideology, Bracher developed quoting Himmler's notes in a conference with Hitler on June 19, 1943, glorified the extermination of the Jews as a "historical task." However, this was kept secret. Himmler again and again reminded his executioners "not to recoil from the most brutal logical consequences: the murder of women and children." The SS should "wipe this race off the face of the earth," but since the mass of the Germans were "not [yet] ready for this", "carry the secret with us to the grave." This would demand many "sacrifices" and high "idealism" which, according to Himmler, was required of SS henchmen. Hitler did not put down into writing "this most secret objective" of his career. Himmler praised this extermination of the Jews, "this silent activity" as "a glorious page of our history."[22] As early as March 1941 the Army Command had been notified by order of the Führer about the powers and "special assignments" held by Himmler. By early 1942, according to precise bureaucratic "program reports" on the "state of liquidation," more than one million Jews were murdered in this fashion. According to Bracher, the idea of gassing the Jews went back to World War I and to old sentiments over Hitler's gas poisoning in 1918. The SS bureaucracy continued to employ Aesopian language, referring to deportations to concentration camps as "emigration," "evacuation," "special treatment," and "disposition." For Hitler the "final solution" had "priority" before everything else. After June 1942 special Commando units burned and incinerated the victims of mass shootings in an effort to "remove any traces of the crimes."

The "Murder Vocabulary" of the Third Reich

Commenting about the infamous Wannsee Conference held on June 20, 1942, which decided on the Holocaust, Bracher wrote that its resolutions "cold, primitive, bureaucratic," combine the vulgar philosophy of National Socialism with the murder vocabulary of the SS-state. Even among themselves, Himmler and the SS leadership continued to use euphemistic language. The Army Command, especially Keitel, on the whole acquiesced in the extermination of Jews, at least closed its eyes to what was happening. "The Army became the accomplice of a policy which a majority of its officers, frequently against their better judgment, followed to the end in blind obedience to the leader." Actually the victory of the SS over the Army, obvious after the summer of 1941 even to outsiders, had in fact been decided at the beginning of the war when the Army accepted the SS murder system. This mass murder was defended even in Hitler's "testament" when he fanatically clung to his "basic idea," admonishing all who came after him, "leaders of the nation and followers, also in future to hold fast to the race laws" and "to relentless resistance against the poisoner of all peoples, 'international Jewry'." "The reality and irreality of National Socialism were given the most terrible expression in the extermination of the Jews."

Before continuing the analysis of the Holocaust writings by some other German historians in the 1970s it should be helpful to compare the conclusions reached by non-German scholars abroad. They were quite similar, if not identical, with the conclusions reached by Bracher.

This historic record makes clear Hitler's and the top Nazis' long-range planning of mass murder which they disclosed in numberless threats and solemn declarations prior to and after Hitler's seizure of power. On the other hand, the record also shows that they were bent on concealing definite plans of the annihilation of the Jews, hiding behind mere "prophesies," to escape in case of the defeat of their military adventures personal responsibility for their crimes.

Hitler's "Wish" and Camouflage. Broadening of Responsibilities: Himmler and Heydrich

Even in communicating with his most trusted advisors Hitler often concealed his ultimate intentions of mass murder, cloaking his goals for the outside world and even for the German people. After the war General Alfred Jodl, Chief of the OKW Operations Staff, referred to the camouflage tactics of the Führer in regard to the "Final Solution" of the Jewish question as a "masterpiece of concealment." By August 28, 1941, when Hitler's euthanasia program was officially discontinued, at least 80,000 mental patients and about 10,000 concentration camp prisoners had been killed. Internal communications referred to the "gassing processes" as a mere "disinfection."[22]

Himmler and other Nazi bosses referred repeatedly to Hitler's "wish" and "will" that the "Jewish race in Europe be exterminated,"[23] Three times in 1944, the last time on June 21, 1944, did Himmler refer to Hitler's commanding position regarding the Jewish question, saying: "It was the most dreadful assignment and the most awful commission that an organization could ever receive, the commission to solve the Jewish question."[24] As Fleming points out, this soldierly order can only have been given to Himmler by Hitler, "no one else stood between them in the chain of command."

Both Hitler and Himmler showed "tactical prudence" not to assume ultimate responsibility for atrocities and murders, Himmler even tried to involve high-ranking SS-leaders in collective responsibility.[25] Almost everyone involved in the mass murder, including the Army leadership, was anxious to establish its own innocence. Field Marshal Keitel repeatedly recalled the assurance that the Führer had given to him, to disassociate the armed forces from anything that would "taint" it in the eyes of the public and the world. Hitler himself made a point of never inspecting extermination camps. Yet he was the driving force in the extermination process. Julius Streicher, the very personification of Jew-hatred, wrote on December 25, 1941, in *Der Stürmer* that there was "only one solution: the extermination of the race whose father is the devil."[26] Whereupon Hitler three days later in his headquarters observed: "Streicher's picture of the Jew is too idealized. The Jew is much more common, much more bloodthirsty and satanic than Streicher painted him," which proved, in Fleming's view, "Hitler's unlimited and pathological hatred for the Jews, the very core of the dictator's *Weltanschauung*."

Referring to the notorious Wannsee Conference when the implementation of the annihilation of the Jews was decided, Heydrich pointed not only to the order given to him by Göring but also to Hitler's agreement that the Jews be "evacuated" to the East. The meaning of this was clear. At the Jerusalem trial Eichmann testified that the "discussion" mentioned "killing, elimination, and annihilation."[27] All this was revealed to representatives of the different ministries and SS agencies. In August 1941 Himmler referred to Hitler's explicit instructions regarding the exterminations, that the Führer's orders had the "force of law,"[28] and promised that the occupied East will be cleared of Jews (become "judenrein").

At a meeting in Prague in May 1942, Heydrich alluded to a personal order from the Führer about the killings. Himmler himself on other occasions referred repeatedly to Hitler's orders in speeches before large audiences, not only to SS officers but also to regular officers of the army. But in documents to Hitler himself, no reference was permitted to the "final solution," the ultimate goal of ruthless murder being carefully avoided in writing. Instead, reference was made repeatedly to "the Führer's wish." Hitler's presence and intervention in the matter of Jewish extermination was always unquestionable and visible at every stage. Hitler talked about annihilation of the Jews virtually during his entire career.

The Führer spoke to the Czech Foreign Minister F. Chvalkovsky on January 21, 1939, and in the *Reichstag* on January 30, 1939, at a time when other prominent Nazis focused on expulsion and Jewish emigration. On the whole, the radicalization of Nazi policy toward the Jews can be clearly discerned, though the period especially between 1933 and 1939 had its ups and downs. In an address to the Party's district leaders Hitler reiterated the point that "the final aim of our policy is crystal clear to us." At the same time he disclosed his tactics of hiding his intention to destroy "the enemy." He rather wanted to push him into "a tight corner" and "then deliver the fatal blow."[29] on January 26, 1944, Himmler revealed to several hundred high-ranking Army officers that when the Führer gave to him "the order to carry out the total solution of the Jewish question," he "at first hesitated to have my worthy SS-men" to execute such a "horrid assignment," but since it was a "Führer's order," "I could have no misgivings. In the meantime, the assignment has been carried out and there is no longer a Jewish question." In the words of S. Friedlander, in his introduction to Fleming's study, "messianic faith and an apocalyptic vision of history" was "at the heart of the political, bureaucratic and technological system of an advanced industrial society. A bureaucracy occupied center stage, indifferent to the destruction but pushed by its leader." What was occurring was the "almost immediate disintegration of the German political, institutional and legal structures as well as of the moral forces. No important obstacles stood in the way to the Nazis in Germany, in the other European countries and in the entire Western world."

Jochen Thiess and Dietrich Adam Uwe

Let us turn to the discussion of the Holocaust by two other German scholars of the 1970s, Jochen Thiess and Dietrich Adam Uwe. Jochen Thiess's *Architekt der Weltherrschaft. Die Endziele Hitler's* (1975) is based on a dissertation accepted at the University of Freiburg. According to Thiess, Hitler already in the early years 1920–23, was "pained by the unfair distribution of the world," the large extent of the empire of Britain and Russia; the former with its limited number of inhabitants practically ruled one-fifth of the entire globe.[30] In several articles in the *Völkischer Beobachter*, starting January 1, 1921, Hitler had declared the establishment of a Jewish world state a great danger and spoke of the "struggle for the victory of our own race" In other articles (January 27 and 30, 1921) in the same daily Hitler "strove for goals," which, he claimed, "the [Jewish] foe strives for."[31] The implementation of "Jewish imperialist plans for world domination" was possible "through the dictatorship of a ruthless minority." Hitler admitted that Germany was relatively small, but so was England and so was Jewry. Hitler believed that the Germans had a chance of ultimately dominating entire continents, possibly the world, especially if they make themselves the "Aryan avant guards" of Europe and the entire world against the "judaized" Soviet Union and the United States, the latter already threatened by Jews.

In other speeches Hitler, according to Thiess, tried to conceal German claims "for world domination" by pointing again to the struggle against Judaism which allegedly strove for this very goal. Germany would play the role of the savior and would make true the proverb "Am deutschen Wesen soll die Welt genesen" [The world should prosper emulating German ways]. The Jew, in contrast, Hitler had developed in an oration in April 1923, decomposed nations through propagation of the principles of democracy and the teaching of Marxism. The Soviet Star, for Hitler identical with the Star of David, the symbol of the synagogue, must be combatted with the swastika.[32]

Dietrich Adam Uwe studied contemporary history and "Politologie" at the University of Tübingen and served in the latter field at the *Pädagogische Hochschule* in Reutlingen. In 1979 he published the book *Judenpolitik im Dritten Reich.* In his oration of January 30, 1941, Hitler, Uwe developed, had threatened the entire European Jewry. The speech, according to the author, revealed that he wanted to shift responsibility for the widening of the European war on the Jews, an "imaginary opponent," while his "prophecy" that the Jews would not survive a new war, such as he plotted against the Soviet Union, disclosed his will in the event even of his failure against the USSR to crush the invisible "Jewish world enemy" with vengeance.[33] Hitler aimed at a terrifying, well organized and executed killing action of unimaginable dimensions.

But Nazi measures taken as late as the summer of 1941 show that the planning for the elimination of European Jewry was still imperfect. In October 1941 the so-called Madagascar plan of forcing Jews out of Europe and having them settle in Madagascar was widely discussed in Nazi and official circles, including by Eichmann, but probably thought of only as a temporary solution. Alfred Rosenberg wished to push the Jews westward beyond the Ural mountains. Hitler himself prohibited any public discussion in detail of the Jewish problem. Until the beginning of the war against Russia, the final orders relating to the Jews were not carried out, but thereafter they were executed with "unknown rapidity." With the proclamation of the "final solution" Jewry emerged "without protection, without rights, without the least certainty to survive the next day or the coming weeks."[34] What took place under the Nazi regime was a battle between conservative authoritarian and totalitarian forces, the latter led or represented by Hitler himself. Supported by the elimination of German Jewry from the economy, the termination of equality of rights and life in general of the German Jews—-which marked the first years of the Hitler regime–the Führer made in the end the "insane" decision of starting the process of annihilation.

The question as to the character of the past German-Jewish relationship and of the depth of German anti-Semitism was addressed by Julius Schoeps, son of the historian Hans Joachim Schoeps, himself a professor of Political Science at the University of Duisburg.

Julius Schoeps was a descendant of the Jewish philosopher Moses Mendelssohn and the businessman David Friedländer, who in 1809 was the first Jew who became City Councilor in Berlin. Julius Schoeps quoted the historian and Israeli philosopher of religion Gershom Sholem, who had developed the thesis that there had never existed a German-Jewish symbiosis, only a very one-sided Jewish-German dialogue. Despite German hostility, the Jews had striven toward emancipation and acculturation. But German Jews did not succeed in being fully accepted. With the year 1933 the German Jewish liberal road came to an end. Max Liebermann, famous painter, eighty-six years old, in a letter to the Hebrew poet Chaim Bialik and Meir Dizengoff, mayor of Tel-Aviv, voiced the view that the nullification of the emancipation by the Third Reich and of the dream of assimilation oppressed all German Jews severely. "As difficult as it turned out to be, I awakened from the dream which I dreamt my entire long life."[35]

The German "*Alltag*," "Good" and "Bad" Times

A prominent feature in the *Historikerstreit* of the 1980s was the endeavor especially of neo-conservative but also of other German historians to focus attention of scholars and of the general public upon the German *Alltag*, the daily life of Germans under the Nazi regime. This tendency had actually preceded the feud. It was designed to divert attention from Nazi barbarism and outright murders to the allegedly innocent life of the "little man" who knew little or nothing about the crimes committed during the Nazi era. Many German historians and journalists had long bared the truth about the vicious character of Nazi rule. German public opinion, however, less critical, preferred to look the other way. Also a popular historiography had tried to hide the terrible aspects of national-socialist crimes and focused upon allegedly positive aspects of the Nazi era, the modernization of the 1930s and the "peaceful" prewar period, the Autobahn, the Volkswagen, the mass entertainment, etc. Many of Germany's populist writers pointed out that, while there were "bad times," there were also "good times" during the Nazi reign. They focused on the daily life and emphasized the *Volksgemeinschaft*, and the full employment in the Third Reich, and other positive phenomena. After 1945 this notion embraced the view of "normality" in the Third Reich. Some German people tried desperately to separate the murder of the Jews from the daily experience of the average man.

During the last years, according to Detlev Peukert, a younger East German historian, a more accurate study of the memories of contemporaries had been undertaken and numerous new documents have convinced scholars and the public that this "apologetic distinction" between the "decent daily life" of the "little man" and the incomprehensible mass murder at Hitler's obvious command was without foundation. The national-socialist terror and Nazi domination of public and private life were fully recognizable not only in 1933, but during the following years up to the *Reichskristallnacht*" of 1938 and the outbreak of the war. In wartime, according to Peukert, the mass murder in the East and in the death camps became "evident to all who could observe reality. Only he who closed his eyes saw nothing."[36]

Normality and "Terror"

In their exchange of letters the Israeli historian Saul Friedländer and the Munich historian Michael Broszat had focused on the distinction between Nazi terror and the "normality" of the German *Alltag.*[37] History has actually shown close links between both phenomena, though some German historians were set on separating the two. Actually it was the terror which was used to establish "order" in the daily life of the average man. It resulted in dispatching so-called workshy (*arbeitsscheue*) people and criminals into concentration camps, in the arrest of alleged habitual criminals, and the "clearing" of the highways from tramps, vagabonds, and gypsies. It was based upon the forcible sterilization of hundreds of thousands suffering from hereditary diseases, including the death of thousands of women. So-called "anti-social elements" too were banished into concentration camps, including gays and lesbians. Himmler's concentration camps needed steady reliable workers, but they were actually maltreated. Millions of foreigners were subjected to "annihilation through work." In all these cases officials, orderlies, attendants, and scientists took part in their arrest, transport, imprisonment, and torture. The scientists claimed that deviant behavior was allegedly hereditary, but could be eradicated through "racial hygiene."

"Social" racism against all not belonging to the community (*Gemeinschaftsfremde*) and "ethnic" racism against so-called *Fremdvölkische* [of alien nationality] were closely linked in National Socialism, as also exemplified in the persecution of gypsies.[38] The chief Nazi ideologist Professor Dr. Robert Ritter, associated with Heinrich Himmler, endorsed the thesis that social character and criminal disposition originated through a mixture of gypsy blood, thus offering the justification for the persecution of gypsies as well as the "elimination" (*Ausmerzung*) of all "conspicuous individuals." Detlev Peukert saw the "key" for the mass murder concept in the use of the most modern techniques of mass killing in combination with the "teachings of racist biology." He admitted that German society even decades after the destruction of the last gas chambers had not come properly to grips with the involvement of broad segments of people, "of scientists and nurses, of employers and soldiers, of concentration camp guards and railroad personnel, who accompanied the cattle vans with their human prisoners," and the sinister role of the camp physicians.

The New Ideology: "Europeanism and Neutralism"

National Socialism had deprecated any kind of internationalism, subordinating it to its new gospel, the exultation of nationalism. But after World War II German nationalism, having adjusted itself to new circumstances and new times, appeared in new ideological colors. The circumstance that ultraconservatives presented themselves in a new garb, that of Europeanism, was nothing but camouflage, deception, and plain opportunism. The boosting of Europe was fashionable in the post-war era, especially after 1954 when the idea of the joint European defense began to flourish in the Cold War era. It received a setback in 1954 after a negative vote in France. German Rightists had pointed to the "European conception" of the SS which had been more than willing to accept volunteers in the struggle against Asiatic Bolshevism. According to the Rightists, the *Waffen-SS* had already realized European integration within its ranks. What the Nazis during the war and their followers thereafter favored was not a supranational Europe, but one in which Germany was to be once again the dominant power in Europe. The German Rightists were not converts to internationalism or cosmopolitanism, but extreme nationalists who aimed at subterfuge which would facilitate the domination over European nations! As the nationalist author Hans Grimm voiced it: The generation of *Frontsoldaten* felt during the Great War "the obligation to break a lance for one joint European family of nations, even to sacrifice our blood and life."[39] While fighting at Leningrad or Stalingrad and later in defense of German soil, they struggled "for Germany and thus for Europe" "against slavery and arbitrary rule." As they wrote:

"We say 'yes' to Europe, but not to one under leadership of Churchill-Spaak," "not to a Europe which ties itself to an extra-European and anti-European power." Though Hitler had stressed the "community of blood" at least of the Germanic peoples of Europe, the European appeal of National Socialism did never gain wide and genuine acceptance among German chauvinists either before or after 1939. For all practical purposes the European propaganda of National Socialism was primarily designed to attract foreign volunteers and mercenaries to the cause of Germany's domination over Russia and Europe. Extreme German nationalism gave itself an all-European appearance in the expectation that it would help to secure victory under the sign of the swastika. After Germany's post-war unification the numerical German superiority in relation to the rest of Central and East Central Europe made the camouflage of Europeanism attractive to many Germans.

Neutralism rejected the post-war alignment of the Federal Republic with either the West or the East. But this political attitude stressed primarily the political and intellectual independence of Germany from all ties with the Western Powers. Thus neutralism, despite its flag, had always an inclination toward the East, ignoring the domination of the DDR by the Soviet Union. The neutralist movement rested upon an inaccurate assessment of the threat from the East. It also disliked and resented the policies of the West.

The post-war history of neutralism started in 1950–51 with a circle of former *Hitlerjugend* leaders in Hamburg. The best known personality of the circle was a former *Oberbannführer* Wilhelm Jurzeck who became a leading activist against the rearmament of Germany. He even linked up with different ideological, political, and religious groups comprising Heinemann, Pastor Niemöller, and others. In later years too the political significance of the neutralist movement exceeded that of rightist extremism. It was by no means identical with it, despite some congruence between the two currents.

There was an indisputable "continuity" of the post-war radical Right with pro-Nazi right-extremist ideas.[40] The *Sozialistische Reichspartei*, as the seizure of documents in connection with the trial of some of its leaders before the West German Constitutional Court revealed, attempted to appeal primarily to former Nazis. With other organizations such as the *Waffen-SS-Traditionsgemeinschaft* (HIAG), the Ludendorff followers or the *Stahlhelm* was the "personal continuity" clearly established. The right extremists were not prepared

pared to repudiate their own political and ideological past. They asserted that this was a sign of their loyalty to National Socialism and testified to the steadfastness of their thought and character. National Socialists who managed to flee their country by the end of the war for Latin America were among those most stubbornly clinging to the past, while others who remained on German soil showed some readiness to accommodate to the new political conditions. This is shown in the early writings of Arthur Erhardt and Hans Grimm. In the post-war era German Rightists modified their vievs either for opportunistic reasons or out of fear of the consequences of full endorsement of National Socialism in a new and hostile environment. They also made some concessions to the change of public opinion in Germany which made the toning down and moderation of expression strongly advisable.

Nazi Atrocities, World War II, and the German Military

Some German military leaders have raised questions about several war policies of Hitler. During the war they did not protest against horrendous Nazi violations of international law. The first *Blitzkrieg* had silenced any oppositional movement on the part of Germany's military élite. Most importantly, the high-placed officers accepted without resistance Hitler's announcement of March 30, 1941, that in carrying out "the racial ideological principles of his conceptions for a war in the East" the front soldiers were to take "an active part."[41] The hostile image of "Jewish Bolshevism," of Bolsheviks and Jews fighting allegedly in close comradeship, helped to suppress any hesitations on their part. The so-called *Kommissarbefehl* [command relating to the commissars] and the *Barbarossabefehl*, the numerous orders to the army to fight alone or in close cooperation with the *SS-Einsatz* units against the gangs in East and Southeast Europe were loyally carried out, leaving little doubt about the active participation of regular German troops in the mass murders. War prisoners of Soviet-Jewish background were without exception liquidated, as were also Jewish prisoners of war of other nationalities. An OKW directive of July 17, 1941 provided for the surrender of "all politically dangerous elements" among the prisoners of the SS, though it was well known what this surrender actually meant.

As said, the ideological perception of close cooperation between Bolsheviks and Jewish partisans was widely shared by the *Wehrmacht* which closely cooperated with the SS. Leaders of the German economy provided no protection to the Jews. To the contrary, German industry participated in the exploitation of this helpless mass. Nearly all great German combines which operated in concentration camps had loaned from the SS an army of human working slaves. The prospect of "liberation" from Jewish competition and the so-called "Aryanization" of Jewish entrepreneurs by the state and new private owners attracted much support.

Within the SS system of domination the churches assumed a special position which was also reflected in their attitude to the Jewish question. Broad segments of the clergy welcomed the Nazi seizure of power expecting that a German-Christian *Volksgemeinschaft* would materialize. Gradually, however, with the churches themselves becoming the target of national-socialist assaults, and the distinct racial anti-Semitism which questioned Jesus and the first Christians, commenced some church resistance. Only some lower clergy began to protest against the persecution of Jews. But the church leaders remained silent and proved even incapable of offering the protection of the church to Jewish converts.

When the government introduced the Euthanasia program providing for the killing of insane people, the Catholic Church reacted sharply as the protesting letters of the bishop of Münster, Graf von Galen, showed. Hitler declared thereupon the Euthanasia program terminated, though he continued it in secret. There was a direct road leading from euthanasia to the assassination of the Jews. But in the latter case neither the church nor the German population was prepared for a public outcry against the murders. Neither the economic elimination of German Jewry or its expulsion, both of which occurred until 1941 publicly, produced any massive resistance or merely disapproval by the German population. As one J. P. Stern observed: "The population knew as much and as little as it wanted to know."[42] In the German Resistance the Jewish question played only the most marginal role. This holds true also of the noted *Denkschriften* of Carl Goerdeler, a key figure in the German Resistance.

In a short article in the *Tribüne* Gerd Ueberschär, "Hitler war nicht der Alleinschultdige," which well summed up the role of the SS, the *Wehrmacht*, and of Hitler himself, based his contribution on research about the development and activities of the *Einsatzgruppen*, of the *Sicherheitspolizei* and the *Sicherheitsdienst* (SD) of the SS which carried out the mass murder in the conquered eastern territories, entrusted to them by the Führer, Himmler, and Heydrich. Those measures received approval by prominent German military leaders such as General Field Marshal von Brauchitsch and numerous others. Actually, the poison of anti-Semitism was widely disseminated long before the start of the war. It had spread hatred among many German officers and soldiers. Thus, the murder of the Jews was in the words of General Fieldmarshal von Reichenau and his command of October 1941 seen as "a harsh but just penalty for the Jewish *Untermenschen* [subhumans]." Within little more than half a year until the spring of 1942, *Einsatzgruppen* murdered about half a million human beings. The author pointed to the essays produced by participants to a congress in Stuttgart about the "murder of European Jews during World War II" which was published by Eberhard Jäckel and Jürgen Rohwer. The book, Ueberschar emphasized, proved beyond a shadow of a doubt that "not only the SS, the SD and the police but also the army, the railroads, the industry" and other administrative agencies helped create the preconditions for the execution of the Holocaust.[43] As the Stuttgart *Oberbürgermeister* Manfred Rommel,[44] son of Field Marshal Rommel, emphasized, the annihilation of Europe's Jews through the Third Reich constituted "the darkest chapter of the history of man."

Ueberschär rejected the apologetic thesis that Hitler had "known nothing" about the murder of the Jews. Without the knowledge and approval of the Führer, other Nazi bigwigs such as Himmler, Heydrich, Göring, or Goebbels alone could not have proceeded with the mass murder. Of course, the final solution was carried out in "strict secrecy" and in "tarned language," Jäckel assumed that a written command of Hitler's may not have been issued.[45] Hitler's decision and command occurred through several agents only orally, but the Führer was not the only individual responsible. The crimes did not occur in a social vacuum, a conclusion reached also by Hans Mommsen.[46] According to A. Hillgruber, the annihilation of European Jews shipped to the East was not a consequence of a situation which forced Hitler into action but rather an essential part of his program. it was the war which offered the Führer the chance to commit mass murder of the Jews. But the death camps and annihilation in the East constituted a planned and integral part of the conduct of the war by the Third Reich.

Officials of the "Final Solution"

Why did so many Germans permit themselves to become participants in a gigantic crime and be led to ruin by a maniacal personality? Anti-Semitism alone may only partly account for it, plain fear of inactivity or of possible resistance, and hopes for rewards also unquestionably played a role. In Hans Mommen's view, a "technocratic hierarchical mentality dominated the outlook of many others." Raul Hillberg in his seminal study *The Destruction of European Jews* (first ed. 1961) developed the concept of the "machinery of destruction" which uninterruptedly grinds on involving an ever-wider group in its murderous enterprise.[47] This machinery was developed already in 1941. Hillberg concluded that Hitler's decision of mass murder was reached before the summer months of 1941, prior to the start of the war against Russia.

Christopher Browning in *The German Foreign Office and the Final Solution* (1978) has discussed the role of the Nazi bureaucrats, including that of the chief of the respective section in the *Aussenamt*, Martin Luther, a plain careerist.[48] He was no doctrinaire or racist like Heinrich Himmler, no dreamer of a future "Aryan heaven on earth" nor an old fighter like Goebbels, determined to cling to Hitler to the bitter end. Martin Luther, according to Browning, was an "amoral" technician of power, anxious to anticipate the will of the Führer in regard to the Jews. To Luther it was superfluous to wait for the specific orders from the Führer. "Initiative from below obviated the necessity for orders from above." According to Michael R. Marrus, "it was similar with the development and production of the Nazi invention of the gas van, which was first used in the so-called euthanasia program against mental patients." Heydrich had ordered scientists attached to the Führer's Chancellery to design a vehicle using exhaust gas for the planned murder. Hitler left details for the killing of people to others. Numerous officials contributed in a sinister manner to the implementation of the "final solution."[49]

National Identity

In *Mein Kampf* Hitler had endlessly repeated the slogan that the national identity of the Germans was threatened. National identity under the Nazis had a negative meaning, as marked by hostility toward non-Germans. Hitler's concept of Germany developing into a world power was indissolubly linked with the mass annihilation especially of the intelligentsia of Slavic peoples, the mass killing of European Jews and the crushing of the German opposition. During the First World War, however, the internal "enemy," the Jews and the Reds, were still spared.

In the history of European national states emerged a miracle weapon to bring about national identification: modern anti-Semitism. "He who wishes national identity must want exclusivity, the exclusion of others." Thus, Wilhelm Ribhegge of the University of Münster in 1987 zeroed in on the "national identity" of the Germans, a favored theme before the feud of the historians in the mid-1980s erupted. Many neo-conservative German historians have condensed their thoughts in expressions such as "identity of the Germans," the "joint identity of the German nation," "the collective heritage of German history" and similar slogans.

It seems strange, wrote Professor Ribhegge, that even historians who have initiated and practiced Anglo-Saxon methods of German history have focused upon the alleged peculiarities of the national character of other peoples. They indulged in vague and dark allusions about national characteristics. He raised the question: How could one seriously discuss for months whether the crimes committed under National Socialism were "unique" or "comparable"? German historians were good, Ribhegge developed, when they produce incredibly long editions of source materials for German history. But they are mostly bad and helpless when they write generally comprehensible accounts of history entirely avoiding value judgments.[50] A good historian will not sacrifice making moral judgments. A "history totally shying away from ethical judgments was an absurdity." This was certainly valid for making necessary judgments about the Holocaust.

Nazi Population Policy

A number of German and non-German scholars have focused attention on Nazi population policy of Eastern Europe. Its evident goal was to bring about vast population movements and radically alter the demographic structure of the region. Non-Germans were to be eliminated from the new territory of the Reich, while *Volksdeutsche* from various parts of Europe were to be resettled in the East. In the fall of 1939 Himmler, already master of a huge political apparatus known as the *Reichssicherheitshauptamt* (RSHA), had succeeded in bringing under his control a number of agencies concerned with resettlement and racial matters. Outright killing was a major instrument in the achievement of these goals. Millions of non-Germans, especially Poles, Russians, Ukrainians, and Byelorussians as well as other national groups were the targets of this slaughter. It did not involve and aim at the murder of all members of these nationalities, but especially its leading strata. Total annihilation of a people was reserved only for Jews, but the dimension of the murder of other peoples was also unprecedented. Thus seen, the extermination of the Jews, though unique, was only a part of a vaster project aimed at the racial reordering of much of Europe.

Nazi policy in the East aimed at the construction of a vast pan-German empire, territory destined for German *Lebensraum*. In this region non-German nationalities, considered inferior to Germans, would be reduced to a serf-like status, but Jews would be totally excluded from this area. Taking account of the large number of Jews in Eastern Europe, the hostile sentiments widespread among the native peoples, the Nazis operated there with little restraint in their anti-Jewish policy.

IV

THE "HISTORIKERSTREIT," 1986–87 JÜRGEN HABERMAS AND THE MAJOR PROTAGONISTS OF NEO-CONSERVATISM AND REVISIONISM: E. NOLTE, F. HILLGRUBER, K. HILDEBRAND, M. STÜRMER, AND J. FEST

After the "Wende" right-wing publicists and researchers increased the publication of patriotic and nationalist articles in the German press, they were soon joined by known university professors. One of the most widely read articles that appeared in the *Frankfurter Allgemeine Zeitung (FAZ)* on June 6, 1986, was Ernst Nolte's "The Past Will Not Pass Away."[1] Many historical events darkened the image of Germany. Though fascism was unlikely to make again any headway in Germany, Germany's obsession with her past diverted attention from pressing contemporary issues such as the bitter struggle in Afghanistan. At the same time the Erlangen University Professor of History Michael Stürmer, frequent columnist for the *FAZ* and close advisor to Chancellor Helmut Kohl, authored a series of articles searching for national identity. Facing "a campaign of fear and hate" originating in the East, this propaganda undermined German national self-confidence. Differently from other Western states, only 20 percent of Germans showed pride in being Germans. Andreas Hillgruber, Professor of History at Cologne University, voiced the fear that East Germany, attempting to regain a positive relationship with Germany's historical traditions, constituted a threat to the Bonn Repulic. It might become the new "Piedmont" in Central Europe.[2]

Expansionism due to revision of the boundaries of Germany through unification of West and East Germany and directed beyond it against Poland and Czechoslovakia was still widespread in rightist and neo-conservative circles and especially among former expellees. In 1985 other developments, especially the Bitburg controversy, added appreciably to the volatile situation in the Bonn Republic and also the historical profession.

The Bitburg Controversy: A Prologue

As Raul Hilberg, a leading scholar of the Holocaust, writing about Bitburg, remarked, Chancellor Helmut Kohl in 1985 was determined to lead the German people out of the "psychological isolation,"[3] out of the "desert." In 1984, when the leaders of the Western Powers met celebrating the anniversary of the wartime landings in Normandy, Kohl understandably was not invited to the ceremony. But he was partly consoled by his meetings with François Mitterand at a Verdun cemetery. Yet anything which only resurrected the First World War was not considered by the Germans the right commemoration. For this purpose Chancellor Helmut Kohl invited Ronald Reagan, President of the U.S. to meet him, choosing the military cemetery of the town of Bitburg. After protests were raised against Reagan's planned visit to Bitburg, the President announced that he had scheduled an additional visit to Bergen-Belsen. However, this only aggravated the protest; while going from the mass grave of the Jews to the graves of the SS-men—about forty-seven SS were buried there—he seemed to be unaware that the SS had been involved in the killing of millions of Jews in Eastern Europe.[4] President Reagan, however, insisted that all, the murdered and the murderers, were both victims. Protests were then voiced not only by Jews but also by majorities in the U.S. Senate and House of Representatives and many groups. On the other hand, German polls showed that three-fourths of the German population were in favor of Reagan's visit and a great majority in the *Bundestag* opposed any cancellation.

From the beginning, U.S. policy in the post-war era toward the Nazi problem was to reduce the number of those held accountable for past crimes. The U.S. had rejected the concept of "collective guilt." The groups not to be pursued during the occupation consisted of the great majority of civil servants, bankers, and industrialists, generals, diplomats, and judges. Among those, however, declared to be criminal organizations were the Gestapo, the Security Service and all SS-men except draftees who had no choice in the matter and who had committed no crimes.

Actually, it was not only the SS and associated organizations but also the German *Wehrmacht*—the name of the armed forces during the Third Reich—which was deeply involved in the mass killings of the Jews. But for years the Germans had tried to create an image of the *Wehrmacht* as a military organization fighting only in the defense of the German homeland, the successor of the pre-war *Reichswehr* and the forerunner of the post-war *Bundeswehr*. The *Wehrmacht* had been dismantled in 1945, but the German army was reborn in the early 1950s. But historical truth, now widely acknowledged by German historiography, was that the functions of the military were not sharply separated from the SS. Toward the end of the war over two million Red Army men, prisoners in Germany, had died, the result of deliberate starvation and exposure.[5]

For a long time after the war, the German public was allegedly unaware of the manifold function which uniformed members of the German army had performed in the annihilation of the Jews. The German Army in the East had established many Jewish ghettos. It gave "logistic support to the "*Einsatzgruppen*" and helped chasing Jews and locating them to be shot. Military governments in France, Serbia, and Greece issued anti-Jewish economic regulations. Officers of the German army signed contracts with German firms which employed Jewish slave labor and transport officers of the army were responsible for dispatching trains to the death camps. The German army transferred Jewish Soviet prisoners of war to the SS which shot them. General Keitel and Jodl were found guilty of these war crimes and were hanged in Nuremberg, and other German generals were tried before U.S. military tribunals.

Bitburg, it was observed, produced no winners. American Jews were perturbed since the president, despite all the protests, had gone to Bitburg. After the visit, Germans complained about the power of the American Jews who had managed to reduce the visit to eight minutes. President Reagan could not extricate himself from the dilemma which he himself had created. For the great majority of the Germans, official expressions of repentance and initiatives of providing reparations, seemed, according to Saul Friedländer, to be a sufficient *Ersatz* for memory.[6]

This silence was broken during the 1960s when German youth began to rebel against the older generation. But later on this youth rather focused the outrage less on the deeds of their parents and more on the American war in Vietnam and on Israel's policies *vis-à-vis* the Palestinians. They still resented matters at home, especially that many former Nazis had found safe and even respected places in the Bonn Republic. But they showed little understanding for the precarious situation of the Jewish remnant from the Nazi slaughter which, battling for dignity and independence of Israel, encountered bitter hostility in the Mideast, being threatened in their national and individual existence.

Some Dissonant German Views, 1985

In the early months of 1985 on the fortieth anniversary of Germany's military breakdown, several major German figures took different positions on the past in the *Bundestag*. President Richard von Weizsäcker was clear-cut that May 8, 1945 was "a day of liberation." "It liberated all of us from the inhumanity and tyranny of the national socialist regime." Golo Mann, author of a history of Germany in the nineteenth and twentieth century, considered a liberal, the son of Thomas Mann, was, however, critical of commemorations that "reopen wounds."[7] In a short essay he compared the defeat of Nazi Germany with that of Napoleonic France, though briefly admitting the criminality of the Third Reich. Regarding World War II, he focused, however, on the massive loss of the German population expelled from the East and the Allies' harsh conditions imposed thereafter.

Rudolf Augstein also questioned whether Germany should continue to commemorate anniversaries of Nazi crimes.[8] In a longer article he tried to develop that, Hitler aside, it was the Bismarckian Reich that had to be destroyed. Even without Hitler, World War II would have come about. While quite critical of the Imperial Germany of Bismarck, Augstein also took the Allies to task: "Whether the Allies committed fewer crimes was not at all certain." Equally misleading was his assertion that Hitler's crimes were directed primarily "against foreign countries and against the numerically much stronger foreign Jews than against the German Jews who numbered only about half a million.

Golo Mann had zeroed in on the terror and death accompanying the German expulsion from the eastern territories. The same emphasis on the terrors and injustices of the late wartime expulsion of Germans was voiced, though somewhat suppressed, by a vote in the *Bundestag* on June 13, 1985. On the positive side, it made the denial that persecution was meted out by the Nazi regime an offense. But after insertion of a few critical words in the resolution of the German parliament, it stressed that persecution was also perpetrated "at the hands of another system of violent and arbitrary domination,"[9] words which were directed not only against the Soviets but also against the

Allies and their methods of warfare against the defenseless German civilian population through fire-bombing, especially the destruction of Dresden.

Jürgen Habermas and the Main Protagonists of "Revisionism." Habermas' Opening Salvo, July 1986

The criticism of the neo-conservative historians was not commenced by fellow historians but by the Frankfurt philosopher and sociologist Jürgen Habermas. A man of broad interests, who belonged to the Frankfurt School of Marxist sociologists, he was politically not associated with the communists. His national as well as international reputation was well established. On July 11, 1986, Habermas delivered the first broadside on Ernst Nolte's theses. The article "Eine Schadensabwickelung. Die apolegetischen Tendenzen in der deutschen Zeitgeschichtsschreibung" was published in the liberal weekly *Zeit*.[10] Habermas pointed therein to the interrelationship between the thesis of the conservative politician Alfred Dregger and history professors such as Andreas Hillgruber, Klaus Hildebrand, Michael Stürmer, and Ernst Nolte, between the "ideological planners" and the Bonn Government's Museum projects, and warned against the "new revisionism."

Habermas first zeroed in on the Cologne historian Andreas Hillgruber and his pamphlet *Zweierlei Untergang, Die Zerschlagung des Deutsschen Reiches und das Ende des Europäischen Judentums* (Berlin, 1986). In Hillgruber, Habermas discovered the clichés and the rhetorics of the war pamphlets and criticized in particular the notion of the reconstruction of the destroyed "European center." Habermas also took Michael Stürmer to task for elaborating on consciousness and identity. Historians like Stürmer wanted a revisionist history to serve the rebirth of a conventional identity. Such "ideological planners" pleaded for a "unified historic image" and rejected a pluralism of historic interpretations,

The expulsion of Germans from the East was by no means the "reply" to the Nazi crimes in the concentration camps. Hillgruber rather held that it had been the goal of the Western Powers in the case of victory to wrest the greater part of the Prussian-German eastern provinces from the Reich. The Allies were rather moved by selfish considerations and by their distorted image of Prussia. The Western Powers recognized too late that through the advance of the Russians all of Europe became "the loser of the catastrophe of 1945." The alliance of the West with Russia was thus a crucial mistake. The German eastern army had been for centuries a protective shield of the German population and of the home of millions of Germans.

In the second part of his treatise, Hillgruber, in only twenty-two pages, juxtaposed the "destruction" (*Zerschlagung*) of the Reich to the "end" of European Jewry.[11] As if the "end" had come "naturally"! The gas chambers were described as more effective means of "liquidation." Here the author aimed to prove that the mass murder of the Jews was "exclusively a consequence of the radical race doctrine"! As if this hypothesis offered an excuse for unprecedented crimes! Hillgruber disavowed the liberation perspective which applied only for the surviving victims of the concentration and death camps and not for the German nation in its entirety. The Bonn historian focused on the concrete fate of the German nation in the East and on the desperate efforts of the German Eastern army and the German navy in the Ostsee to protect the population of the East against the "orgies of vengeance by the Red Army," the murders and the arbitrary deportations, and to keep open the flight to the West. Habermas was "stunned" why the historian of 1986 should deal with the thought and sentiments of the affected East German population forty years after the event. All this was to be illuminated from the perspective of the courageous German soldiers and the desperate German civilians. Hillgruber wanted to prove that the expulsion of the Germans from the East was by no means the "answer" to the German crimes committed in the concentration and death camps. Turning to Allied war goals, he claimed that in the case of Germany's military defeat there was never a chance to improve the destiny of the East Prussian and other East German provinces. The disinterest of the Western Powers in this question was due to a "cliché-ridden image of Prussianism," The Western Powers, according to Hillgruber, were blinded by their war goals which embraced the destruction of Prussia. They recognized too late that through the progress of the Russians "all of Europe was the loser of the catastrophe of 1945."

In the latter part of his essay, Hillgruber dealt with the "end of the European Jewry" (*Judentum*). While previously Hillgruber had focused on the central role of the East German population, he avoided giving prominence to the fate of the Jews. He made Hitler alone responsible for the "Final Solution," but failed to judge the "frightening" fact that the mass of the German population had assumed a passive role. That a civilized people permitted monstrous deeds, Hillgruber tried to explain by pointing to generally human weaknesses (*allgemein Menschiiches*)—hardly a convincing explanation.

If not the Nazis but German Nationals and members of the *Stahlhelm* would have come to power in 1933, the Nuremberg laws and all other measures which were passed in the Third Reich would also have come about, since this was in agreement with the feelings of a great part of German society. But in 1941 Hitler alone had conceived the physical annihilation of the Jews, since only through such a "social revolution" the world power status of the Third Reich promised durability. Habermas questioned whether Hillgruber shared the view of this alleged connection. Hitler, Hillgruber also claimed, was "isolated" in the concept of the annihilation of the Jews—a thesis which acquitted even Göring, Himmler, and Heydrich, or lessened their guilt. But Hillgruber himself was apparently unconviced of the correctness of this analysis. The "mass of the German population" had a "premonition" of the "gruesome events." Hillgruber was deeply terrified about the high percentage of academicians among the Nazis.

In another contribution, "Zwischen Mythos und Revisionismus," Hillgruber underlined the importance of historical revisionism because the history of the Third Reich was largely written by the victors and by Jewish authors. He pointed to alleged threats of annihilation by Jews—a mere figment of invention. Yet, according to Hillgruber, Hitler, "long before Auschwitz" had good reasons for his conviction that the enemy had "wanted to annihilate him." He had pointed in this context to the alleged "declaration of war" of Chaim Weizmann, the Zionist leader, before the Jewish World Congress in September 1939 when Nolte had presented this view—which in his opinion had justified Hitler to treat "the Jews as prisoners of war"—to his Jewish guest, the Israeli historian Saul Friedländer at an evening meal, the latter demonstratively left the table.[12]

As far as Nolte was concerned, Habermas referred to his mention of Pol Pot in Cambodia, the Gulag of Stalin, to some nineteenth-century European personalities and events, and concluded that "the so-called [!] annihilation of the Jews during the Third Reich was a reaction or a distorted copy, but not a first-hand event or an original." While pointing to the contrasts between Marx and Maurras, Engels and Hitler, he considered them "still related figures" despite the gulf between their intellectual status and character. Habermas ridiculed Nolte's "comical background philosophy," the thought of eccentric spirit. Some "unappetizing examples" of his writings show that Nolte in regard to anti-Semitism "far surpasses the playwright Fassbinder" against whom the *FAZ*, which published Nolte's article on June 6, 1986, had come out previously. The theory of Nolte, a disciple of the philosopher Martin Heidegger (whose Nazi leanings were well known), helped in general "manipulation." The Nazi crimes lose their singularity because they are not made comprehensible as a rejoinder to the still continuing Bolshevik threats of annihilation.[13–14]

Nolte had referred to the circumstance that the history of the Third Reich, to a large degree, were written by the victors, had created a "negative myth" by comparing it with a "disgusting" picture which a victorious PLO would paint after a complete annihilation of Israel. Long before Auschwitz, Hitler had good reason for his conviction that the foe wanted to "annihilate" him. In view of Hitler's alleged conviction of being personally threatened by the Jews, Nolte considered their destruction merely the "reaction" to the Jewish menace.

As a contribution to the 1986 Römerberg talks, the *FAZ* on June 6, 1986, had published a belligerent article by Nolte which had started the polemics. Nolte, according to Habermas, reduced therein the singularity of the annihilation of the Jews to a mere technical innovation of gassing them. He pointed out that the Gulag Archipelago had preceded Auschwitz. Nolte also held that the SS-men of the death camps were in a way also "victims." The Nazis also killed Poles, many of whom were "virulent anti-Semites." Did the killing of both Jews and some Poles, who by chance were also Jew-haters, minimize the Nazi-crimes against the former?

While acknowledging Nolte's past scholarly contributions, Habermas questioned his long-winded conclusions that National Socialism must be placed in relation also to the fears and the crisis which were caused by the "Industrial Revolution," and his bizarre assertion that the annihilation of the Jews must be related to the Russian October Revolution as "its most significant precondition." Similarly irritating to Habermas was Nolte's remark about the process of Western "modernization," which made Marx, Maurras, Engels, and Hitler[15]—men of rather different intellectual caliber as well as of character—"related figures."

Pointing to the energetic attempts of the Bonn government to awaken and reinforce the historic conscience of the population and to revive the national identity, Habermas rejected the Erlanger historian

Michael Stürmer's endeavors to create a "unified historic image" of Germany. Bonn's great intellectual achievement of the post-war era was the opening of the *Bundesrepublik vis-à-vis* the political culture of the West. That opening has been achieved through overcoming the "ideology of the center which our revisionists with their geopolitical ballyhoo [Tamtam] of the old European '*Mitellage*' [central location] of the Germans [Stürmer] and of the reconstruction of the destroyed European center" (Hillgruber) were tying to revive.

Finally, Habermas observed that there had emerged after 1945 a pluralism of historic interpretation and methodological approaches.[15] Aiming at the leading conservative and nationalist lights of the traditional German historiography, he asserted that the old "conscience of the mandarins" had not survived the national-socialist period, since they had been found guilty by their powerlessless and even their "complicity with the Nazi regime." Revisionists were therefore miscalculating when they believed that they could choose an "especially suitable historic image" from a purposefully reconstructed past.

"The only patriotism which does not alienate us from the West is a constitutional patriotism," He "who wishes to revert to a conventional form of national identity destroys the only reliable foundation of our tie with the West."[16] The declaration of war against German revisionism was clear and unencumbered.

Ernst Nolte

Criticisms of Jürgen Habermas was directed to a substantial degree against the Berlin historian Ernst Nolte. Nolte, born in 1893, had studied philosophy at Freiburg University where he was influenced by Martin Heidegger. He obtained his doctorate writing a dissertation about "Selbstentfremdung [self-alienation] und Dialektik in deutschem Idealismus und in Marx." Between 1953–1964 he worked as a classical philologist in school administration. An outsider among historians, a teacher (*Studienrat*) at a secondary school in Godesberg, he published the important work *Faschismus in seiner Epoche* (1966).[17] At the suggestion of the historian Theodor Schieder he had habilitated* in 1964 at the University of Cologne. His book was based upon an analysis of German National Socialism, Italian Fascism, and

* Habilitation required a postdoctoral thesis as a qualification for university lecturers.

the *Action Française* as variants of fascism. In his study Nolte considered fascism as an extreme but understandable reaction to the Russian October Revolution and to the Bolshevik threat to Germany, In an essay "The negative vividness [*Lebendigkeit*] of the Third Reich" (1980) he developed the major outlines of his interpretations.

Though on questions of university policy, which in the late 1960s assumed a major role in the *Bundesrepublik*, Nolte had been engaged on the Right, he was generally known as a loner and eccentric. For one semester he had served as visiting professor at the Hebrew University of Jerusalem. But subsequently he performed a volte-face on the Jews.

Three Faces of Fascism (1966)

According to Nolte's *Three Faces of Fascism*, Hitler's *Table Talk* exposed in a most startling way the determination with which he always wanted war and the lack of scruples he displayed when financing it. Hitler's "world dominance" was not the resuit of a single act of conquest and not to be understood as a subsequent permanent state of peace, but as a constant state of war, with the assurances of ultimate German dominance. The German notion, according to Nolte's interpretation of the Führer's thought, was that the German people was to verify its own life through the death of others.[18]

Nolte concluded that fascism in its most extreme form had committed a crime which was beyond comparison [!] with anything the world has ever seen, even including Stalin's reign of terror against his own people because it was "at one and the same time rational to the point of perfection and irrational to the point of excesses and because it regarded its victims to longer as human beings but either as creatures of the devil or tools without rights." He indicated one man bears the legal responsibility "for a crime of such unprecedented magnitude." But, often wavering, Nolte also pointed to the international aspects of anti-Semitism, without however offering any explanation why it originated and grew to monstrous proportions just on German soil. Was total mobilization inside and outside of Germany—a display that could have only one implication—"not universally taken for what it was, 'a [German] declaration of war'? How could the Germans, he had then asked, "once known as a nation of thinkers," seriously suppose that their Führer was a wizard who alone among earth-dwellers knew how to create employment and economic recovery out of nothing, while producing quantities in unproductive weapons?

In any case, how could Nolte reverse the role of Germans and Jews, making the former innocent victims of the latter's militancy, victims of a Jewish "declaration of war"?

Nolte accorded to the millions of Hitler's victims "the highest of all honors," implying that those "who were exterminated as bacilli" did not die as unfortunate victims of a repulsive crime, but as "deputies [!] in the most desperate assault ever made upon human beings." What honor!

In Nolte's study *Three Faces of Facism*, Hitler admittedly was "no hero" to the author. The Führer "in the most monomaniacal core of his being," did over the length of time not change "one iota of his thought,"[19] Also, Nolte rejected the "all too transparent apologia" which saw in Hitler and only in "his unusual, not to say abnormal personality" the *causa efficiens* of the whole sequence of events.[20] He rightly stressed the Führer's Austrian background and the influence upon him of Georg von Schönerer, the pan-German leader, Karl von Lueger, the mayor of Vienna, Adolf von Lenz of Liebenfels—the latter the author of numerous anti-Semitic pamphlets—and of the first national-socialist German Workers Party founded in Trautenau in 1904. Though the Germans were the leading nationality in Austria, Schönerer, like Hitler later, feared or pretended to fear that the Germans were in danger of being "slaughtered."

Questionable Utterances

Next to some insights, there were many questionable utterances and dubious comparisons in Nolte's work about fascism. Referring to the assassination of Councilor von Rath by Hershel Gruenspan in the German Embassy in Paris—which was the catalyst unleashing the Nazi pogrom in November 1938, the misnamed *Kristallnacht* and the burning of the synagogues all over Germany—Nolte wrote: "By making thousands of Jews answerable for the deed of one man, the leaders of the [German] state were preparing the soil for the deeds of one man." The isolated act of one young desperate Jew against one German was thus compared to Hitler's planned mass assault upon the Jews—a genocidal act which could not have occurred without the knowledge and assistance of hundreds of thousands of Germans! Still the emphasis in Nolte's work on fascism lay not in his inept comparison of Gruenspan with Hitler, but in different directions. On the whole, Nolte escaped criticism for the scattered yet clearly anti-Jewish implications in his early book.

In this work on fascism Nolte called World War II "the most atrocious war of conquest, enslavement and annihilation known to modern history."[21] In this context he did not wish to blame Hitler alone for all the atrocities committed. Thus he wrote; "One cannot accept the theory that not only personal criminal tendencies of Hitler and some of the 'arch-villains' of his coterie were responsible for the atrocities." In his view, Hitlerism and racism were inseparable. Auschwitz was "firmly embedded in the principles of national-socialist race doctrine." On the other hand, Nolte seemed gratified that none of the defendants in Nuremberg made "any attempt whatsoever to justify the extermination measures" and that no one "testified defiantly to the necessity of the war for the conquest of living space and its unprecedented methods." He hurriedly drew the apologetic conclusion that "these men had been better people than most of the world had assumed."[22] That obviously had not been the judgment in the Nuremberg trial and of world public opinion.

Germany and the Cold War – Foreign Critics

About a decade after his first book, Nolte published *Deutschland und der Kalte Krieg* (Stuttgart, 1974).[23] While insightful in some respects, it was also marked by long-winded digressions about antiquity, the formation of the U.S., and other unrelated topics. Nolte also made some bizarre observations, such as that the national-socialist regime prior to 1939, if compared with Soviet communism, could be called "a state under the rule of law, a liberal idyll" and that the U.S. during the Vietnam War initiated "basically an even more cruel service of incarceration than Auschwitz"! He also asserted that Zionism in origin and goal was "very close" to its sharpest enemy, anti-Semitism.[24] In the opinion of a noted German scholar, those were hardly permissible errors but total misjudgments.

According to Nolte, Hitler was not only an anti-Communist and anti-Semite, but he also wanted *Lebensraum* for the German people; the latter concept did not merit the ridicule which it has often encountered. After all, both the Russians and Americans had in the nineteenth century conquered vast lands and Hitler's drive for living space was principally not different from that of both these peoples. In this work Nolte, dealing with Zionism, held that the Zionist criticism of the "Luftmenschentum" [people not culturally and territorially rooted] of the Diaspora and of assimilation Jews "was not infrequently similar to the description of "a parasite-like exploitation" and to the "simultaneous invectives of the anti-Semites." Allegedly the Zionist ideal of combining "plow and weapon in one hand" was not very far removed from the "ideal of their foes." Zionism appeared to Nolte obviously as a "reactionary movement," aiming at the restoration of the conditions of antiquity and directed against modernization and modernity, though it was simultaneously a movement for the liberation of the suppressed Jewish masses of Eastern Europe. Nolte vastly exaggerated and distorted the extent of the "agreement" between Zionism and anti-Semitism and suppressed their deadly hostility, Jewish rebirth and revival against destruction and annihilation. He also saw in the emigration of Jews to Palestine the possibility of the emergence of a "racial state." A "racial state"—this was the Arab and Soviet denunciation of Zionism at the time of the publication of Nolte's *Germany and the Cold War.*

Though Nolte admitted the anti-Jewish deterioration of British policy in the immediate post-war era, he criticized the "great terror campaign" of the Jewish "Self-Protection" organizations against the mandatory power. David Ben-Gurion's proclamation of the state of Israel and the announcement of plans of unlimited immigration into the new state was practically a "declaration of war" against the Arabs. The disciples of the nineteenth century Zionist writer Moses Hess, who was also a socialist, adopted the concept of a "racial war—culminating in accusations of "racism."

In the U.S., Nolte was taken to task by Felix Gilbert of Princeton and Peter Gay of Yale University. The former judged Nolte's work *Deutschland und der Kalte Kreig* as "myopically Germanocentric" and regarding major points of interpretation "disturbingly vague and unsupported by hard evidence,"[25] as a "massive and sophisticated apology for modern Germany." Peter Gay took Nolte to task for the "tortuous syntax, his evasive conditional phrasing, his irresponsible thought experiments" which make it "virtually impossible to penetrate to his own convictions."[26] Nolte tried to divert attention from the Third Reich by pointing to "crimes committed by others." Rejecting his anti-American line, Gay found "a world of difference" between the Third Reich's calculated policy of extermination and the SS's "ill-conceived, persistent, often callous prosecution of a foreign war." Nolte's frequent "speculations even transcend competitive trivialization."

A later criticism by the British historian Richard Evans fits in quite well with the foregoing earlier American assessments. Evans held that many of Nolte's views have been presented "in a manner that is often obscure, sometimes confused, occasionally downright contradictory." "Isolated" affirmations of condemnations of Nazism were "completely undermined by numerous claims and suggestions to the opposite effect." The German echo to these criticisms was still rather feeble.[27]

The dispute of German historians about Nolte's views in the *Historikerstreit* erupted in 1986 when Nolte published in the *FAZ* an article "Vergangenheit, die nicht vergehen will" on June 6, 1986, and continued with the publications of his pamphlet "Das Vergehen der Vergangenheit" the following year against his critics. While he encountered distinguished opponents, a few noted historians rushed to his side defending him. To the surprise of many, the prestigious *Historische Zeitschrift (H.Z.)* offered a review of Nolte's latest work by his colleague Klaus Hildebrand, a historian at the University of Bonn, who praised it as "pioneering."[28] Both Hildebrand and Joachim Fest, the latter a well-known biographer of Hitler, hurried to the defense of Nolte. Shirking responsibility both for the start of World War II and for the Holocaust and laying it on the shoulders of Bolshevism fitted in well with the post-war goal of German neo-conservatism. It was designed to deepen the gulf between East and West and to make the German Federal Government's alignment with the Western Powers more acceptable to its own people as well as to the Western Powers.

Joachim Fest Rushed to Nolte's Defense

In 1986 Ernst Nolte's most recent comments were not and could not be presented orally, since he had taken extreme positions. But the *FAZ* in the name of freedom of speech published Nolte's notes on June 6, 1986. Three months later, against the rising criticism of Nolte's views by liberal scholars, Joachim Fest one of the editors of *FAC*, came out in support of Nolte. According to Fest, Hitler himself had averred that the practice of the revolutionary opponents of the Left had been his alleged model[29]—a questionable assertion and a palpable device for diminishing, if not radically shifting the responsibility for mass murder. Fest also concluded that Hitler's genocide was not the first and probably also not the last mass killing in history. Therefore, the "submissiveness of the Germans" in acknowledging guilt for the mass atrocities should finally cease.

Nolte's analysis of the ideological origins of Zionism in *Germany and the Cold War* (1974) was marked by almost complete absence of quotes from Zionist champions such as Moses Hess, Theodor Herzl, and others. Since Zionists sharply criticized the existing Jewish "Luftmenschentum" as well as Jews who were in favor of assimilation, Nolte had jumped to the conclusion that Zionist "invectives" hurled against Jews were "very similar" to those of the anti-Semites. This view ignored the actual Zionist motivation and the real thrust of Zionist critique of the Diaspora existence and character of many Jews. Nolte also pictured Zionism as a "reactionary movement against industrialization and modemization " He overlooked that Zionism aimed at self-determination and self-government and warned to eliminate the consequences of long-lasting persecution and suppression. Nolte also claimed that Zionism would lead to a "racial state"—a repetition of the extremist Arab and anti-Semitic Soviet propaganda. The latter found expression in the "Zionism is Racism" U.N. resolution, only much later rescinded by the U.N. Following racist attacks on the Jews by the Nazis, Nolte became engaged in denouncing Jewish regeneration taking the form of Zionism. In Nolte's view, Zionism in its alleged fight against the ideas of Enlightenment belonged unmistakably to "national-socialist movements."[30]

Again, almost a decade later, appeared Nolte's third book *Marxismus und Industrielle Revolution* which, to some critics' surprise, he declared the last volume of a trilogy, though the three books actually addressed different topics. In the last-named book he dealt with the Marxist "doctrine of annihilation" of classes, the inner core not only of communist practices but also of all fascist movements and of German "radical fascism" in particular. He saw in Nazism an even more radical movement, namely "radical annihilation." In the *FAZ* (25 November 1978), Nolte then developed more fully the thesis that Hitler's destruction of Jews must be seen "ultimately in connection with a contemporary deed,"[31] the annihilation of the Germans in Russia, also with a second large annihilation, that of the Kulaks, a social rather than an ethnic group. The inhuman expulsion of the Germans from the Volga as well as of other Soviet nationalities of Southeast Russia during World War II at the approach of the German armies was of course not the work of the Russian Jews nor was it comparable to the Nazis' wholesale extermination of the Jews. But Nolte claimed that National Socialism mirrored "the Russian Revolution and also Marxism," As H. U. Wehler later observed, the thought processes and interpretation of a scholar "as stimulating and provocative" as well as "egocentric" who "because of his education and his thinking style felt to be an outsider in the historical profession, should have been [long] known to everybody who read his most important books."[32]

In his work on fascism Nolte had called World War II "the most atrocious war of conquest, enslavement and annihilation known to modern history"[33] and had been certain that the destruction of the Jewish "race" was "cold-blooded murder" and "will be counted for all time among mankind's most extreme experiences of horror." In that context, he did not blame Hitler alone for all the atrocities committed, as he did later on.

Let us go back to *Germany and the Cold War* (1974). Ben Gurion's declaration that Israel would open the doors for the dispersed Jews of the world was "actually a declaration of war against the Arabs."[34] Such a declaration of war" was a favored thought of Nolte. Later, in 1986, he was to speak again of a "declaration of war," one by Chaim Weizman against the Third Reich, after the latter had attacked Poland in September 1939, without declaring war! For a diplomatic historian to resort to such distortions of facts, is almost unprecedented. Nolte found it also difficult to understand that Israel, the recipient of German reparations to cancel (*wiedergutmachen*) "the debt" of the Third Reich allegedly insisted on "prohibition" of showing a positive picture of a German in an Israeli movie for fifteen long years! It is difficult to believe that Nolte personally had examined Israeli movies over such a period. In any case, he found the apparent ingratitude of Israel revolting, though it followed the mass murder of six million Jews. The author found German expansion during World War II not different from Russian or American expansion of the nineteenth century, pointing to the suppression of Ukrainians and Indians respectively.[35] However, Nolte was full of understanding for the Arabs who after 1948 remained irreconcilable, using a language regarding "Jewish world conspiracy" which in his own words was "very similar" to that of the Nazis.

That Nolte was invited to teach at the Hebrew University in Jerusalem in 1983 nevertheless remains indeed most puzzling, since his bias toward Jews, Judaism, and Zionism had become pronounced. This hostility was expressed again in an article published in 1986, an opening phase to the "*Historikerstreit*" in Germany.

"The Past Which Does Not Pass" - (1986)

It was Nolte's polemical essay "Vergangenheit, die nicht vergehen will,"[36] published by the *FAZ* on June 6, 1986, which had commenced the dispute among German historians. Ernst Nolte pleaded therein to leave the discussion and analysis of the Nazi past to the historians, since some past developments had adversely affected contemporaries' judgments, the author's assumption being that all historians will shy away from "black-white pictures" of the Nazi era and that the time for revisionism had come.[37] The "memory" of the "Final Solution" had most contributed to the "non-passing of the past," to the continuous demand for an "endless debate about National Socialism." The talk about "guilt of the Germans" recalled in Nolte's view the talk of the "guilt of the Jews"—despite the total absence of actual Jewish domination and "atrocities" committed by them. The attention given to the "final solution" diverted attention from the killing of "unworthy life" and the treatment of Russian prisoners of war, not to mention "ethnic murder" in Vietnam and Afghanistan. Nolte avoided, however, a clear answer to the question of his own attitude to the latter crimes. Historians' unequal treatment of historic events had produced a "paradoxical and grotesque" situation. Occasionally some Jewish organization's speaker had exaggerated a rash utterance of a German deputy as a symptom of anti-Semitism. Nolte referred approvingly to a Jewish movie director who had pictured as likely that also SS-men of the death camps were "victims, in a manner." Revisionism and historiography had always belonged together. But he disclosed his motives when he raised the question whether revisionism might not lead to "justification of Hitler or at least to an exculpation of the Germans?" He concluded that no German could justify Hitler if it would be only on account of his commands of annihilation against the German people of March 1945"—as if the misdeeds against other nations and the annihilation of the Jews did not count! Nolte lauded those who had overcome mere polemics and had painted a more objective picture of the Third Reich and of its Führer," as did Joachim Fest and Sebastian Haffner. Nolte made a point of occasionally retreating and making apparent concessions to his critics only to accuse them in the next breath. He focused upon a rumor that opponents of Bolshevism had faced torture in Soviet jails by hungry rats and pointed to such "Asiatic deeds" which allegedly had caused anxiety to Hitler. This explained the Nazi racial murder. In his June 1986 article, Nolte suggested that Hitler followed in the footsteps of Stalin.* He reiter-

* It was characteristic of Nolte that he clothed his often shocking theses into rhetorical questions, thus leaving an exit open to himself.

ated that Hitler and the National Socialists acted out of paranoic fear of what the Bolsheviks would do to Germany and to Europe. The Germans and Hitler himself may have considered themselves potential "victims" of an "Asiatic" deed. Such fear, in the author's view, apparently assuaged Germany's guilt, Nolte propagated the theory that the Third Reich merely reacted defensively to an alleged Jewish threat—represented by less than 1 percent of the entire German population! Irrationality aside, Nolte adopted here extremist rightist views, if not outright Nazi doctrine, by identifying Bolshevism with Asia and Asians and contrasting German superiority to alleged inferior Russian and Bolshevik capacities and low-type morality. Thus the atrocities committed in the East during the war became by a sleight of hand not only not German, but were declared to be Asiatic in origin. There was an indisputable attempt of denying the "singularity" of the Holocaust, and shifting ultimate responsibility for it to others.

A brief consideration appears in order in this context. The Holocaust admittedly surpassed anything that traditional vulgar anti-Semitism had propagated. The mass murder actually would never have been possible without preceding centuries of segregation, vilification, and persecution of the Jews by the Germans. Nor can Nolte's accompanying thesis that the Holocaust was the result of Germany's, respectively of the Nazis' or Hitler's anxiety, lest the handful of defenseless Jews kill millions of armed Germans if the latter did not resort to preventive murder, be taken seriously. The Nazis' propaganda turned matters upside down, of course. According to National Socialism it was the Jews who wanted to dominate the world, not Nazi Germany. The Jews had started World War II, not Hitler! The Jews were Germany's misfortune, to recall Heinrich von Treitschke's often-repeated nineteenth century phrase, not National Socialism the bane of Jews and of Europe.

Continuation of the Polemics: Criticism and Defense of Nolte

While the Hitler biographer Joachim Fest sharply accused Jürgen Habermas, he himself tended to ignore Nolte's missteps. He based Nolte's judgment of the *Cheka* upon a single utterance at the end of

---

He asked whether the Nazis and Hitler did not commit an "Asiatic deed." Was not the class murder by the Bolsheviks the logical and real precondition of 'race murder' by the Nazis?[37]

1918, in the midst o the Russian Civil War, by the Latvian Martyn Latsis, one of the first Chiefs of the *Cheka*—rather questionable evidence. Fest also ignored Andreas Hillgruber's relative indifference toward the mass murder of the Jews as contrasted to his deep sorrow over the expulsion of the East Germans in 1944–45.[38] He deplored the heaps of corpses in Nazi death camps, but raised the question whether they were absent in Soviet gulags. He appreciated the centuries-old German-Jewish cultural symbiosis and regretted the collapse of an old *Kulturvolk* into inhumanity. Fest, like Nolte, claimed, that Hitler took the communist foe as a model, but quoted the Führer's pledge that he would resort to a ten-fold greater terror. Hitler had learned not only from the Russian Revolution and its threat of annihilating its class enemies, but had also inherited the "early anxieties and phantasies" of the German Austrians of being overwhelmed by non-Germans. Reports from Russia which reached Hitler through Baltic German refugees were "certainly exaggerated," but they seemed credible to him. The leadership of some Jews in the Munich Räterepublik gave these "anti-Semitic obsessions" new strength. Fest did not entirely discard that communism, as distinguished from the "*völkish* sectarians" who had preached their crude philosophy in numerous tracts and cheap pamphlets (*Groschenhefte*) since the turn of the century, had a remarkable intellectual and humanitarian origin. But against this Fest claimed that the Nazi reference to "annihilation" (*Vernichtung*) had not quite a literal meaning. Who will decide whether these utterances were not mere "verbal excesses"?

Fest admitted that national-socialist thought originated in "inferior ideological garbage." He still concluded that communism acted perhaps out of "good conscience," while National Socialism pursued its "murderous business" with less good conscience. Fest defended Nolte when he wrote that in his view the murdered Jews could find solace having died as "representatives" of a struggle against humanity itself.

There can be little doubt that Fest went to extremes in his apologetic attempts *vis-à-vis* Nolte, Hildebrand, Stürmer, and Hillgruber. This undoubtedly undermined the impact of his criticisms of Habermas, He also vigorously denied that these historians formed a "conspiracy." But it is indisputable that they and others who rushed to the defense of Nolte often came close to being apologists of the Third Reich.

Though pleased about such support as he received for his article of June 1986, Nolte reentered the arena in 1987 with the brochure *Das Vergehen der Vergangenheit. Antwort an meine Kritiker im sogenannten Historikerstreit.*[39] In this rejoinder to his critics, Nolte emphasized the need for an all-European and even a global perspective about the twentieth century and developed the concept of "a global civil war" which had allegedly raged ever since 1917. He later elaborated about this notion in the book *The European Civil War, 1917–1945.*

The European Civil War

In a chapter "Genocides and the Final Solution of the Jewish Question," in the study *Der Europaische Bürgerkrieg 1917–45, Nationalsozialismus und Bolschewismus* (1987),[40] Ernst Nolte reiterated some major points he had made earlier during the 1986 polemics, comparing the mass murder of the Jews with other genocides and pursuing the same questionable tactics of raising often pointless questions and avoiding giving clear-cut answers. In his view the beginnings of the genocide may be found already in the First World War when Armenians were killed by the Turks. In 1939 the Poles had started it when allegedly killing thousands of German citizens and Stalin had continued it with the deportation of the Volga Germans which was in violation of the non-aggression pact. It would never have occurred without the preceding Nazi aggression against Russia in 1941. One may "assume" that no less than 20 percent of the deportees died in the process. One must also "raise the question" whether E. Beneš' plan of the "transfer of the Sudenten-Germans" did not amount to "ethnic murder."

The "Final Solution" began with the boycott of Jewish businesses on April 1, 1933, On the other hand, Nolte questioned whether Hitler since 1993 or even since 1923 had a "firm plan" of exterminating the Jews. In practice, the Nazis since the Haavara agreement with the Zionists in 1935 had taken the side of the Zionists against the Arabs. Nolte questioned whether the mere deportation of the Jews from Germany and other European countries to Poland was actually "part of the process of annihilation." The German people considered the Jewish deportation "inevitable," since as late as "autumn of 1941 there lived in Berlin alone the amazingly high number of 70,000 Jews." Nolte even tried to defend the *Einsatzgruppen of the SS*, since some of their leaders pleaded allegedly for a "better treatment" of the Russian and Ukrainian populations. He again asked "preliminary questions" whether the *Judenaktionen* were not "a German countermeasure recalling the era of the German civil war" during the Weimar period. Even the mass murder at Babi Yar near Kiev found a defender in Nolte. Germans had apparently, "without further examination," identified Soviet partisans with Jews. The actions of the *Einsatzgruppen* were only examples of a "preventive" method of waging war. A great part of many "hundred thousands" of people killed were Jews, which Nolte found a source of "amazement" (*auffallend*). One cannot deny, he concluded, the annihilation at Auschwitz and Treblinka, which was also directed against gypsies and Slavs. If Hitler had let European Jews "evacuate" from Germany to Poland, so that they would live there in ghettos, he would not have been anything but a "wind-bag" (*Schwätzer*). Needless to point out that Nolte in this publication surpassed himself in insensitivity, poor judgment, and bad taste, not to mertion distortion of facts.

Nolte finally raised the rhetorical question whether "Archipelago Gulag," the class murder of the Bolsheviks had not preceded Auschwitz. "Were Hitler's most secret acts not to explain that he had not forgotten the account of the prison?" One feared to raise questions of this kind because they dated back to the Cold War and had been anti-Communist fighting theses. Yet the Nazi mass murder cannot be separated from the preceding Bolshevik murder, since a "casual connection" between the two was "likely."

Nolte had tried to explain Hitler's and the Nazis' fear and hatred of Bolshevism as the result of Germany's experience with the communist threat emanating from the Russian October Revolution. Yet in his work on fascism he had admitted that Hitler's hatred of Marxism had "originally nothing to do with the Bolshevik Revolution"—it actually preceded the latter—and not much to do with the social-revolutionary elements in Germany. Hitler's antagonism was directed at Social Democracy. The latter was also the Austrian politician Georg von Schönerer's chief adversary and was the pretended enemy of German influence in Austria. It was Austrian socialism that in the earlier work had blocked German *Lebensraum* policy. Furthermore, in his work on fascism, in contradistinction to German nationalists and to Nazis in particular, Nolte had held that a comparison of the treaty of Versailles with the preceding German dictate of Brest Litovsk, imposed upon Russia in March 1918 and that of Bucharest thereafter, put the Versailles treaty "in a favorable light." Indeed, the Versailles treaty separated 6.5 million from Germany, about half of whom were German by nationality. The treaty of Brest Litovsk, in Winston Churchill's words, cut off 66.5 million people from the Russian Empire.

Nolte propagated the view that placing the Holocaust and twentieth century German history into a larger framework and pointing to atrocities by other nations was likely to diminish German responsibility for unprecedented crimes. Placing these Nazi outrages into an even larger framework, that of world history, for instance Pol Pot's atrocities and those of Idi Amin would make Nazi excesses stand out even less and make them appear less "singular."

Nolte's critics rejected the making of comparisons with the record of other nations. Comparisons should only be made with members of the European family of nations, especially with developed West European, other Central and North European countries, their prevailing cultural standard and moral code, but not with illiterate tribes and their brutal tyrants representing low types of development. The purpose of "relativizing" and "historicizing" Nazi crimes by making the foregoing improper comparisons and making the point that the Nazi Holocaust was not a "unique phenomenon" in world history was also achieved if National Socialism and fascism in general were primarily seen as the unavoidable response to Bolshevism. Yet however brutal the latter was, historical truth was in the view of some of Nolte's critics distorted by placing Bolshevism and Nazism on the same moral plane. The former's theoretical, though not actual opposition to racism and chauvinism aside, mass murder on the Nazi scale, the most barbaric genocide in death camps, had, whatever communism's crimes, not been resorted to by the Bolsheviks.

Nolte's critics also stressed that proof was lacking that Hitler, in resorting to mass murder and in aiming at the domination of Europe and the world, was deliberately copying Lenin's and Stalin's totalitarian methods. Hitler had no such model, as the study of his writings and speeches made abundantly clear. Though he was impressed by Stalin and his organizational talents, an unbridgeable abyss separated their philosophies. Hitler deprecated Bolshevism, rather than secretly admiring and emulating it. There was no evidence of a link in Hitler's and the Nazis' mind between the Soviet discrimination against individuals of the Russian upper classes and their maltreatment and the national oppression in the USSR with the unprecedented mass annihilation of the Jews. Soviet excesses were committed in the heat of the Civil War. Hitler's atrocities were carried out in "normal" times, though intensified when World War II darkened the skies, making atrocities at the moment less visible.

Actually German historians who have tried making such comparisons have, in the judgment of their German colleagues, produced no hard evidence of comparable mass atrocities in Russia's post-World War I civil war. Nolte's own references to M. E. Scheubner-Richter and Alfred Rosenberg as witnesses were limited to accounts by these ideologically biased German Baltic refugees rather than to genuine Russian sources. Nolte also wrote that "the European bourgeoisie threatened with extinction and having grown half-insane [?] out of fear," in this "madness" "turned against a part of itself" by attacking Jewry. This "analysis" was again full of dubious observations and generalizations. It was not the "European" bourgeoisie but its German section which turned against the Jews, helped along by many of the German intelligentsia and strongly supported by lower class elements. Unquestionably, some non-German extremists to win Nazi favor climbed on the anti-Semitic bandwagon.

Nolte offered no valid explanation why Hitler turned the Bolshevik "class murder," which was never total, into total "racial, biological genocide." The only apparent "explanation" for the identification of the objects of his fury and obsession, Bolsheviks and Jews, was ideology and racism. Hitler and his coterie simply considered anti-Semitism a most effective propaganda ploy to make all Jews the scapegoat by exploiting the Jewish descent of many of the Bolshevik élite. They ignored that the mass of Russian Jews, despite the lure of equality and opportunity, did not embrace the Bolshevik program, but on religious, national, cultural, and economic grounds actually opposed it.

Andreas Hillgruber

The other historian who emerged in the very center of historic dispute was Andreas Hillgruber. Born in 1925, of the University of Cologne, he had written his dissertation about German-Romanian relations between 1938 and 1944. While serving as director of a gymnasium in Marburg, Hessen, he wrote his postdoctoral thesis (*Habilitationsschrift*) about "Hitler's Strategy. Politics and Military Leadership" in 1965. After a stint in Marburg he was called to the University of Freiburg in 1968. During a student unrest in 1967 he was involved in irritating disputes and bitter confrontations and apparently moved to the conservative side. In 1972 he joined the history faculty at the University of Cologne. He became increasingly involved in polemics with the "Left" and alleged "*Tendenzhistoriker*" and also against their alliance with *Sozialhistoriker*. Though he authored numerous smaller booklets, his critics wondered why his long announced modern political history had not yet seen the light of day. Still, at the time of the start of the *Historikerstreit* Hillgruber had acquired international recognition in the field of Nazi foreign policy and military policy.

Long before Hillgruber wrote his disputed piece about the Holocaust in 1986, he had penned a chapter in *Deutsche Grossmacht- und Weltpolitik im 19. und 20. Jahrhundert* (Düsseldorf, 1971) entitled "Die Endlösung und das deutsche Ostimperium als Kernstück des rassenideologischen Programs des National-Sozialismus,[40]* which had appeared first in the *Vierteljahrshefte für Zeitgeschichte* (1972).

Germany and Two World Wars. From the German Eastern Imperium to the Struggle of the Continents

Hillgruber's work *Germany and the Two World Wars* appeared first in 1967, with a second edition published in England in 1981 (Cambridge and London). Bethmann-Hollweg, according to Hillgruber, was outmaneuvered by supporters of the "new policies." With the "quasi-dictatorship" of General Erich von Ludendorff emerged a "new set of war goals," "grandiose" plans for the East. "A basic axiom for the 1918 eastern policy held that it was entirely possible for Germany to take all of Russia in its grasp and keep the giant empire in an enduring state of dependency."[41] This stood in direct contradiction to the exaggerated estimate of Russian strength that had so distressed both the German government and military in the years prior to 1914. After the Russian Revolution, the Russian Empire was considered unstable, and with some skillful help from the outside could be "broken apart." The *völkisch* settlement and colonization plans that were then proposed for the East were not entirely new, but only in 1918 did they fully dominate the highest leadership of the Reich.

---

* See also Hillgruber, *Der Zusammenbruch im Osten 1944–45 als Problem der deutschen Nationalgeschichte und der europäischen Geschichte*, 1985

In November 1918 German troops were in control of much of the East, from Finland to the Ukraine. "Hitler's long-range aims fixed in the 1920s, of erecting a German Eastern Imperium on the ruins of the Soviet Union was not simply a vision emanating from an abstract wish." For a short time the German Eastern Imperium had already been a reality.[42] "World Power or Decline"—these were the alternatives posed by Friedrich von Bernhardi in his enormously popular book *Germany and the Next War* (1912) as the consequence of a coming struggle between European powers. Hitler carried it to a new extreme with his pronouncement "Germany will either be a world power or there will be no Germany." "The wave of irrational aspirations carried him along and prevented the emergence of a soberly conceived German policy of moderation."

Hillgruber developed that the "decisive and totally novel" formation of the Nazi program was "the complete permeation of originally crude Machiavellian objectives by the most radical variety of anti-Semitism." Hitler drew on the "theory" of the world-wide Jewish conspiracy as propagated in the Protocols of the *Elders of Zion*, a forgery which was widely disseminated in *völkisch* circles in Germany in 1919–1920. The wide-ranging political aims of Hitler's foreign poiicy were subordinated to a central goal, the eradication of the Jewish "archenemy." After gaining power in Germany and consolidating his rule in Central Europe, Hitler would lead the Reich to a position of world power. This should be accomplished in two stages, first through controlling all of Europe by gaining vast stretches in Eastern Europe. Then after adding a colonial realm of Africa and by building a strong Atlantic-based navy, Hitler would make Germany one of the four remaining world powers, the others being the British Empire, the Japanese sphere in East Asia, and the U.S. The final struggle of continents between the two leading world powers, the Germanic Empire of the German Nation and the U.S. was a war Hitler anticipated for generations after his death. If the Germans would fail, he expected Germany to be condemned to insignificance in world politics.

As far as the continental European phase of his program was concerned, the conquest of European Russia was for Hitler "inextricably linked" to the extermination of the Jews, the "bacilli." Bolshevism meant to the Führer the consummate rule of Jewry. Russia's defeat and the extermination of the Jews were "inseparable" for him Hitler built on Ludendorff's expansive principles of the latter part of

World War I. But his ultimate aspiration in power politics, Germany's position as a world power, went far beyond the earlier program of Ludendorff. His "enormous schemes and particularly their connection with racism were the program of a single individual."[43]

Hillgruber seemed to disregard that the Nazi program, though not known to the last detail by the German public, was widely accepted by it. He admitted that in parts, regarding the revision of the Versailles treaty and the creation of a Greater Germany, his goals overlapped with the aims of the old German leadership "and the phantasies of a large part of the German public that had never assimilated the loss of the war."

The Destruction of the Russian Empire and the Annihilation of the Jews

What Hitler, according to Hillgruber, aimed at was the destruction of the millions of Jews in East Central Europe. He wanted to gain colonial space for German settlers in the best agricultural region of Russia and in areas strategically significant for Germany. He aimed at the decimation of Slavic masses and their subjection to German domination in four state formations: the Reich Kommissariate Ostland, Ukraine, Moskowien, and Kaukasien, all under the leadership of German "viceroys." The masses should forget any memory of the Russian *Grossstaat* and blindly obey their new "masters." Russia should be robbed of her very center and Moscow and Leningrad should be razed to the ground. Russia should be dominated and exploited. Yet these ultimate German plans for Russia should be carefully concealed. Russia should be conquered in a world *Blitzkrieg* and Jews should be exterminated. Only then was there a chance for securing German world power.

As Hillgruber continued, Hitler revealed his thoughts to the Croatian Minister of Defense on July 21, 1941: "If there were no longer Jews anymore in Europe, the security of European states would not be disturbed any longer." Ten days later, on July 31, Göring ordered Heydrich to submit to him "preliminary procedures" leading to the "final solution" of the Jewish question.[44] These measures were communicated to top Nazi authorities at the Wannsee Conference. The latter endorsed that Europe "from the West to East" should be cleansed of Jews (become *judenrein*). Thus began, according to Hillgruber, the second phase, 1942–44, of the annihilation of European

Jewry. In this period a greater part of the old German leader élites participated in the annihilation of the Jews.

On the German Army and the Elimination of the Jews

The German army fought against the West more or less according to the rules of international law. But Hillgruber conceded that Hitler in fighting against the East ordered that the army disregard all principles of international law and the rules of the Hague relating to the waging of war. This was made clear in an address to about 200 to 250 higher German officers in the Reich Chancellery on March 30, 1941. Commissars and GPU-people were criminals, they were told, and ought to be treated as such, otherwise Germany would face another war thirty years hence. Hitler's order to the security police and the SD to undertake behind the front special tasks appeared for the first time in a military document and was adhered to as a direct order from the Führer.[45] The command for the shooting of all Jews was given orally to the leading officers of the *Einsatzgruppen* and *Einsatzkommandos*. It also included the execution of communist functionaries, of so-called inferior "Asiatic people," and of Gypsies.

In accordance with such an order the top commander of the Sixth Army, General Field Marshal von Reichenau[46] proclaimed "the complete destruction of the power and the elimination of the Asiatic influence in the European cultural region." "The German soldier in the East was not only a warrior according to the rules of the art of war but also the bearer of a merciless *völkisch* idea and avenger for all beastly misdeeds which had been administered to Germans and kindred peoples." Hitler called this order of von Reichenau "excellent." Similar was the order of General von Manstein of November 20, 1941, which called Jews the intermediary between the enemy in the rear, the Red Army, and Red Leaders. Therefore "the Jewish-Bolshevik system must be uprooted once and for all." As Hillgruber concluded, "the federal support of Hitler's racist-ideological *Ost-Programm* through the old [military] leadership of the higher officers represented by Manstein cannot be overlooked." The top leaders of the army—which previously already had been deprived of its political power—failed in preserving the soldierly ethics. They followed the slogan "My honor means fidelity" to become unthinking tools of every command of the Führer.

The results of numerous military actions were listed in the known "Ereignismeldungen USSR" by the chief of the Security Police and the SD as well as in Himmler's personally signed *Meldungen an den Führer über die Bandenbekämpfung.* Again, Hillgruber reached the conclusion that the leaders of the German army, though overwhelmingly indirectly, became the accomplices of the Security Police and the SD. When Hitler on March 31, 1941, with unusual frankness had proclaimed before high officers his resolution to wage a racial-ideological war of annihilation in utter disregard for international law, von Brauchitsch, chief commander of three armies contemplating and preparing for the invasion of the Soviet Union considered it hopeless to dissuade Hitler to cancel this fateful order.[47] Though Hitler in the winter of 1941–42 had already recognized the probability of the failure of his plan for conquest and victory against Russia and revealed it in the most narrow circle, he still was anxious to accomplish the other good which he had "prophesied" as a result of war already on January 30, 1939, "the elimination of the Jews [*Ausrottung*] in Europe." During the summer campaign of 1942 military necessity demanded that he move all forces in Russia against Stalingrad and the Caucasus. But railroad transports with Jews continued to dispatch these victims to the Polish annihilation camps. Thus, the plans of German *Grossmacht* policy ended in crimes of monumental dimensions. At the end of the Nuremberg trial General Field Marshal Keitel admitted his personal guilt:

> It is tragic to acknowledge that the best which I had to give as a soldier, obedience and loyalty, were exploited for not recognizable intentions and that I did not see that there were limits also to soldatic fulfillment of duty.[48]

This, according to Hillgruber, raised the question of how it was possible that the traditional circles controlling power and having responsibility "in Germany—next to the generals also the leading groups in administration, diplomacy, and economy—followed National Socialism even when the qualitative transformation of its policy to the strikingly criminal became apparent, and assisted in the state-organized crimes." In the end, Hillgruber, however, claimed the "atrociousness of the events makes it difficult to judge the perpetrators and those entangled [*verstrickt*] in an adequate manner and to render justice to its millions of victims." One would have thought that the very dimensions of the crimes made their perpetrators guilty beyond the shadow of any doubt.

Still, in the 1970s Hillgruber judged the Holocaust events in a fair manner when he condemned the participation of leading German cadres and élites in committing unprecedented misdeeds. The tone and content of this work presents a striking contrast to the apologetic and self-serving comments and evaluations of the same historic events by this same historian only a decade later. This holds true also for his special focus on anti-Semitism.

Hillgruber's Bird's-Eye View on the History of German Jew-Hatred

Prior to the nineteenth century the Jews had been the perennial target of anti-Semites, and for very different reasons. Despite Bismarck's support for Jewish emancipation in 1969 in the North Germanic Confederation on the eve of the Franco-Prussian War and of Germany's unification, the German conservatives soon began to develop second thoughts about it. German liberals, long the best friends of the Jews, favored a more rapid assimilation of the Jews and a few, like the progressive historian Theodor Mommsen, recommended baptism to them. Many Christians of various denominations also resented the continued attachment of the Jews to Judaism and favored their early conversion. Even to many Socialists, the Jew remained alien, a representative of capitalism and individualism. Racial anti-Semitism, appearing in the last decades of the nineteenth century, retained and further developed all earlier prejudices, and, in addition, introduced racist mythology, pointing to the allegedly evil and unchanging character of the Jewish "race." It demanded the abolishment of emancipation, depriving the Jews of German citizenship, and came out for even more radical anti-Jewish measures.

According to Hitler, Jews were the eternal enemies of the Germans and their rivals in regard to the domination of the world. He claimed to believe in an international conspiracy of the Jews as expressed in the falsified *Protocols of the Elders of Zion*, accusing the Jews of aiming at the disintegration of nations. He claimed that the victory of the Bolsheviks had been completed and had resulted in their domination of Russia. The "democracies" in Western Europe and in the Weimar Republic were early stages for Bolshevism, since Jews had already won a substantial, though not yet dominating, influence.

Hillgruber recalled that already in *Mein Kampf* Hitler had compared Jews to parasites and germs (*Bazillen*) and had voiced regret that during World War I 12,000 to 15,000 of "Hebrew corrupters and demagogues" had not been killed, poisoned by gas. Then millions of other peoples' sacrifices at the front would have been avoided. The Jewish Bolsheviks were proclaimed the "deadly enemy" and the military conquest of Russia for the purpose of gaining new "living space" and bringing about the annihilation of the Jews were in Hitler's program indissolubly tied up with each other. Thus anti-Jewish measures were an imperative in the field of foreign policy and of military strategy. In 1945 Hitler asserted that he had underestimated the extent of Jewish influence in England and blamed the Jews for England's rejection of his outstretched hand.[49] In the months prior to the attack on the Soviet Union Hitler, in a small circle, clearly revealed the main lines of his thought, showing the continuity of his goals. He suggested the "elimination" of the Jewish-Bolshevik commanding élite including its alleged biological roots,

In the writings on the Holocaust before the eruption of the historians' feud in 1986, Hillgruber had displayed objectivity, but in writing *Zweierlei Unterganag*, deepening the historians' dispute, Hillgruber showed a complete underestimation of the roots of anti-Semitism and of its depth. But it was only in the late nineteenth century and during World War I that, in his view, it became part of the nationalist ideology and of the doctrines of the Fatherland Party. The latter, founded in 1917 by retired Grand Admiral von Tirpitz and widely supported, represented a new anti-Semitism which was based on a racism and which supplemented in the decades of the nineteenth century a centuries-old religious, economic, and social Jew-hatred. The "final solution," however, was Hitler's decision and responsibility.

Though Hillgruber did not fully acquit the German people for its past indifference to the Jews, he clearly tried to lessen its guilt. Yet the very title of Hillgruber's essay showed his indifference to the fate of the Jews as compared to his condemnation of the fate of the Germans who were expelled or fled from the East. Everything considered, Hillgruber's attempt to place most, if not all, responsibility for the annihilation of the Jews on Hitler alone remained utterly unconvincing. Other Nazi leaders such as Goebbels, Himmler, Göring, Streicher, not to list many others, were also fanatical Jew-haters and the executors of the Holocaust.[50]

Hillgruber's "Zweierlei Untergang" (1987)

It was Hillgruber's writings in 1986, especially his coming to the defense of Nolte and his publication *Zweierlei Untergang* which made him a major figure in the "*Historikerstreit.*" According to Hillgruber, Europe's chance to become a world power was contingent on German leadership. He was sharply critical of alleged British territorial plans during World War II, going back to the British Foreign office memorandum by Sir Eyre Crowe, which was later endorsed by Prime Minister Winston Churchill. The British and the Allies, through Russian and American intervention in Europe and later by dividing Germany, split not only the latter but Europe in its entirety. Apparently, Germany had never "intervened" in Europe when she crossed her own borders—Europe was her natural playground.

In the foregoing essay Hillgruber advocated the domination of Central Europe by a strong united Germany. But he was critical of the Resistance conspirators of the summer of 1944 who thought that a conservative Greater Germany might be able to lead Europe. In his view, they were completely unrealistic. He admitted that had they succeeded with their *Putsch*, they might have saved those Jews who were still alive and other inmates of the camps. But Hillgruber rather praised the ethical convictions and the sense of responsibility of the military opposing the rebels, while criticizing the latters' attitude. The military opposition wanted to demonstrate resistance to the tyrant and his regime. An early end of the war would have definitely been in Germany's interest and would have brought the hopeless war to an earlier end.

"Polarization": Criticism of Hillgruber by Colleagues and the Press

In its earliest stage the *Historikerstreit* involved the philosopher and social scientist Jürgen Habermas and the historian Ernst Nolte, the latter being quickly seconded by the noted diplomatic historian A. Hillgruber. Habermas, promptly retaliating in a reader's letter to the *FAZ* on August 1, 1986, observed:

> He [Hillgruber] does not want to identify himself with Hitler and Resistance fighters, but with the inhabitants of the population in the East. This was not the legitimate view for a historian writing decades after the event.

"Apologetic tendencies" became clear when Hillgruber already in the title of his article juxtaposed "the aggressive destruction [!] of Germany through external enemies to the end [!] of European Jews'—"end" rather than brutal murder and annihilation. It was strange that Hillgruber, a renowned historian, had long escaped criticism by his colleagues. He had first published his views only in dailies and journals such as *Die Welt*, the *FAZ* and the *Rheinisher Merkur*, and had voiced them on television. But Karl Dietrich Erdmann, the editor of a scholarly journal, *Geschichte in Wissenschaft und Unterricht*, invited him to express his opinion in its pages. Hillgruber complied, but lost no time denouncing therein the politically motivated campaign "to undermine his reputation."[51] Other conservatives entering the arena charged that the critics had quoted incorrectly and that they were dogmatists. Conservative historians claimed that it was not they who had started the dispute, but Habermas. While defending scientific independence against leftist "absolutism," they were raising the ante by claiming that they were battling political agitation, calumnies, and lies. They ignored the political support of their views by Chancellor Helmut Kohl, various members of the federal government and leading politicians, some larger media, and the Foundation of the Union of Employers.

In *Das Argument* (May 1987) Fritz Haug quoted Hildebrand that the historians had loosened an "avalanche."[52] As Thomas Nipperdey saw it, the guilt of the historians as well as the public were "polarized."[53] The following election in the *Bundesrepublik* in January 1987 produced a backlash for the Right but also a gain by the Liberals. One columnist for *Die Welt* lambasted the dispute over Auschwitz, which was a focus in the polemics, as a new "Gesslerhut," referring to Schiller's *Wilhelm Tell*, a sign of alien domination which every German historian allegedly had to pay respects to. This language followed the pattern of discourse of extreme Rightists against the Federal Republic. The concepts fought over continued to be history, singularity, identity, and freedom to ask questions. One editorialist concluded with the critical refrain, "We need history again" means practically "we must finally forget."

Among the critics of Hillgruber was Wolfgang Mommsen, Director of the German Historical Institute in London since 1984. Having returned as professor to Düsseldorf, he asserted that the defeat of national-socialist Germany had not only been in the interest of the European peoples against whom Hitler had waged war and who were destined to be suppressed,[54] exploited, and partly even annihilated, but of the Germans themselves. His twin brother Hans Mommsen accused Hillgruber of "relativizing" the crimes of the Third Reich. He also thought that his *Mitteleuropa* concept opened the way for "revisionist misunderstandings." Martin Broszat, Director of the *Institute für Zeitgeschichte* in Munich, did not think that Hlllgruber deserved being charged with minimizing the misdeeds of National Socialism through the hurried linkage of the two contributions in *Zweierlei Untergang* about the Eastern front and the murder of the Jews. But he accused him of having adopted a distorted perspective, which had an exculpating effect. The theory of Hillgruber was also subject to detailed critique by the East German historian Kurt Pätzold of the Humboldt University of Berlin.

The relative restraint of many of the professional historians toward Hillgruber was not shared by the press. *Der Spiegel* condemned the patriotic concoctions (Klitterei) of Hillgruber[55] and ridiculed "conscious-creating (*sinnstiftende*) writings, a fashionable neo-conservative term, used especially by Michael Stürmer. Richard Augstein, *Spiegel's* editor, criticized the author's widely shared views according to which the "willful break-up [*Zerschlagung*] of the Reich" was only "the reply to the misdeeds (*Untaten*) of the national-socialist regime."[56] Hillgruber, he charged, acted and wrote like a "constitutional Nazi." Otto Köhler in an article in *Konkret*, "Kohl befiehlt, wir folgen"[57] accused Hillgruber of uncritically endorsing neo-conservatism, Michael Brumlik, professor of education at Heidelberg, called Hillgruber's book in *FAZ* as signaling the turn of conservatives to "hard aggressive nationalism." In cynicism and brazenness Hillgruber, in his view, surpassed anything which on the part of serious scholarship had appeared, recalling pro-Nazi attitudes.

Hillgruber and Chancellor Kohl

At the very height of their dispute, Hillgruber was chosen to interview Chancellor Helmut Kohl. The latter elaborated that his expression "grace [*Gnade*] of late birth" regarding his own birthday "did not signify a repudiation of responsibility [*aussteigen*] for our history."[58] To Hillgruber's question whether the European NATO allies would assume responsibilities in non-European regions to lighten the burden of the Americans who had world-wide obligations, Kohl declined military responsibilities but accepted political ones: "The *Bundesrepublik* was no hegemonic power, but it was an economic world power," which he claimed nobody suspected to harbor hegemonistic inclinations. In his question-and-answer discussion Kohl voiced his understanding of the perilous consequences of German unification, then considered possible only in the remote future. He voiced the view that the North-South conflict would be "more important than the East-West conflict," "more dynamic, more dangerous." The chancellors vision embraced the political unification of Europe, not only that of Germany.[59] The emerging "Grosseuropa" will be oriented toward the West. In this new Europe a policy of neutrality will be excluded, even Switzerland and Austria will relinquish their neutrality.

Hillgruber wanted the Federal Republic of Germany to restore relations with the DDR and East European states. Though he in other context proclaimed that the old conception of *Mitteleuropa* under German leadership was historically finished [*erledigt*],[60] Helmut Kohl in a TV talk with Hillgruber considered that the "construction of *Gesamteuropa* [!] was our main task." "To Europe, as I understand it, belongs Poland, the CSR, Weimar and Dresden and Leningrad." The formula "Silesia remains our future" was a slogan which the Bonn government had adopted in 1985. Obviously, unification quite aside, these formulations had most dangerous implications for Germany's neighbors, raising not only the specter of revisionism, but also making territorial claims beyond it. But Kohl's assessment of World War II and of the importance of the militay struggle in the East in 1944–45 not only for Germany but for Europe in its entirety was not likely to calm the numerous non-German neighbors either. While the latter were unlikely to forget that the great war was a Nazi attempt to enslave them and all of Europe, Kohl held that at stake in 1945 was only "vengeance" by the various European peoples for the misdeeds which were committed in the name of Germany in Poland and elsewhere! Such views had actually been promoted for decades by the rightist and revisionist German press organs. In accordance with it, the German Resistance fighters were seen merely as accomplices of Bolshevism or, at best, as unrealistic dreamers. Had the July 20, 1944 Putsch against Hitler succeeded, the war would have come to an earlier end, apparently a terrible defeat for Germany. The German rightists ignored that an early end of the war, lost in any case, would have also saved the life of hundreds of thousands of Germans.

Analysis of Hillgruber's Thesis

The weaknesses in Hillgruber's thesis were quite apparent. His focus on the end struggle 1944–45 was of course most arbitrary. After all, the war had started in September 1939 with a treacherous attack on Poland. It was the latter which waged a defensive struggle and Nazi Germany which engaged in blatant aggression. And it was the latter which waged a defensive struggle and Nazi Germany which engaged in blatant aggression. And it was the latter which aimed at the suppression of the Slavic peoples up to the Ural mountains. Soviet troops, however, had succeeded in blocking the German armies and pushing them westward. Hitler's and the Nazis' gamble, mass murder and enslavement of all East European nations and their resettlement projects—to all of which Germans had offered no effective resistance—resulted ultimately in most severe losses for the Germans in the Baltic area, in Poland, and the rest of Eastern Europe.

Though German aggression against Poland, unleashed on September 1, 1939, could hardly be denied, German rightist circles in the post-war period have attempted to disavow German aggressiveness against the Soviet Union, trying to picture the war as a defensive struggle. Nazis and neo-Nazis have condemned Stalin rather than Hitler as the main culprit in unleashing the Second World War. Martin Broszat criticized Hillgruber since he had not offered any new research results justifying the drawing of a new conclusion.[61] The only claim presented by him was that Great Britain fighting Nazi Germany aimed at the elimination of Germany as an economic and political power. This was not caused, he went on, by the crimes of National Socialism, but rested on independent and selfish British motives. Yet nothing appeared more comprehensible than the reduction of German power after the harrowing experience of two world wars started by Germany which nearly brought her victory.

Hillgruber clung to the legend that Hitler's opponents had fixed their goal on the disintegration of "our German Reich." Actually, as the *Neue Züricher Zeitung* put it: "Hillgruber does not acknowledge that all consequences of the German collapse had one central cause, namely the war which Hitler had unleashed." He simply ignored the German "war of aggression" which had begun in September 1939. Despite his knowledge of detail, "Hillgruber suffered from a total blackout in this regard." He spoke of Allied "vengeance," but downplayed the crimes committed by German troops between 1941–44 using in this connection a "passive grammatical construction." He ignored the need of evacuation in time the threatened German population in the East, emphasizing "holding out (*durchhalten*)" and voiced anxiety over the "orgy of vengeance" by the Red Army as well as confidence in Nazi propaganda of Germany's ultimate victory and in Hitler's illusions in miraculous weapons which would turn the tide. The Swiss paper also accused Ernst Nolte of "minimizing (*verharmlosen*) "the

Holocaust, of plain suppression (*Verdrängung*) of the historical truth and of reiterating slogans of the "gemütlicher Stammtisch" (friendly table of the regulars).

Klaus Hildebrand, Life and Work

Klaus Hildebrand, born in 1941, professor of history at Bonn University, was an admirer of Andreas Hillgruber, the older productive colleague. He wrote a massive dissertation (1967) on the thought and activities of Hitler and the NSDAP regarding the colonial question (1919–1945), a work which showed a close relationship to Hillgruber's thought. He authored his post-doctoral thesis *(Habitilationsschrift)* "Prussia as factor of British world policy 1866–1870." In 1973 he wrote on *The Foreign Policies of the Third Reich* and in 1984 he turned to German history between 1963 to 1969, *From Erhard to the Great Coalition.*[62] This book was widely criticized; it shared Hillgruber's bias about Social Democratic foreign policy as well as opposition to the student movement of the late 1960s. Rather suddenly he found himself supporting many of Nolte's theses. In 1984, relating to the renewed debate about the disputed German *Sonderweg*—which the Germans of the nineteenth and twentieth centuries had chosen—a diverging from that of Western Europe and North America, Hildebrand reduced the *Sonderfall* to Hitler alone. He also demanded the "historization" of National Socialism. Actually, "historization," the interpretation of which differed widely at times, had been demanded in the last quarter of the twentieth century by Martin Broszat, Hans Mommsen, and others. Hildebrand, however, raised the question whether comparisons with Stalinist Russia or "with Cambodian 'stone-age communism' " would not be inappropriate.

In an article in the *FAZ* on July 31, 1986, Klaus Hildebrand finally entered the arena of the historians' feud, polemizing with Jürgen Habermas.[63] Four months later, on November 22, 1986, he published another essay on the historical dispute in *Die Welt.* He sharply questioned Habermas' objections to the second half of Hillgruber's booklet relating to the "end" of European Jewry. He accused him of falsifying quotations and of asserting his own "intellectual hegemonic position." He charged even Broszat and H. Mommsen with "evil representations" and rejected Christian Meier's judgment that the Nazi annihilation surpassed that of the Soviets' elimination of the Kulaks.

Hildebrand's Preventive War Theory. Who Commenced the

War, Hitler or Stalin?

In the *H.Z.* in early 1987 Klaus Hildebrand tried to place Hitler's attacks on the Soviet Union in 1941 in a new light, exculpating the Führer. Comparing the foreign policies of Stalin and Hitler, the long-range expansionist territorial goals and far-reaching plans of both. Hildebrand made it appear as if Hitler's attacks—"flight forward" to avoid an inescapable threat—had a defensive motivation. An even more extreme and less disguised attitude was taken by the military historian Joachim Hoffmann[64] who claimed that Hitler's aggression against the Soviet Union was aimed at preventing Stalin's allegedly planned offensive against the Third Reich. Hillgruber had repudiated the preventive-war theory, while Hildebrand took a dubious position. While speaking of the Nazi "surprise attack (*Überfall*)" on the Soviet Union, he hinted at the latter's aggressive and expantionist distant goals rather than impending plans.

Serious historiography has not embraced but rather repudiated the preventive-war theory of the Nazis. The last thing Stalin thought of in 1941 was an attack on the Third Reich, which had demonstrated its military strength in the campaigns against Poland and northern and West European states. In the purges on the eve of these wars, Stalin had virtually decapitated the Soviets' own military leadership. He displayed military weakness in the war against Finland. In the first weeks and months after Hitler's attack on the Soviet Union in June 1941, Stalin again clearly revealed his lack of military preparedness. His major goal in 1941 was to stay out of the war, preserve Soviet neutrality and let the Third Reich and the Western powers fight each other to exhaustion.

About Other German Historians of the Holocaust: Uwe D. Adam, M. Broszat, and H. Mommsen – Intentionalists and Functionalists

The reader opening Klaus Hildebrand's *Das Dritte Reich* (Munich - Vienna, 1979)[65] must have been most surprised by the failure to include a special chapter about National Socialism's Jewish policy, of the escalating persecution, and the final annihilation of German and of much of European Jewry. Of non-German works on the Holocaust, only Lucy Dawidowicz's study, *The War Against the Jews*, is mentioned. Nor are other major non-German works about the mass murder of the Jews listed. A work by Uwe Dietrich Adam, *Die*

Judenpolitik im Dritten Reich, (1972)[66] focusing on Nazi anti-Jewish hostility during the so-called "peaceful" period before 1939, furnished the primary source and focus.

According to Adam, the deportation of the Jews during the war into the occupied territories of the East and the resulting chaos had aggravated the "specific lack of planning" by National Socialism. The "organizational incapacity" in the East had had an impact upon the racial policy of Hitler, Both of these factors allegedly underlined the improvising character of the Nazi annihilation of the Jews.[67] Supposedly this diminished the magnitude of Nazi crimes.

Hildebrand also seemed to side with U. D. Adam in other respects. He reminded the reader that the command of Hitler to murder the Jews "has so far not been found." As if Hitler had had no interest in avoiding or suppressing any final written command of this kind and limiting himself to mere oral orders. Though Hildebrand did not deny Hitler's responsibility for the ultimate Jewish tragedy, he saw the "finally determining measure" for the mass murder in the "institutional structure of the Third Reich," in a functionalist interpretation.

Hildebrand briefly referred also to another functionalist historian, Hans Mommsen, who was less interested in exculpating Hitler than in accusing the German élites for the murderous decision. According to H. Mommsen, the "final solution" was an outgrowth of the complex structure of the decision-making process in the Third Reich. Thus, according to Hildebrand's and Hans Mommsen's reputed motivation for the Führer—however different their points of view were—it was the unfortunate wrong structure of the Nazi state, not primarily Nazi decisions, which were the real cause of the mass annihilation of the Jews.

Hildebrand rejected Broszat's thesis that Hitler considered the problem of anti-Semitism a "central" one. Broszat had also stressed the uncontrolled dynamism of the Nazi regime which pushed it toward improvisation and inherent radicalism as decisive for the annihilation of European Jewry. According to Hildebrand, the mass shootings of Russian Jews could not be sufficiently explained by Broszat's functionalist interpretation, "They were carried out at Hitler's [apparently oral] command and were implemented according to plan."

Though Hildebrand in *The Third Reich* (1979) referred to the Nazi murder of the Jews, he still appeared strangely brief as well as detached. In summing up, he quoted approvingly, and correctly, Karl Dietrich Bracher that the roots of Hitler's thought and of the Third

Reich, despite some all-European conditions of his dictatorship and that of National Socialism, was a "German phenomenon." The roots of his thinking lay in the German problems of the nineteenth century. Hitler was primarily a German and Austrian occurrence, though in the words of Bracher he represented a "warning"for all nations and politicians to avoid "a destructive delusion of power and a barbaric regime."[68]

Hildebrand made reference to different views as to Hitler's timetable and secret command to annihilate the Jews. It was always closely connected with his preparations for war against Russia. According to E. Jäckel, this decision of the Führer was made in the summer of 1940, while H. Krausnick dated it March 1941, and A. Hillgruber traced an oral order to the end of May 1940. About Hitler's decisive role, Hildebrand continued, there could be "no doubt" concerning his personal activity and full responsibility.

What was plainly objectionable in Hildebrand's discussion of the various interpretations of the mass murder of German and other European Jews was his attitude and that of many post-war Germans of rejecting responsibility for the Nazi atrocities. After all, they had not occurred in distant centuries, with no witnesses or evidence left behind. Yet the deliberate detachment of many German jounalists and historians from the crimes committed by their compatriots, relatives, or acquaintainces, was designed to create a misleading impression, as if the Germans of the 1970s and 1980s were not the descendants of the Germans of the 1930s and 1940s in whose name unprecedented crimes had been perpetrated and had no reason to trivialize what had occurred. Hildebrand himself talked nonchalantly of "mass murders," but none apparently were committed by "murderers." While Hildebrand treated all Germans with velvet gloves, he managed to express little commiseration and empathy for the murdered Jews.

The national-socialist propaganda, stressing the defense of "Festung Europa" against Bolshevism and Western plutocracies was, Klaus Hildebrand admitted, nothing more than concealing one's own intentions for conquest. He denounced the Nazi "state of injustice," though he also rejected the idea of the Resistance, which to him had the "odor of high treason." The same kind of contradiction marked his rejection of the Holocaust; "The most disgraceful [*abscheulichste*] and most vile of all the crimes of the Third Reich" to which the "more friendly sides [!] of its development were always subordinated" was genocide. In this regard the "historic singularity" of the Third

Reich can hardly be denied.[69] Yet again, according to Hildebrand, comparable events outside of Europe have perhaps so far not been fully considered with this observation. Hildebrand opened thus the door widely to future revisions which led him ultimately to side with Ernst Nolte. It remains still something of a puzzle that he was able to suppress his earlier views.

Michael Stürmer, Helmut Kohl, and Geopolitics and "Zielsetzung"

Michael Stürmer, born in 1938, had written his dissertation about "Koalition und Opposition in der Weimarer Republik von 1924 bis 1928" under the Social Democratic Marburg historian Erich Mathias. He worked subsequently on the topic "Government and *Reichstag* in the Bismarck state from 1871 to 1880." After teaching in Darmstadt he moved to the Gesamthochschule in Kassel and in 1973 to the University of Erlangen. Since the early 1970s, he shifted politically to the Right, following the so-called "Tendenzwende" since 1974—75. Through his doctoral advisor he sought and found closer contact as "ghost-writer" and advisor to the CDU rising politician Helmut Kohl. Thereafter, his teaching career aside, he engaged in extensive journalistic work and became more widely known through his lectures throughout the country and his role as "Praeceptor Germaniae."

The topics which attracted him most were the interpretation of disputed historic problems such as nation, creation of identity, integration, and the rediscovery of geopolitics, the magic formula of Germany's *Mittellage* [central location],[71] which became a key for the explanation of German historical trends. At the same time he firmly supported the concept of an alliance with the West and opposition to a German *Sonderweg* between the capitalist and democratic West and the "socialist" East. He focused upon two concepts, the modernization of Imperial Germany and the geopolitical notion of Germany's central position in Europe. According to Seeley, an English expert on German history, the degree of internal freedom of a country depends on the external pressures on its borders, a concept also elaborated by Karl Haushofer, the propagator of German geopolitics. Already before 1986, the date of the outbreak of the *Historikerstreit*, Stürmer's politics combined a defense of Bonn's west-oriented German foreign policy and of neo-conservative domestic policy.

J. Habermas' critique in the summer of 1986 was directed not only against Nolte but also against some of his fellow travelers, including Michael Stürmer. All the more surprising was Stürmer's relatively long silence after the criticism of his concepts of *Zielsetzung* [determination of goal] and identity. The latter concept derived from psychology of the young generation and referred to a complex individual and social psychological process until the youth, outgrowing his adolescence, developed his own unchanging personality. The concept went back to Erik H. Erikson who had gained considerable influence at Harvard University. The concept of identity was applied to numerous phenomena including countries divided in the post-war period like Germany and Korea, and others.

The external geographic situation of Germany, a country of open frontiers, has "determined the constitutional development of Germany." It was certainly not possible to think that it was not dependent on the intellectual, economic, and strategic geography. "Hitler's war had created the conditions for the penetration of Russia to the Elbe," though the division of Germany and of Europe was not an "inescapable" consequence of the war. Quoting Lenin, Stürmer held that "to him who possesses Germany, belongs Europe." The dispute over Germany "is not yet at its end." Defending Adenauer's German policy of linking up with the West, where alone security can be found, he affirmed that German unity was the price—as it turned out, only a temporary one—for democracy and freedom. As many other Germans lamenting their people's fate, he concluded that "German history was one of misfortune." This self-pity, after a hurricane which caused greater misfortune to other peoples, was characteristic of many a German reaction not only by rightist nationalists to the outcome of the war.

Christian Meier, Conciliator and Critic. At Trier (October 1986) and in Jerusalem (1987).

In 1986–87 the bitterness of the historians' feud steadily escalated. The conservative Munich historian Christian Meier, presiding officer of the *Historikerverband*, admonished in his opening address at the 36th *Historkertag* in Trier in early October 1986 all historians to "extreme caution" in carrying on the dispute, expressing the fear that historical science would be adversely affected by a deepening of the break. It was "not possible that historians refuse to enter the same room in which certain other historians stay to avoid the temptation to shake hands with them." Trying to play the role of a mediator, he acknowledged that neo-conservative historians had the right to raise questions. Comparisons between the misdeeds of Germans under Hitler and those of the Soviet Union under Stalin were by no means illegal or improper, to the contrary, they could be 'useful.' He conceded, however, that "German crimes were in a sense singular that they quantitatively exceeded comparable crimes of other peoples." Yet the remembrance of them, in his view, hindered by no means "walking upright."

Christian Meier had tried to enlist Michael Stürmer to publicly defend his concepts of the "Mittellage" and of "Sinnstiftung." The latter, rather surprisingly, declined participating at the Trier *Historikertag*, whereupon Hans-Ulrich Wehler too, on the opposite side, also declined. In his opening address at Trier, Christian Meier made clear that such a dispute would be not only scientific but also political.[72] He clearly criticized Stürmer and rejected ignoring both Habermas' concerns and asked to respect his "caliber." He emphasized against revisionist critics that nobody had decreed a "prohibition of raising questions," as Nolte had charged. It was "important for a country that in the ethically most sensitive period of its history no cheating [*schummeln*] occur, but the truth be acknowledged, how bitter it may be." Meier most aptly raised the question:

> What advantage would it be for us, if the annihilation of Jews is comparable to Stalin's liquidation of the Kulaks or the extermination by Pol Pot? Should we not measure ourselves rather with other yardsticks?

Meier finally asked what kind of conclusions German historians were to draw from German history. About a month later he reiterated some of these questions in the *FAZ*, which proved rather embarrassing to revisionist historians. To work off the "burdensome in our Nazi-past through relativizing will not succeed."[73] What moved Hillgruber to identify himself after this event with the German soldiers defending East Prussia "will probably remain his secret." No doubt the historian may be influenced by his personal experiences. Meier wrote apparently in reference to Hillgruber's East Prussian origin—however, one should have to restrain one's sentiments. Though in recent times the disgust with the Nazi regime had grown, the new conservative attitude toward history, especially in the case of Michael Stürmer, was noticeable. It was clear that Stürmer wished to "use history as an instrument" to serve his purposes.

On the eve of the *Historikertag* in Trier, the conservative Hans

Martin Schleyer-Stiftung had arranged a sort of competitive convention in Berlin for October 2–3, 1986, choosing the strange topic "To whom does German History belong?"[74] It was Michael Stürmer who had picked this peculiar theme.

In his article Christian Meier voiced his conviction that German history would also belong to non-Germans. In any case he found the question "perverse." Hans-Ulrich Wehler similarly ridiculed the notion that German history could be stolen from its possessor. Surely there were "no claims of property rights." It hardly needed an explanation why the history of any country cannot be reserved for the historians of the nationality and state concerned, and that historians of a different nationality or citizenship cannot be legitimately excluded from engaging in research and writing about any topic of their choice. In any case, Christian Meier's criticism of the revisionist German historians was open and vigorous and had clearly repelled their main thrusts.

German historians were later invited by Israeli colleagues to a discussion of the *Historikerstreit* in Jerusalem. But after first accepting, they bowed out. Apparently those invited felt uncomfortable because they considered it opportune to reach first an agreement among themselves on the issues raised. But Christian Meier later accepted an invitation to discuss the problems involved in Tel-Aviv in the spring of 1987.

In his lecture in Tel-Aviv entitled "At a turning point of German Historical Memory," referring to the annihilation of more than 5 million Jews,[75] Müller stressed that "the *Wiedergutmachung* [compensation] was the only way that the *Bundesrepublik* could gain a place of esteem among the nations." It had to "negate that which between 1933–1945 Germany represented." Responsibility, which belongs to freedom, was unthinkable without assuming such responsibility also for the past. The meaning of past German crimes was actually embedded in the fundamentals of the *Bundesrepublik.* Part of the common identity was a relatively stormy historical memory which expressed itself "in most German crimes against other peoples." "The old question is still open whether we and how we acknowledge what we brought about between 1933 and 1945. The unique thing that happened in those twelve years was not the accumulation of injustice and crime, not even the acknowledgment of the criminal character of the Nazi regime" but that "a country, a people, represented through its government arrogated to itself the decision whether an entirely different people [whose membership, on top of it, arbitrarily determined] may live on earth or not." "This people, incidentally, never showed hostility to Germans, to the contrary in most cases it met it almost with love." Yet "this people was killed like vermin." "There exists no parallel." This was "an entirely new crime" against humanity.

Some Germans, however, denied and "suppressed the uniqueness" of their crimes. Some "like to retreat in calculation of misdeeds [*aufrechnen*] which we [Germans] suffered. Yet through these crimes history has become a different thing. Therefore we cannot think of our fallen soldiers at a national memorial without thinking of those whom we have battled, maltreated, and murdered and giving them an honorable memory."

Since the end of the war, Christian Meier continued, new problems have been added to the old ones. The overwhelming majority of Germans living today have not been participants in national-socialist crimes. Should there not be made an end to the charges and "self-accusations," as they are often referred to? Should Germans not, as one political leader suggested, "step away from Hitler's shadow?" Responsibility forced Germans "to acknowledge this [recent German] history as ours."

According to Christian Meier, while there did not exist anything like a "collective guilt," Germans still had a "definite responsibility for that which was done by us and in our name . . . ,therefore even the younger people among us must keep alive the memory of the crimes. This we owe to the victims." An attempt "to escape responsibility through relativisms and excuses will be doomed." "If we recall our relationship with the worst parts of German history, we shall make it easier for others to spare us."

Descendants of those who bore responsibility for the Holocaust will admittedly have a difficult time. But this process of communication, especially with the "new Jewish generation," appeared to Meier "extraordinarily important." Forty years after the end of the war the possibility of the Nazi war, of shootings, of threats, and quick condemnation of human beings heavily oppresses us, as does its inhumanity." While German soldiers met their duties during the war and were courageous, on the other hand the number of those who permitted themselves to commit "wrong deeds" was on the German side "much greater" than in other armies. "There is probably no need to be ashamed of our parents and grandparents." Yet on the other hand, "we can take them on only relatively few cases as models."[76]

Domestic Summary

While the historians criticized by Habermas shared common ideas, they were in other respects moving in different directions. Hillgruber, an empirical scholar had not much in common with the phenomenologist Nolte nor with M. Stürmer's *Sinnstiftung* and philosophy of identity. Nor had the two latter much in common with Nolte. In the past they had all rejected the barbarism of the Nazi regime and none had disavowed in an outright fashion Nazi crimes. On the other hand, there was in the early 1980s, whether the *Wende* was primarily responsible or not, a marked clearly noticeabale shift in the position of all these historians. Instead of focusing on anti-Semitism and geographically on Austria and Germany, Nolte claimed to perceive the model for Hitler's poisonous thoughts and murderous actions in Bolshevism. Similarly, Stürmer's emphasis on Germany's *Mittellage* and geopolitics in general seemed to acquit Nazism of many of its evils by tracing the latter to mere geography. Hillgruber's focus on "perfidious Albion" and its sinister war plans of wishing to destroy Germany tended to ignore that British plans were the unavoidable reaction to Germany's strivings for hegemony over Europe and her indirect but apparent threat to the British Isles.

The subjects of Habermas' critique might have easily prevented some if not most of their retaliatory responses if they had shown some restraint. If the publisher of Hillgruber's pamphlet and not the author himself had chosen the dubious contrasting heading and subheading of his booklet in 1987—"destruction" of Germany and the "end" of European Jewry—the author could have rectified it in his reply. He might have done so in any case. But virtually all historians who had become the targets of Habermas' criticisms questioned his scholarly qualifications and the validity of most of his criticisms. They complained about his "campaign" against their scholarly prestige, accused him of Stalinist "purifications" (*Säuberungen*) and show trials. They criticized his "censorship" and tried to trivialize the Jewish persecutions and final annihilation of Jews in twentieth-century Europe. They talked about "Frageverboten," though nothing of this sort had been in Habermas' mind. In a letter to the *FAZ*, Stürmer raised questions about Habermas' research methods and his alleged falsification of quotations and went as far as to disavow his own interest in *Identitätsstiftung*, a specialty of his for several years. Habermas was even told that what he actually would have needed was a historic

"Proseminar" which, unfortunately, had not been part of his training. It became rather clear that the scholars wounded by Habermas' critiques were out to exclude him from continuing participation in the scholarly and public exchanges. Hans-Ulrich Wehler, comparing the *Historikerstreit* of the 1980s with French and English scholarly exchanges in the post-war period, reached the conclusion that many of the German discussants lacked the basic respect for the intellectual and scholarly status of their adversaries.

Escalation of the Dispute: Old Ideologies and the New Right

Following Jürgen Habermas' attacks against Nolte and associates, these revisionist historians had gained some notable defenders among colleagues, in the press, and in the political arena. After the summer of 1986 the dispute assumed a markedly shriller tone. Hans Mommsen held that the recent West German debate about National Socialism revealed the repression over many years of an uncomfortable historic legacy. A neo-revisionism and nationalism, as Habermas called it, had surfaced. After 1945 the memory of domestic policy of the Nazi regime and of the persecution of the Jews had receded into the background. Hans Mommsen now charged that Nolte had painted a wrong picture of the Third Reich as an "unfortunate countermovement" against the threats against German society by Bolshevism, exaggerating the latter's importance for post-World War I Germany.[77] Nolte thus ran the risk of becoming identified with the more assertive neo-fascist currents in the *Bundesrepublik*. The neo-conservative philosophy at present had acquired some political relevance due to the vigorous support of these tendencies through prominent speakers for the CDU-CSU. German nationalist and revisionist groups had registered increasing influence upon the government coalition, shifting it to the Right. The previously homogenous critical image of the Third Reich has increasingly vanished.

Alfred Dregger, presiding officer of the CDU-CSU *Bundestag* representation, had claimed on November 11, 1986, that most German soldiers knew nothing about the terrible wartime events and crimes. He complained that the Allied formula of unconditional capitulation was not only directed against Hitler but also against the German people. He thus repeated arguments recently advanced by Hillgruber.

The historian and social scientist Arno Klönne drew attention to the recent election for the *Bundestag* and its connection with the historians' debate, the cultural revolution of the Right and the neo-revisionist threats. Rightist forces had recently scored also in France and Italy. In Germany the new Right harked back to the tradition of pre-fascist conservative revolutionaries. The Thule Seminar in the Reich held up F. Nietzsche, O. Spengler, E. Jünger, Martin Heidegger, and Carl Schmitt among its intellectual fathers.[78] The Right's gain in intellectual reputation offered no guarantee against gliding into fascist thinking.

The ultra-conservative and nationalistic waves on the Right influenced in turn many in the scholarly camp who also adopted a neo-conservative line, as for instance the prestigious *Historische Zeitschrift.* In 1986 (volume 247) the *H.Z.* felt the need to have a non-German citizen, Peter Stadler, in "Rückblick auf einen Historikerstreit-Versuch einer Beurteilung aus nichtdeutscher Sicht"[79] attempt to make a judgment about the historians' dispute of 1986–87. While criticizing some aspects of Nolte's position, the author considered his view "quite defensible," pointing to the Turkish mass murder of Armenians during World War I as well as to Stalin's annihilation of the Kulaks, the latter of course not a national group. Hillgruber was merely taken to task because of his unfortunate choice of words. Stadler even defended the German people which, while having succumbed to a dictatorship, came face to face with a "natural [!] catastrophe." In the 1960s the Holocaust was still considered a "malevolent invention," propaganda by Nazi ghosts. Compared with it, Stadler saw in the *Historikerstreit* of the 1980s "a certain progress." Stadler's "non-German" interpretation of the dispute in the *H.Z.* had clearly an apologetic tone.

V

GERMAN SCHOLARLY CRITIQUE OF THE "REVISIONISTS"

Back in 1952 the historian Theodor Heuss, President of the *Bundesrepublik* between 1949 and 1959, referring on occasion of the "week of brotherhood" to suggestions to stop talking about National Socialism and the Holocaust, rejected the idea. Silence would be too comfortable for the German people, "Who would possess the impudence to tell Jewish people 'forget this'."[1] A third of a century later, some of the revisionists in the *Historikerstreit* actually reiterated this very suggestion. But a majority of German historians repudiated it, since the task of history, evidently, is to uncover the truth, not to bury it. Having liberated the historical profession from past prejudices, they took up the challenge raised by nationalist colleagues and commenced their Philippic against them.

Hans-Ulrich Wehler, professor of history at the University Bielefeld, had served also as a guest professor at Harvard, Princeton, and Stanford. In a hard-hitting polemical booklet Wehler castigated the attempt of minimizing and relativizing national-socialist policy of mass murder with the help of its "bizarre constructions." In his view, the end of the historians' dispute was nowhere in sight.[2]

What was primarily involved in this feud was, according to Wehler, the dispute about the place of National Socialism, its war of annihilation and its significance for the present and future of the *Bundesrepublik.* At issue were "the adventurous attempts of relativizing its limitless misdeeds through misleading comparisons," the alleged loss of a stabilizing historical consciousness and the attempts of neoconservative historians and publicists to contribute to the awakening of a conservative national feeling of identity. "Apologetic tendencies" among some historians of the most recent German era had clearly surfaced and had "already produced effects."

The author's polemic was directed against the apologetic interpretations of Hitler as the sole or "main culprit" of the Holocaust in order to exculpate the old German power élites, the army, the bureaucracy, the judiciary, the railroads, as well as the silent mass of all those knowledgeable (*Mitwisser*) of national affairs. The feud of German historians was only within narrow limits a scientific and scholarly dispute. In the main it was a political struggle centering on the political conscience of German citizenry unleashed by a conservative *Machtpolitik*. Wehler focused on the main actors, Ernst Nolte, Andreas Hillgruber, Michael Stürmer, and Klaus Hildebrand. The conflict had smoldered already for several years, but burst into open flames in 1986–87.

Wehler ridiculed the "comparative attempts" of some of the foregoing historians to refer to the "rat-infested prisons" of the Chinese *Cheka* and what one of them called "the Hitler era" of every great nation. He saw in Alfred Heuss' remark in his book *Versagen und Verhängnis* and Hillgruber's approval of the latter's "eccentric" judgment that the expulsion of Germans from the East was the "most grievous" consequence[3] of World War II, the true motive for the latter's excursions. If in 1986 he pictured the loss of Germany's eastern territories as the most atrocious consequence of the war, what then, asked Wehler, was the

> Holocaust, this unique mass annihilation of more than 6 million Jews? Where are the 21 million* [sic] of Russians killed in consequence of a barbaric war which Hitler's Germany unleashed for four years against Russia? What can be said about the fact that every fifth Pole and Yugoslav has perished during World War II? And what about the mass liquidation of children, women and old people, of Slavic 'Untermenschen' and Gypsies?[4]

Where was, Wehler finally asked, "the balanced judgment" which one has the right to expect from a historian of the national socialist regime and of the Second World War?

Wehler focused upon several issues on which German historians have taken an opposite point of view. First, the massacres of the tribal warriors of Idi Amin or the Red Khmer Pol Pots, performed with modern weapons, were, he asserted, absolutely incomparable

---

* Later revised Russian official estimates spoke of 28 million victims.

with the industrial annihilation machinery of the Third Reich. Of the asserted causality between Stalin's Gulag and the Nazi annihilation camps has, as one year of the dispute has shown, "not much" been proven. The few German historians who have pointed to the Russian model have not demonstrated a solid knowledge of Soviet history or of the struggle against the Kulaks in particular. Most of the Russian peasants had had the option of survival in the collectives; no Jew, however, in the annihilation camp possessed that option.

Another major issue separating the neo-conservative historians from the great majority of historians was the question of German identity. According to the neo-conservative ideologues, the German Federal Republic lived day in and day out like a "country without a history." Wehler, however, disputed that West Germans had lost their identity, no one has destroyed it. West Germans looked upon the German Federal Republic as the center of their new loyalty. Only neo-conservatives spoke of the threats to Germany, her destabilization, and the erosion of German identity. The maturity of the citizens of the *Bundesrepublik* must depend on their self-criticism, on freedom from arrogance, and on the desire to freely confess the burdens and "sins" of the past.[5]

A third major source of the dispute among historians was geopolitics. The Nazis had been greatly influenced by Karl Haushofer's geopolitics, which stressed the crucial significance of geographic factors for their policy. In recent years some historians have revived geopolitics in substance, avoiding the term by replacing it with an innocent-sounding phrase; Germany's *Mittellage* (location in the center of continent). In 1981 Michael Stürmer had talked about the history of Prussia and Germany "loaded with the curse of geography." A few years later he wrote about the "temptation of the middle." Since the mid-1970s Klaus Hildebrand has elaborated upon the "threatened" position of the "traditional *Mittellage*." Germany to him was the "failed Great Power," which had entertained "Ideas of the Grossraum" (large space conception) and most recently he lamented that the "European center, smashed during the war," had become a "victim" of the catastrophe of 1945. According to Stürmer, the central location of Germany and the German "Sonderweg,"[6] the peculiar road traveled by Germany, were virtually identical. Yet Germany, Wehler stressed, lay by no means alone in the middle of the continent. Bohemia, Austria, and Switzerland lay also, and in their entirety, in mid-Europe! But their history had a different course from that of Germany. Wehler found it strange that none of the recent authors considered it necessary to distance himself emphatically from the vocabulary as well as the model of the older *Geopolitik*.

Earlier, in 1949, Friedrich Meinecke, glancing back into the "tortorous paths [*Irrwege*] of German history," had already remarked that it was the geopolitical situation of Germany "which forced upon us the alternative either to remain a region of depression or one of glorifying power [*Machtstaat*]." Wehler ridiculed this belief and that of recent historians to see "fateful forces like the Destinies [*Nornen*] at work." Wehler also rejected Nolte's "causal analysis" of alleged Soviet "Asiatic" annihilation practices and the Nazi Holocaust as well as his account of Chaim Weizmann's and the Jewish Agency's supposed "declaration of war" as "intellectual contrariness [*Bocksprünge*]."[7]

Hitler and National Socialism according to Wehler must be judged primarily as a product of German and German-Austrian history.[8] Only thereafter may European history, to which Nolte and others have pointed as the broader framework, be considered. Nolte had placed Germany's "guilt" primarily upon Marx and Lenin, the Russian Revolution and the alleged Bolshevik policy of the annihilation of an entire class, the bourgeoisie, and the upper class. Nazi ideology, racism and extreme chauvinism, and Germanomania were virtually excluded as primary motivating factors of their crimes. Against Nolte's view, according to Wehler, must also be held that Hitler had developed the anti-Marxist ideology long before the Russian Revolution and the Russian Civil War. The same holds true of the rabid anti-Semitism which had occasionally emerged already in the nineteenth century in both Germany and Austria. Its origins lay thus in German and German-Austrian thought rather than in imitation of Russian Jew-hatred. Numerous other sources may be found in the German rather than in the Russian past. Wehler accused Nolte and other neo-conservatives of having refused to make the slightest concession to their critics. In conclusion, Wehler held that the critical self-examination of the *Bundesrepublik* has been successfully upheld in the historians' feud against their rightist opponents.[9]

Jürgen Kocka Upholds the "Singularity" of the Holocaust

Other weak points of Nolte and the revisionists were critically examined by the historians Jürgen Kocka and Heinrich August Winkler. According to Kocka, Nolte through relativistic comparison of the Holocaust with the Turkish annihilation of Armenians, the Stalinist mass terror, and the Pol Pot praxis of outright killings in Cambodia wanted to "take away the singularity" of the Nazi mass murder of the Jews. This attempt was by no means novel.

Some German historians have attempted to relativize or even deny the national-socialist crimes. But, according to Kocka, the strategy of repressing bad memories can be successful only if the high price of moral "cost"[10] is paid. There is evident injustice for the victims in renouncing the calculation of the crimes. The concept of totalitarianism had drawn attention to undeniable similarities between National Socialism and Stalinism such as their common hostility *vis-à-vis* the liberal-democratic constitutional state. But Nolte had blurred the "qualitative difference between the bureaucratic, passionless perfect systematics of mass murder in the highly industrialized *Reich* of Hitler and the brutal mixture of civil war excesses, mass 'liquidations,' slave labor and starving in the backward country of Stalin."[11] The "singularity" of the German development cannot be eliminated through the foregoing comparisons with Stalin and Pol Pot, and was "shameful." It would be more proper to compare Hitler-Germany with the Western Powers. Such a comparison has nothing to do with "arrogance" and "mind of the master race" (*Herrenvolk*) but with "taking seriously our European tradition from which Enlightenment, human rights, and constitutional-political structure cannot be separated." How can one consider national-socialist annihilation of the Jews as a defensive mechanism against threatening annihilation by the Soviet Union with which one concluded pacts until 1941?

H. A. Winkler: "The Greatest Crimes of the Twentieth Century"

The Freiburg historian Heinrich August Winkler similarly rebuffed Nolte, who offered "no shadow of a proof" for his absurd assertions about Auschwitz. No other German historian had so far demonstrated "so much empathizing" for Nazi crimes as Nolte. Germany belonged to the West, Winkler asserted, rejecting like Kocka and Wehler the comparison of Nazi Germany with the dictatorships of the Third World. It must be measured "by the norms of the West." In this light the murder of the Jews was "the greatest catastrophe of the twentieth century." He who excludes Germany from the western cultural circle "breaks with the West anew." This should terrify "even German conservatives."

Revisionists who try to minimize the terrors of National Socialism and deny its crimes have made much noise throughout Germany. What they assert cannot, in the long run, shape Germany's true historical image. The revisionists may succeed, however, in arousing doubts about unfortunately firmly established facts of National Socialism. According to Winkler, there were admittedly "fools" who want to make Germans believe that the Jews in the Third Reich did not fare so badly. They complained that one had taken from the German nation its history. Some people wanted a German history of which they could be proud. Instead of writing true history, some writers created "new myths," the positive myth of "an honorable national history which would balance out the dishonest parts of it, the history of the Third Reich."

Winkler raised the question why the "greatest crime of the twentieth century was committed just by you Germans." On occasion of the Bitburg Ceremony the Second World War was transformed into a "normal European war." Criticizing three authors and the *FAZ*, which had opened its pages to them, Winkler ridiculed that Hitler, fearful of the Asiatic will to annihilate, had himself committed an "Asiatic deed." The *FAZ* was responsible for the "national-apologetic" waves which recently swept over Germany. It led to the truism cultivated at the German table of regulars that all history was one of crimes, not excepting German history.

Concluding with the question what is to be learned from German history, he replied: "We must learn to live with it without trying to make a deal with it." Germans have the duty to demonstrate "solidarity with the victims of German arrogance. primarily Jews and Poles."[12]

Eberhard Jäckel Rejects the Thesis "Post hoc, ergo propter hoc."**

The Stuttgart Professor Eberhard Jäckel was author and editor of several books about Hitler and his *Weltanschauung*. He did not hold back with sharpest criticism of Nolte and fellow travelers, His article "Die elende Praxis der Untersteller, Das Einmalige der national-sozialistischen Verbrechen lässt sich nicht leugnen" in the *Nürnberger Zeitung*, 20 September 1986,[13] revealed the main thrusts of his writing. He rejected what Joachim Fest called the "miserable

---

* "Thereafter, therefore because of it."

practice" of looking for motives of the opponents, but reversing this charge accused the opponent of alleged falsification of quotations Tacitus himself had not written "sine ira et studio." According to Jäckel, the murder of the Jews was unique since never before had a state, with the authority of a responsible Führer, resolved and announced to kill without exception a certain human group including the old, women and children and infants and transformed this resolve into deed with all possible means of the disposition of the state. According to Nolte, the Gulag had preceded Nazi practices. But Jäckel rejected the logic supposedly inherent in it and Nolte's conclusion that a "causal connection" between the class murder of the Bolsheviks and the racial killings of the Nazis was "probable." According to Nolte and Fest, Hitler's decision to annihilate the Jews was "determined by anxieties." It was unique.

Fest had quoted a *Cheka* chief,[14] but, according to Jäckel, failed to prove that it was Bolshevik theory and practice to kill the entire bourgeoisie "as a class." Himmler, however, in a declaration of October 6, 1943,[15] had specifically justified the impending killing also of women and children to avoid the latter's subsequent vengeance. In any case, the question of the uniqueness of the Holocaust—which he did not doubt—was in Jäckel's opinion not critical in judging the mass murder. "Shall the *Bundesrepublik* in that case not pay reparations, the Chancellor not bow his head in Yad Vashem or [German] citizens feel better?"

Nobody disputed that persecutions, expulsions, and murders had taken place throughout history and that these excesses could and should be historically examined. But it was also indisputable that the murder of people originating "in our country" should not be relativized by questionable parallels which were not clearly defined.

Martin Broszat: To Whom Does German History Belong?

Another historian, the senior member of the *Munich Institut für Zeitgeschichte*, Martin Broszat, was one of the most severe critics of Ernst Nolte. In view of the collegiate manner long prevailing among German historians, Broszat welcomed the sharper tone of the recent Habermas polemics as a breath of fresh air.[16] He felt, however, that the weakest points of Habermas' attack was his lumping together politically agile professors like M. Stürmer and K. Hildebrand with the easy going A. Hillgruber and the great eccentric (*Eigenbrötler*) E. Nolte.

In these last days, Broszat developed, there had been formed under the auspicies of the Schleyer-Stiftung a circle of historians of modern times under the leadership of K. Hildebrand and with M. Stürmer and A. Hillgruber as additional resource persons. They planned a symposium on the strange topic "Wem gehört die deutsche Geschichte?" [To whom does German history belong?]. The selection of active participants as well as the timing—one week prior to the Trier *Historikertag*—point to the programmatic intention to take issue with the "troublemaker" (*Störenfried*) J. Habermas. Nolte, though a resident of Berlin, was not invited by Hildebrand to this Berlin symposium, which showed the latter's attempt to distance himself from his colleague.

Nolte, according to Broszat, "in arrogant contempt" of empirical historical occurrences, had transgressed acceptable boundaries. Some arguments of his came close to "splitting hairs."[17] Broszat referred to Nolte's "Mythos" essay as "perhaps the most offensive piece" of his publications. The "spinning of a yarn" [*fabulieren*] about the letter of Chaim Weizmann, noted Zionist leader who had allegedly "declared war" against Germany, could have been expected from a "radical" rightist journalist, one with lacking education. But Nolte should not have been permitted to use it for dubious purposes, Klaus Hildebrand too, Broszat continued, should confess that he had overlooked some of Nolte's writings when he had praised him in the *H.Z.* Yet Broszat himself had already supported a "historization," whatever its meaning, of the Hitler era by comparing it with Stalinist Russia and Pol Pot's "stone-age communism."[18]

Broszat did not think that Hillgruber deserved the accusation of wishing to play down the misdeeds of National Socialism even though the distributor Wolf Jobst Siedler, in connecting his two essays about Germans and Jews in *Zweierlei Unteraang*, written from an apologetic perspective, has not published a magisterial work. The link-up between the two themes—"destruction" of Germany and the "end" of European Jewry—was missing.

Broszat criticized M. Stürmers "diversions,"[19] but questioned whether he merited Habermas' "vehement attack" since he was neither a "Deutsch-Nationaler" nor a political Romantic, but a decided protagonist of skeptic rationalism and proponent of the Atlantic Alliance. He admitted, however, that Stürmer had also voiced in *Dissonanzen des Fortschritts* contrary views. Among the latter's questionable opinions Broszat rejected the view that history promised to be a "guide to identity," that it was imperative for the survival and progress of the *Bundesrepublik* and that it was essential to have a unified plan for the teaching of *Kultur* to assure continuity and consensus.

In Stürmer's view, history had the function of replacing religion and must be imposed by the state for the sake of a general democratic agreement. When Stürmer talked of the "straight walk" of the Germans, it reminded Broszat of the politician Alfred Dregger's observation in the *Bundestag* that Germany will not be able to survive without a "basic patriotism." Habermas had aptly remarked that, according to Stürmer, Germans should no longer display shame. What stood behind all this were politically ambitious élites wishing to exhibit the pride of being bearers of culture.

Broszat held that Stürmer's endeavors were attempts to engage in "transparent diversionary maneuvers."[20] All this was marked by a "gross lack of clarity, rationality, and precision clothed in pretentious language," which suggests but does not show "depth of thought and significance." Though Stürmer had somewhat retreated from his extremist stance in the *FAZ* of 16 August 1986, Broszat considered it "indisputable" that he had assigned to history the "task of guiding social and political integration of the German nation."

A German-Jewish Dialogue

Broszat had dealt with the Jewish question in earlier years. In 1989 the German bi-weekly *Tribüne* published a series of letters of 1987 exchanged by Broszat and the Israeli historian Saul Friedländer. The correspondence bore the dates starting late Sepember 1987 and ending in December, and focused on the topic of the "historization" [*Historisierung*] of National Socialism. Broszat referred therein to his article in the journal *Merkur*, "Plaidoyer für eine Historisierung des National-Sozialismus," on occasion of the fortieth anniversary of the end of the Nazi regime and Friedländer's polemics in Germany and abroad, expressed in various articles and speeches.[21]

In his first letter Broszat admitted that the concept of a "*Historislerung*" of National–Socialism had many meanings; it could be easily misunderstood and mislead. Historic understanding cannot stop before the national-socialist era merely because of the massive crimes and catastrophies which the regime had generated and which had produced political-moral condemnation. Broszat claimed that his concept of "historization" was different from the romantic-idealistic view of "*Historismus*" of the nineteenth century. He rejected the historic opinions of "a Heinrich von Treitschke" which may have led to giving moral justification to brutal power. Broszat failed, however, to make his caption clear as well as his desire "only to understand." He himself appeared to realize his quandary when raising the question: "Where is the dividing line between condemning unspeakable crimes and understanding?" Broszat admitted that the history of the national-socialist era cannot be determined by German historians alone. "In view of the persecution of millions of human beings of non-German nationality, any exclusive claim of German interpretation must be rejected. For the persecuted of all countries and nations of the Nazi era and their descendants the Nazi regime is not a historically dead past. It would be absurd and arrogant if Germans demanded a waning of their memory, whatever German historiography, operating on a scientific basis, may arrogantly claim."[22] The German claims to have the only assured, exclusive approach to truth and "science" are bound to encounter plain disbelief. Such claims would surely be haughty and ludicrous.

In his reply Friedländer, hardly satisfied, pointed to the tone of urgency in Broszat's first "plaidoyer" which created the impression as if he had become impatient with the alleged lack of a "critical understanding" of this era. Referring to an article by Hermann Rudolph "Falsche Fronten?" Broszat acknowledged the need of respect for the remembrance of the "victims" of the national-socialist regime, but he called their memory "mythical." Friedländer challenged Broszat: "You juxtapose to the rational discussion of German historiography the mythical remembrance of the victims." Was the murder of millions a "myth"?[23] Broszat recalled that the history of the Nazi era was first written by historians who for political and racial reasons had been forced to leave Germany. He implied that the victims of Nazism and their descendants after four decades still continued a kind of non-scientific memory. But according to Friedländer, Broszat himself had previously expressed his admiration for such pioneers of the analysis of National Socialism as Ernst Fraenkel, Franz Neumann, and Hannah Arendt, who were all Jewish emigrants. Friedländer also recalled that "the most recent debates have been carried on by a great majority of those historians who on the German side belonged to the Hitler-Jugend generation, sometimes also by individuals whose families were burdened by accusations of personal participation in past crimes. And he raised the question whether this German background in presenting the Nazi era did not pose as many problems as that of the victims.

In his rejoinder to Friedländer, Broszat, pointing to the "criminal core" of National Socialism, has accused the German bureacracy, the German army and the German churches as having served the preservation of Nazi domination in Europe. Even "non-participation" and mere "passivity" had been factors stabilizing the regime. Broszat questioned that his view did justice to Germans or was leading to real historic comprehension. He also felt that Friedländer's strong doubts about almost all more recent perspectives of the historic description of the national-socialist era—for instance, the concentration on daily events or the social-historic preservation of the 1933–1945 period—were prejudicial. He asserted that the judgment about the "national-socialist crimes" will not be "changed" in any way by these approaches, but claimed that it will be better understandable why such "large parts of a civilized nation erroneously succumbed in so strong a measure" to Hitler and National Socialism. Broszat thus defended the focus of *Alltagsgeschichte* upon which he and his collaborators in the Munich *Institut für Zeitgeschichte* in the framework of the Bavaria-project had concentrated. While it was important for historians to distinguish between "good" and "bad," he supported the view that it was also imperative to show a "sympathetic interest for the [German] cordemporaries."

According to Broszat, the Holocaust and Auschwitz were a "result of special intensive Jewish memory"—a memory apparently too "intensive" in his view—overshadowed other deeds and misdeeds of the Third Reich. Auschwitz had been made the central event of the Hitler-era. Yet he could not fully accept that the entire national-socialist period has been placed into the shadow of Auschwitz. In his rejoinder Friedländer voiced the fear that "broadening of the historical outlook through insisting upon the normal German *Alltag* and social trends are likely to lead to a misplacement of the right focus." The years 1933–1945 have been marked by the "primacy of policy" rather than by German *Alltagsleben.* Broszat himself, Friedländer recalled, had given his elaborate Bavarian research project the fitting subtitle "Perspective or Trivializing?"

Recent studies by Ian Kershaw about the "Hitler-mythus" and the history of the German *Alltag* by H. and E. Obenaus had proven that the average German knew much more about the fate of the Jews than was claimed by apologists to have been the case. Broszat himself in an article published already in 1983 had written:

> So completely concealed were the persecutions by no means. The basic anti-humane outlook. . ., especially the fanatical hatred of the Jews, was expressed quite clearly and publicly by the leadership again and again on almost every occasion.

And why was the German people even toward the very end of the war so passive? Broszat had previously asserted: "The Germans were conscious that they were 'co-responsible' and 'involved in the crimes' of the regime." As Broszat had then conceded, massive crimes had been committed in the name of the Germans. Such crimes did not support the thesis of their having led a "normal life."

In Friedländer's view, broad sections of the Nazi leadership and parts of their following had the feeling of accomplishing something truly formidable and extraordinary. Referring to Himmler's oration in Posen in October 1943, Friedländer found in it an "intoxication" [*Rausch*], a feeling of an almost superhuman undertaking. He held important aspects of the national-socialist movement as belonging to the categories of a "political religion" in the sense of Eric Voegelin, Karl Dietrich Bracher, James Rhodes, Uriel Tal, and others. On the whole, in his correspondence with Friedländer, Broszat was frequently on the defensive, while in other writings he was sharply critical of the Third Reich and the Holocaust.

Michael Broszat: Hitler, World War II, the "Old" German Élites and the "New" Nazi Élite

Broszat took up the Jewish question once again in the work edited by himself and Klaus Schwabe, *Die Deutschen Éliten und der Weg in den Zweiten Weltkrieg*, published in 1989 in the wake of the *Historikerstreit*. According to Broszat and other West German historians, it was necessary to emphasize the "disastrous historic legacy of National Socialism" and to stress the influence of "German *völkisch* nationalism, imperialism and pan-Germanism" upon Nazism.[24] This legacy of the era of Bismarck and Wilhelm II brought German national thinking and German national policy to the dangerous *Sonderweg* [special road]. In exploring the prehistory of World War II, it was not enough to point to "Hitler-fascism" but to illuminate a piece of the earlier German history of the national state.

Nor was it possible to exclude the German "Teil-Nation" [partial nation] of the DDR, which must also bear responsibility for the "bad legacy" of the German national state. According to Broszat, the "old" German élites, the new élites of National Socialism and the "factor Hitler" were all closely linked in the Nazi era. The old élites followed Hitler at least so long as it appeared that his foreign policy pursued the traditional goals of German revisionism. After 1933 "a Führer absolutism" emerged in the Third Reich and decisions shifted more and more to the "most narrow coterie" around Hitler. For a long time conservative and German national élites have played a major role in disseminating nationalist warlike spirits.

Broszat endorsed this view of H.-U. Wehler and other German historians who have pointed to the spread of a "vociferous power-nationalism" under Bismarck and Wilhelm II among bourgeois and partly also among proletarian circles as a "social-imperialist diversion" from the necessary attempts at "democratization." Next to the nationalism of Imperial Germany flourished already since the 1880s a *völkisch*-anti-Semitic undercurrent. It tried to deepen nationalism in a quasi-religious amd ideological fashion, as becomes clear in the writings of Paul de Lagarde and the pan-German Heinrich Class. Both West and East German historiography have drawn attention to the thought of the *Alldeutsche Verband* which embraced before 1914 all the ingredients of the later Nazi ideology.

After the First World War the German national dreams of a Great Power and World Power were by no means overcome and the policy of "virtually all parties" for a revision of Versailles had become clear. In the struggle against Versailles, the Weimar Republic itself developed secret measures in behalf of recruitment and rearmament. And under the name of "Conservative Revolution" and the *Jung-Konservative* movement developed an anti-republican nationalism. This turned out to be an essential component of the prehistory of National Socialism. Though Broszat did not share the views that the charges against the main representatives of the NSDAP, which the Nuremberg judgment of the International Military Tribunal had conidered a "criminal" organization, could be upheld, he was convinced that the top Nazi leaders had "hardly fewer scruples than Hitler to move to the very brink of war risks." The most prominent Nazi bigwigs were primarily interested in a "strengthening of the German hegemony" already attained and also in the personal enjoyment of their positions of power. But they did not rise to contradict Hitler openly, just as little as old pre-Nazi élites had done, Broszat tried to prove this by producing the unknown portions of the diaries of the

Propaganda Minister Goebbels for the years 1936–39. He also confirmed later the Nuremberg accusations of criminality against Hitler, his "cynical-brute utterances" about his foreign policy and war goals, his racial and "*raumpolitische*" [expansionist] goals.[25]—resting on the alleged need for *Lebensraum*.

Karl Dietrich Bracher: "Singular Inhumanity" and "Totalitarian Manipulation."

Long before the *Historikerstreit* erupted in 1986, Karl Dietrich Bracher had denounced Nazi atrocities and their attempts to conceal their crimes by an "Aesopian" language and by removing all traces of the "final solution" as well as the Wehrmacht's "complicity." In a letter to the *FAZ* on September 6, 1986, Bracher held that the recent major discussion about the comparability of national-socialist anti-communist policy of mass murder contained scientifically "really nothing new."[26] All the essential facts and arguments have been discussed in books in the 1940s and 1950s, not the least the enslaving power of the two dominant radical ideologies, Nazism and Communism. Unfortunately, these insights have been repressed through the virtual taboo of the concept of totalitarianism and through the inflation of the fascism formula—of which, incidentally, both Nolte and Habermas were not quite innocent. It was still important that through comparisons of ideologies and both dictatorship nothing is diminished of the "singular" Nazi inhumanity. Shame on account of the failure of a *Kulturvolk*, which thought itself shaped by the values of Christianity and humanism, and Enlightenment, may help to recognize the perils of totalitarian manipulation.

Responsibilities of Hitler and the Old and New Élites. Rejection of the Bolshevik "Model" by Hans Mommsen

In an article in *Merkur* in September-October 1986, a descendant of the distinguished historian Theodor Mommsen and specialist of ancient Roman history, Hans Mommsen, entered the arena of the German historical dispute. Though he had strong convictions, he at times appeared less critical of Nolte, Hillgruber, and subsequently of J. Fest. While praising Hillgruber's earlier "fundamental" works, he castigated his recent "inacceptable ideological construction." This had brought Hillgruber the reproach by an American historian of German descent, Felix Gilbert, that he was an "ordinary German nationalist."

Shortly after the foregoing article Hans Mommsen published in the *Blätter für deutsche und internationale Politik*, October 1986, the article "Geschichtsbewussein und Relativierung des Nationalsozializmus,"[27] Nolte, according to H. Mommsen, denied the singularity of Nazi crimes. Considering the anti-criticism of J. Fest, who had come to Nolte's defense, serious, Mommsen acquitted him, "one of the most eminent historians of the Nazi-era," of pro-fascist or other extreme tendencies. Mommsen did not object to making comparisons of the Nazi Holocaust with the mass annihilation of other peoples. The basic question was whether "correct or misleading conclusions" were drawn from such comparisons.

H. Mommsen's own comparisons, however, raise several questions, since he did not seem fully to distinguish between the maltreatment of some peoples from the unique, total destruction of the Jews by the Third Reich and that the persecution of the Jews throughout history constituted a singular historical problem. Their annihilation was a special goal in Hitler's sick mind and national-socialist ideology. Mommsen also tried to blame other nations for their Jew-hatred and not "German mentality alone"—again ignoring the totality of the Jews' annihilation by the Nazis. Mommsen voiced his conviction that only "a relatively small number of fanaticized Nazis" adopted "passively the deportations and largely approved it." But he sharply denounced the "cynical and systematic annihilation of unpopular [*missliebig*] peoples and minorities."

There are evident contradictions in H. Mommsen's analysis. While shifting part of the responsibility for the mass murder of the Jews onto the German people, he on the other hand clearly limited it to a "relatively small number." Though he did not by any means acquit Hitler for the decision to murder the Jews, he appears to have underestimated his role, espousing a functionalist interpretation. The real problem, he correctly pointed out, was "that the many people involved in the elimination" [*Ausgrenzung*] of the Jews from German life and society, which marked the beginning of the Holocaust," were actively engaged in it and did not refuse in its participation, "not in membership in the *Einsaktruppen*, the technical implementation of the deportation, the utilization of Jewish wealth," and even "the blending of the gold teeth." He sharply denounced "acts of crying injustice and also rejected the thesis that Bolshevism was the root cause of the Nazi Holocaust. Whatever Bolshevism's crimes, Nazism in the treatment of the Jews and other national minorities was apparently not comparable to it since it surpassed it by far and, in any case, was also not its consequence.

H. Mommsen held that the supposed "conspiracy of world Jewry"—which Nolte had partly endorsed—was an ideological construct. The inner boundlessness, which was especially characteristic of National Socialism, did not permit any compromises and led by necessity to the annihilation of the Jews. In this form it was not typical of the communist system of domination, however tyrannical the latter was. H. Mommsen rejected the notion that Hitler, as Nolte's construct assumed, had borrowed the idea of the Holocaust from Bolshevik writings and practices. Mommsen blamed the *FAZ* for publishing Nolte's thought and for making itself the instrument of *völkisch* radicalism by arousing instinctive fear of "Asiatic hordes"—a characteristic defamation by Nazi racism. The opposition to Nolte's attempt to trace Auschwitz to the Gulag Archipelago has not only aroused the enmity of the descendants of the victims but also the opposition of all whose life's task was to destroy the course of similar developments in the future.

In regard to the Holocaust, Hitler, according to Nolte, did in H. Mommsen's view not encounter serious resistance from the old élites. To the contrary, "the leadership of the *Wehrmacht* made itself rather a willing accomplice" of the policy of annihilation. To place all responsibility, as Nolte did, on Hitler, meant practically to divert attention from the "decisive share of responsibility of the military leadership and of the bureaucratic élites."

H. Mommsen rejected the attempt to explain the persecution and annihilation of European Jews—"the most difficult chapter" of German, certainly also of European history—a chapter which did not vanish on account of universalist contemplations of totalitarianism, "mass murder and mass expulsion." It was not feasible to cover the "shame" over past history by claiming that every people had its "Hitler era." H. Mommsen vacillated between an explanation of national-socialist anti-Semitism on universal grounds applicable to other countries and one based on specific German and Austrian sources.

Wolfgang Mommsen. "The Burden of the Past" and "Intellectual Sincerity"

Wolfgang Mommsen, twin brother of Hans Mommsen, in an article in the *Frankfurter Rundschau* (1 December 1986) with the caption "Neither denying nor forgetting liberates us from the past. The harmonization of the historic image threatens freedom,"[28] offered an overview of recent German historiography of the Third Reich and especially of the Holocaust. Since the end of the 1950s the national conscience of the Germans of the *Bundesrepublik* had undergone important changes. A hybrid nationalism had started with the First World War and terminated with the tyranny of National Socialism and a gigantic war of annihilation. In the early 1960s, Karl Jaspers had declared that the national idea was finished and that the concept of a united Europe should take its place. His optimism was apparently misplaced.

On the whole, W. Mommsen avoided taking a sharply critical attitude in the *Historikerstreit* against Nolte and his fellow-travelers. In his view, "most historical interpretations" contain a "small kernel of truth," though they have different thrusts and also varied political goals. W. Mommsen pointed to the largely positive recent assessments of the personalities of Martin Luther, Frederick the Great, and Otto von Bismarck in both West and East Germany, but questioned their possible utilizations by neo-conservatives. These endeavors were only possible if events are omitted "of which we as a nation have to be ashamed and which are a challenge to "intellectual sincerity." Mommsen considered the Bitburg ceremony a failure and President Richard von Weizsäcker's often quoted 1985 oration a proper acknowledgment of German guilt. He emphasized that Germans could not escape the burden of the past through personal forgetfulness or by claiming exemption due to late birth. W. Mommsen considered Hillgruber's recent attempt to justify the continuation of the war in the East in 1944–45 on the basis not only of national considerations but also from the perspective of the present as "problematical." "We can't deny the bitter truth that the defeat of Nazi Germany was not only in the interest of the nations battling the German troops and of those selected groups of people Hitler's henchmen had doomed to annihilation, suppression, or exploitation, but of the Germans themselves." At least parts of the gigantic events of World War II of direct concern to Germans were "plainly senseless, even suicidal." W. Mommsen considered the assignment of partial responsibility for the outbreak of World War II to other nations questionable.

German history can only be studied in a critical manner, not in an uncritical affirmative fashion. "First command therefore is to see German history in European, even world-wide historical context, rather than, as happened in the past, in contradistinction to other nations." "Political decisions since the post-war era were influenced by Western thinking, and this must continue."

Karl Heinz Janssens' Identical Theme

This was also the theme song of Karl Heinz Janssen, Director of the Institute for Didactics of History at the Westphalian Williams-Universität in *Die Zeit* (November 27, 1986).[29] Though the German people had an urgent need for "normality" and declined being made responsible for the "terrors of the Holocaust," even coming generations, according to Janssen, will have to carry the burden of German history. The German survivors of the war knew of course the connection between the outbreak of the war unleashed by the Third Reich and the national catastrophe which followed, "the unconditional capitulation, division and amputation" of the Reich. Only many years later commenced the Germans' coming to grips with National Socialism. "One should not deceive oneself. . . . The quick integration of the *Bundesrepublik* into the system of Western alliance and into the European community, the *Wiedergutmachung* [payments to Israel and others to millions of persecuted people], the regularly voiced repulsion of the national socialist dominion of violence" soothed the conscience of the nation. But "too much remained repressed." Élites and various professions needed the passing of many years before they admitted their own involvements and their own share of the blame. Among them were the psychoanalysts and jurists. The role of the army in committing the crimes remained a taboo subject until the late 1970s. Industrialists and bankers remained equally silent. These circles believed that the German obsession with guilt should cease. According to Janssen, for forty years the Germans had attempted to flee from the worst epoch of their history. But they will not succeed in living like a people of Schlemihls without a shadow. However young, they must carry with them the heritage of Auschwitz.

The Kulaks and "Genocide." East German Expulsions and Richard Löwenthal

The question of comparability between Soviet maltreatment of its population, of the Kulaks in particular, and the Nazi Holocaust figured large in the German historians' dispute. German historians who have repudiated their comparability have pointed out that Stalin's brutal persecution of Russian peasants was a bloody social revolution, in the course of which force and starvation killed millions. But many survived if they accepted Stalin's collectivization drive. It was no genocide, no murder of a specific ethnic group whose existence was arbitrarily proclaimed to be a threat to the life of others. Stalin's hostility to the Kulaks did not extend beyond the Soviet Union, as Hitler's enmity extended to all Jews beyond Germany's borders. Nor did Stalin aim at the physical liquidation of the *entire* Russian upper classes or the bourgeoisie in Western countries. Both Nazism and Soviet communism were repulsive to the West, but socialism, as it survived in Soviet society, still had a more humanitarian tradition. While in Nazi eyes the Jews were destined to be annihilated, in Soviet eyes no ethnic and national or racial unit was doomed to extinction, though social groups in time of revolutionary transition were bound to suffer. In theory, at least, the Soviets rejected any national or racial discrimination, while the Nazis extolled German superiority and domination over all non-German and non-Germanic ethnic groups to last for a thousand years.

In a letter "Verzerrte Zeitgeschichte" [Distorted Contemporary History] to the *FAZ* (November 29, 1986), Richard Löwenthal, an expert on the Soviet Union, referring to the communication about the mass annihilation, Hitler's and those in the Soviet Union by Georg Reissmüller, pointed out several erroneous remarks of the letter--writer.[30] Like Nolte in 1974, Reissmüller assumed that the Russian and even exclusively European countries had had their "Hitler-era." Religious wars especially had been bloodier than others, insisted Löwenthal. But none of these civil wars consisted of a "one-sided mass annihilation of defenseless people," and Lenin's struggle to preserve power was not of this kind either. This war was carried on by the Bolsheviks against the military alliance of the Social Revolutionaries with Czechoslovak troops in Russia against the rebellion of the Cossacks, against the rebellion of General Denikin and of Kolchak and the Poles after a previous Polish assault. In all these struggles until 1921 heavy losses were suffered on both sides and terrible murders of prisoners took place. Anti-communist Germans fleeing to Germany reported proudly of the atrocious deeds which they had carried out.

What Stalin did after 1929 against the Kulaks was in its systematic inhumanity historically new, and therefore comparable with Hitler's deeds. But Hitler in his perception of the total annihilation of the Jews, Gypsies, and others was certainly not influenced by Stalin's "model." The idea of the total annihilation of Jews was developed by Hitler's mentor, Dietrich Eckart in 1924, and Löwenthal owed the reference to this source to Ernst Nolte's *Faschismus in seiner Epoche*.

Some German historians have pointed to the killings of the German populace in the last phases of World War II by Polish militia, Romanian troops, Czech people's guards and Yugoslav partisans, which amounted to 600,000 Germans, according to a 1969 estimate. Unaccounted for were 2.2 million, though officials held that it would be wrong to list all of those as dead. Nolte himself and other neo-conservative historians implied that it was genocide. The expulsion of the German population from Eastern Europe eliminated in the view of the native peoples their role as a fifth column which had helped the German army in the conquest of their countries. After the conquest they reversed roles played by the Poles and the Czechs, who were now dominant.

In no case was the post-war treatment of the German minorities, harsh as it was and resulting in brutal expulsion, comparable to the annihilation imposed by the Nazis and the German military on the Jews. A majority of German historians have accepted this thesis. It should also be recalled that the Nazi government itself, beginning in September 1939, had started the process of forcibly resettling German people of the conquered regions within the boundaries of the Third Reich. The post-war expulsion of Germans in Eastern Europe was the ultimate result of the German post-World War I drive for the complete revision of the 1919 "dictate" of Versailles as well as of German plans of conquest and resettlement becoming evident in the course of World War II.

"Cumulative Radicalization" or Long-Range Planning?

Some West German historians linked with Social Democrats and Liberals have questioned Hitler's ability to manipulate completely the average German's mind; even a fair number of German conservatives, though agreeing with some facets of Hitler's ideology, did not go as far as he in wishing and planning the extermination of the Jews. Yet neither did they oppose it. Hans Mommsen, of Social Democratic persuasion, has claimed that the Third Reich experienced cumulative radicalism. In his view, if Hitler before January 30, 1939, talked about the total destruction [*Vernichtung*] of the Jewish race, he meant only their removal from the German economy.[31] Apparently, some German historians had never heard the popular song by marching SA and SS-men: "Until Jewish blood spurts from the knife." During the war Hitler referred repeatedly to his blunt threat in January

1939 and other similar utterances at innumerable occasions. Going beyond H. Mommsen's interpretation, the rightist British publicist David Irving[32] claimed that Hitler himself was unaware of the Jews' annihilation—which he consistently demanded and finally executed and of which he was the inspiring mind—until 1942–43. The particular situation during the war and in 1941, after the invasion of the Soviet Union, offered him only a welcome long-anticipated opportunity. As the British historian Richard Evans wrote: "It does in the end stretch the credulity to believe that the will to exterminate the Jews was absent from Nazism before the late summer of 1941."

Other "Forgotten Victims"

In recent years left-wing German historians have focused attention on the "forgotten victims" of Nazism: Gypsies, Soviet POWs, the retarded and the mentally ill among the German populace, so-called "anti-social" elements, German vagrants, prostitutes, and homosexuals. Many of them were killed by the "euthanasia" program two years prior to the start of the extermination of the Jews. Thus, according to these historians and populist writers, Auchwitz has not been quite unique. Detlev Peukert,[33] an East German historian, underlined, however, that the Jews, differently from these groups, were no "social ballast" but fulfilled economically useful functions. Financially they did not burden the German state and society. The Gypsies excepted, they were not killed on account of their racial-biological identity. These groups were "Aryans," though they did not contribute to the war effort. It was only the Jews who, according to the Nazi doctrine, were "parasites," "plotters," and a stumbling block to German domination of Europe and other countries. Jews alone were the racial and national archenemy. No other group of people was subjected by the Nazis to the same fiendish treatment. Only Jews were systematically hunted down all over Europe to make certain that none was to escape and all of them were to be annihilated.

While the historian Raul Hilberg thought that millions of Germans must have had first-hand knowledge of the mass murder of German and European Jews,[34] Nolte claimed to know that the murders were all Hitler's responsiblity and that the German people, as so many leading Nazis and German military leaders later pretended, did not know the extent of the annihilation of the Jews.[35] Students of Nazi administration have made clear that domestically the Nazi regime was not an orderly organization and that Hitler, being "a weak dictator" (H. Mommsen), was reluctant to make firm decisions on domestic matters, leaving it to individual office-holders to fight each other about internal policy. But in some matters relating primarily to anti-Semitism, he was, as among others von Ribbentrop pointed out, unyielding. Even if the view of his henchmen had differed from Hitler's, they did not dare challenging him. They were rather anxious to anticipate his wishes. The average Nazi set-of-mind was long familiar with Hitler's radicalism whipped up by years of his own virulent hate-filled anti-Semitic rhetoric. This type did not oppose the killing but furthered it.

Nolte, as even his defender Immanuel Geiss had to admit,[36] plainly ignored the evidence of Western scholarship regarding the Holocaust. Nor can his claim that the German invasion of the Soviet Union was undertaken to save Western civilization be taken seriously. A perusal of Nazi literature of the 1930s clearly reveals that it was German domination of Europe which was their only concern, not saving European civilization. A Nazi victory would have signified its end. Nolte called the bombing of Dresden, which came after the bombing of Coventry, "genocide." Similar charges relating to the alleged genocide of Germans planned and executed by Poles and Russians have been invented by Nazi propaganda but are not supported by international or German scholarship.

VI

REPERCUSSIONS OF THE "HISTORIKERSTREIT" ABROAD, POLITICS AND THE HOLOCAUST

Political and intellectual developments in Germany have usually affected the outlook in other European countries and beyond the continent. Events and changes in twentieth century Germany have always seized the attention of her neighbors in Europe and even more distant states. The *Historikerstreit* has been no exception. The intellectual disputes had from the start far-reaching implications, since the history of the Third Reich had left its indelible mark on the whole European continent. The revival of nationalism, autocratic leanings, and anti-Semitism and the rebirth even of pro-Nazi ideology among extremist elements of the Bonn Republic, not to mention the region of the former *Deutsche Demokratische Republik* (DDR) has revived anxieties in all of Europe, since most of the continent had experienced Hitler's war and destruction and German occupation and domination. Various European countries have quickly taken notice of the internal German debate by prominent historians and have been alerted by the rise of the intense German nationalism and anti-Semitism among German apologists of the Third Reich. Some learned German academics have shown a desire to soften the harsh image of the Nazi past. The press in Austria, Switzerland, the Netherlands and of the Western Powers, of France, Italy and the United Kingdom, not to mention the U.S., have revived fears and were forced to recall an era of foreign domination and repression.

Reaction in Austria

The Austrian Chancellor Franz Vranitsky has called the period 1938–1945 the "greatest misfortune of this century."[1] These were the years when Austria's independence had been extinguished, first with the approval of many Austrians, soon to be followed by a bitter war in which Austrians sacrificed their lives for the greater glory of the Third Reich and for the goals of Nazi imperialist domination over non-German peoples. Differently from many other Austrians who blamed exclusively the West, the Soviet Union, or Germans for the failure to stem the Nazi tide. Chancellor Vranitsky placed blame squarely on the Austrians themselves, "many of whom actively or passively have contributed to this misfortune." On occasion of the fiftieth anniversary of Austria's annexation, Austrian scholars supported by the government arranged in February 1988 a symposium of commemoration, to which foreign scholars from ten different countries were invited.

The commemoration revived also the question of the long-suppressed pre-war and post-war anti-Semitism in Austria. Though officials minimized anti-Semitism of the West, Jew-hatred was still flourishing in Austria after 1945, though pre-war Austrian Jewry had either managed to flee or had been largely wiped out, being reduced from about 200,000 to 10,000 Jews. The latter were to a large degree refugees from Hungary after the abortive rebellion of 1956. Though an open and frank discussion of the situation of Austrian Jewry in the post-war era was long "taboo," anti-Semitism was not sqashed but had reemerged.

Jew-hatred flared into the open during the Kurt Waldheim affair when the former General Secretary of the U.N., despite overwhelming evidence of his Nazi past and personal knowledge of and participation in anti-Jewish measures, was elected President of the Austrian Republic. The Waldheim affair, among other matters, proved beyond doubt the deep roots which Nazi extremism and anti-Semitism had sunk into Austrian soil. The spirit of extremism had not been stamped out, but had survived after 1945. Austrian school texts still reflected popular prejudices against several strata of Austria's population, foremost Jews, and guest workers. An anti-Semitic journal, *Sieg*, edited by the *Deutsch-Öterreichisches Institut für Zeitgeschichte* (DOIZ), claiming to have 10,000 addresses, denied in the No. 10 issue of October 1990 that a Holocaust had ever taken place.[2] It also declared the *Tagebuch der Anne Frank* a "falsification." Too many Austrians, having personally profited from the Aryanization in Vienna and the loss of Jewish properties and flats, had an unquestionable stake in impugning the obvious. No wonder that in 1988 there was founded the *Liga of the Friends of Judaism* with National Bank Director Dr. Kienzl President; it called itself a "Kampforganisation gegen Antisemitismus."

After Austria's annexation the hatred of Jews, encouraged by political parties for decades, was let loose in all its fury; Jewish shops were plundered, their property and valuables destroyed. In Vienna about 20,000 apartments were bound over to "Aryans," more housing than socialist Vienna could build until 1932. George Clare, a British writer of Austrian origin, wrote after revisiting the Austrian capital soon after the war's end, "In Vienna I entered the additional dimension of a feeling of Austrian innocence." The mood of Austria's population was revealed in a poll instituted by the American occupation forces; 44 percent of the Viennese agreed with "the view that the Nazis had gone too far in the treatment of the Jews, but asserted that something had to happen to curtail [!] them."[3] The Viennese ascribed responsibility for the anti-Jewish policy almost entirely to German National Socialism, not to Austrian greed and hatred. They interpreted the Moscow Declaration of 1943 as releasing Austria from guilt for the persecution of the Jews, the theft of their property, for their deportation and atrocious killings. They tended to ignore the Austrian roots of national-socialist fascism as well as the role of conservative and Catholic anti-Semites for the maltreatment of Austrian Jews.

Attacking some Austrian politicians and one noted bank president for suggestions to take issue with critical accounts of foreign historians about Austria's role in the Nazi era, the Austrian historian Gerhard Botz warned that the apparent suppression of Austria's Nazi past was interpreted abroad as an expression of affinity for National Socialism. "Forms of open and latent anti-Semitism are minimized in Austria since they are here so common."[4] After the Holocaust the Austrian people which "had contributed to [anti-Jewish] crimes, cannot escape" from these charges. An advisory commission of the Foreign Ministry had concluded that the causes for Austria's recent loss of prestige lay allegedly in international economic competition, in Kreisky's* pro-Arab foreign policy, and in Waldheim's anti-Israel U.N. official activities.

The past, Botz held, cannot be repressed for long without causing most severe damage. But a large majority of Austrians had cheered Hitler's *Anschluss*. They had in larger numbers joined the NSDAP than anywhere else in the "Altreich." In 1942 there were 688,000

---

* Bruno Kreisky was the leader of Austria's social democrats.

national socialist members in the "Alpen-Danubian Gauen," which meant that every fourth Austrian adult male was a Nazi. Within the Nazi apparatus of occupation and annihilation there were such men as Ernst Kaltenbrunner, second in command of the SS after Himmler, Odilo Globocnik, Adolf Eichmann, and numerous others, not to mention the occupation chiefs Seyss-Inquart, Glaise-Horstenaü, and Otto Wächter. Simon Wiesenthal, the known "Nazi hunter," has estimated that the killing of "at least three million Jews" must be attributed to the "crimes of participating German and Austrian workers and peasants."[5] During the war Austrians, along with Germans, fulfilled their military duty, with Austrians displaying no less willingness to fight than their German comrades.

The wars unleashed by the Third Reich, Botz continued, were not "normal" wars, nor were their occupation regimes "normal." With all the modern terror resorted to, they were brutal attacks upon many European nations and the world at large. After the completion of the "solution" of the Jewish question, following final victory, National Socialism planned to deport 500,000 Austrians of Slavic ancestry!

Repercussions in Anglo-Saxon Countries and in France

The young British historian Robert Knight in the distinguished London literary journal *Times Literary Supplement* ("The Waldheim Concept: Austria and Nazism") had illuminated Austria's convoluted history during the 1930s and the Nazi occupation 1938–1945, subjecting it to a sharply critical analysis. Thereupon the Austrian Foreign Minister Jankovitsch took Knight to task for his "perverse perspective" and appealed to the Austrian Cultural Institute abroad to correct his views. The *Frankfurter Rundschau* (9 March 1987) commented "that the Austrian problem of feeling their attachment to the Third Reich" has since been solved to a large extent, but criticized the "Austrian tolerance" of anti-Semitism and the indifference *vis-à-vis* the Austrian President Kurt Waldheim's apparent dishonesty. At the end of the war many Austrians had not seen 1945 as a liberation from foreign yoke. During the German occupation Austrians did not live under the terror and persecution which had spurred so many Poles, Italians, and Yugoslavs to heroic deeds. After liberation the two major pre-war Austrian parties had reached an "historic compromise." But the latter was based, according to Robert Knight, upon memory lapses on both sides. The first Austrian denazification law of May 1945 turned out to be a farce, leaving unrepentant Nazis in positions of influence. The situation in the Federal Republic was not identical with that of Austria, but in some respects not too dissimilar. In both countries the *Historikerstreit* had wide repercussions, still showing some pro-Nazi sentiments.

The view of some historians that their feud in the 1980s was superfluous and harmful was energetically repudiated by Frank Schumacher in the *FAZ* on 1 February 1987. The earlier German consent regarding the reprehensibleness of national-socialist crimes had been abandoned. The author also observed that the dispute was followed in foreign countries with greatest attention.

That was certainly also true for the U.S., where the *New Republic* (1 December 1986), the *New York Times Magazine* (16 November 1986), and the *New York Review of Books* (20 November 1986) had partly very critically reacted to the circumstances that a debate was necessary. The *New York Times* spoke not only of German but also of a European "decline of memory."

In his review of four German works on the problem of German historiography of the Third Reich and the Holocaust by A. Hillgruber, M. Stürmer, Thomas Nipperday, and E. Jäckel, dubbed "The War of German Historians," Gordon Craig of Stanford University tried to absolve Hillgruber from the charge of being an apologist of National Socialism, an accusation leveled against him by many German colleagues. He thought it difficult to find "any startling revisionist tendency. But Hillgruber's lack of empathy for the fate of the Jews was evident. On the other hand, according to Craig, it was not always easy to understand what Stürmer was driving at. During the past two years, Nolte, in Craig's view, refused to make clear his own opinion on some critical matters of German twentieth-century history. Craig disclosed the sharp split in the German historical profession on the question of the proper place of the Third Reich in German history. On the whole, American reviews of the *Historikerstreit* were quite critical.

If "Historisierung" meant the opening of the archives and the examination and study of the documents as well as the judicial punishment of the offenses and the moral condemnation of the past, it has started in France long ago. There were a number of judicial proceedings in France against Germans of the *Bundesrepublik*, not to mention judgments in French military courts against the absent Germans. A number of French collaborators also had committed war crimes against humanity.[6] Claus Leggewie in his essay "France's collective memory and National Socialists" has estimated that their number amounted to 120,000 persons. The death sentences carried out in France after liberation probably varied between 2,000 and 10,000. Many were killed by lynching or summary liquidations. The "épurations" were carried out on several levels, especially against a number of prominent literary-cultural collaborators and against leading representatives of French industry, not to mention numerous Vichy-employees. Many archives have still not been opened up to researchers, and the extent of French responsibility for the "final solution" of the Jewish question in France has not been fully established. The most important contribution to historic research about the Jewish fate in France has come less from professional French historians than from Jewish centers of documentation and from historians abroad.

There has not taken place a debate in France comparable to the German *Historikerstreit*, but there were disputes about basic questions as to the prevalence of a homogenous, widely shared historical view. Professional historians were long convinced of the existence of proto- and pre-fascist ideas in France; but it was the Israeli historian Zeev Sternhell who cast full light upon the spread of fascist thought and ideology throughout France and beyond the Rhine into other European countries.[7]

French fascism developed from a complex of nationalist and socialist ideas as an ideology combining leftist and rightist ingredients. The syndicalist Georges Sorel, the theoretician Henrik de Man, Marcel Déat, in the interwar period the left-Catholic Emanuel Mounier and his journal *L'esprit*, and the renegade of the extreme Left, the former Communist chief Jacques Doriot, were prime theoreticians and leaders. According to Zeev Sternhell, French fascism as such was kept away from full power, but it participated as a sort of right wing in the "National Revolution" of the Vichy government in 1940–41, and in the blue-white-red fascism of the period. While Sternhell's theses were criticized for some methodical weaknesses, he has firmly established that French fascism had an existence independent from Berlin and Rome.

French participation in the Holocaust has been amply documented. Jewish survivors and non-French historians have zeroed in on the responsibility of the Vichy government and its various high-placed as well as low-level officers. The Vichy regime may have protected certain groups of French Jews against the Germans, but it played quite a different role in regard to the stateless Jews who after 1933 had fled from Germany and Eastern Europe to France, the traditional asylum of refugees. French fascism displayed a hatred of foreigners in general and anti-Semitism in particular, was imbued with the racial theories of Count Joseph Arthur Gobineau and Edouard Drumont's *La France Juive*.[8] It reached back to the Dreyfus affair and also pointed to alleged links of some French Jews with the claimed communist threat of the early post-World War I period and later with the formation of France's Popular Front. French rightists tried to discredit the Left by accusing all Jews for the asserted close links of some of them with communists and socialists.

Without immediate German pressure, France began, according to Leggewie, passing exclusionary laws banishing Jews from public service and cultural life, and assigning foreign Jews to special camps. In the so-called "free zone," leading French politicians, such as Pierre Laval, purchased a residue of French sovereignty at the expense of active cooperation with the German authorities in the field of discriminatory anti-Jewish legislation. Most incriminating have proved the talks and agreements in June and July 1942 between the SS leadership and high-placed Vichy officials which aimed at making France the first "judenrein" country in Western Europe.

The total number of Jewish victims in France was 80,000. Of these, about one-third were of French nationality, while others were citizens or former residents of Poland and Southeast European countries. Only after the total occupation of France did Vichy's Jewish policy undergo moderate improvement. The French government, it has been estimated, cooperated in the annihilation of one-fourth of all Jews on its territory. On the other hand, Frenchmen also helped in the rescue of the other three-fourths of the Jews. During the Barbie trial, the number of revisionist brochures, denying the assassination of Jews in France during the war and French cooperation with the Nazis, grew by leaps and bounds. The German *Historikerstreit* and the issues disputed aroused in France keen interest in raising questions about the extent of French officials' collusion with the Nazi persecution as well as about the German state of mind and that of the French regime.

Quoting August Comte, "The living are dominated by the dead," L. R. in *Enquête*[9] "Quarante ans après l'effondrement du nazism. Débat historique, débat politique" wrote that the German historians' debate revived by German politicians showed the continued dispute with the Nazi era in the Bonn Federal Republic. Some noted conservative German historians, while not denying the Nazi genocide, had voiced the opinion that it had been possible only against the background of the preceding Stalinist terror, a view which had aroused sharp reaction by other professors and publicists. There was a risk that the dams would break and that the next phase will proclaim "forgetting of terrorism."

Swiss, Dutch, and Italian Dailies

A critical though balanced account of the *Historikerstreit* and the repercussions felt in Switzerland was produced on 18–19 January 1987, in the *Züricher Zeitung* by Fred Luchsinger. As he wrote, "Germans have not yet been reconciled" with "that which since the 1930s and 1940s is attached to the German name." But "the past cannot be extinguished for a long time to come." It was rather evident "that one will have to coexist together with the Germany of the *Bundesrepublik* and that "one depends on a democratic Germany, that without it nothing works in Europe, and that one remains tied to it for better or worse."[10]

There had already opened up a gulf separating the Germany of today and the Third Reich. The ruling generation of today's Federal Republic has hardly its own recollections from the Third Reich. "No active German general of today knows the last war from his own memory." In the *Bundesrepublik* there was still raging a fierce contention about one's own attitude to the Third Reich and a bitter debate whether it should be excluded from German history or whether it belongs to it, whether it was a tragic, false development, an error rather than a harmless episode. But "the past cannot be corrected." Exploring it was "inescapable and imperative," and it is rather questionable whether it can be overcome. There have been many attempts to play it down. Some say that National Socialism should be freed from the "murderous violence and expansionism" and the bad reputation which it has acquired in large parts of world public opinion. In any case after its breakdown, there was built a democratic *Rechtsstaat* and Europe and the world has cooperated with the new Germany. "But this cooperation does not include a retribution of National Socialism, of its policies and its system." The national-socialist image, also that of Wilhelmian Imperial Germany, has centered on the glory and might of the Reich. But present-day German historians had displayed a self-critical capacity, though some individual historians are still attached to nationalist and revisionist biases. The new German historiography stressed German and European developments which harmonize and less with those nationalist reactions either against the French character or against perfidious Albion, which had often marked German historical views in the nineteenth and earlier twentieth century.

The historians' feud was also extensively discussed in the Netherlands, where it aroused "great attention." Reporting about the *Historikerstreit*, the Dutch media placed this debate, carried on not only by professional historians but arresting also the broad public, in the very center of the report about the elections in the *Bundesrepublik* (*Die Zeit*, 14 January 1987).[11] The *NRC-Handelsblad* in Rotterdam published under the heading "Deutschland über alles,"[12] a whole page on the controversy aimed at "formulating a new German national conscience." Even the German Social Democrats could not escape the attraction of national consciousness. The author of the article criticized that extremist conceptions appear to become fashionable in the Bonn Federal Republic. The paper at the same time observed that parallel to this period of "concilliation with the past," a new movement tried to "gloss over" German history. The Germans were interested "on forgetting the past." Other influential circles in the country discuss the controversy about the assessment of the most recent German history more frequently. The *Hague Courant* voiced its concern that there were thus reawakened in Germany "chauvinist sentiments, and the shadows of the past become alive again."[13]

The historians' feud caused in Italy and among Italian scholars "displeasure and astonishment" that Germans could still not agree on the significance of Auschwitz. First, there was an outraged Italian reaction to the theses of the nonsingularity of Auschwitz and the comparability of the annihilation of the Jews with the killings of other people. The Italian-Jewish writer Primo Levi considered the thesis of comparability an intolerable piece of relativism, an attitude which was almost completely shared by the Left and by organizations close to the anti-fascist Resistance. While not embracing the view of the collective guilt of the Germans, there was at the same time no preparedness to doubt in the least the scope and significance of what had happened.

There was agreement in Italy about the difference between the two totalitarian regimes in Germany and Italy. While Italian writers had stressed the need for a comparison of violence and crime in the various countries, the Italian press rejected the causal nexus between Gulag and Auschwitz, which neoconservative German historians had suggested. The leftist press sharply criticized the German historical revisionism and the interpretation of Nazism as "Hitlerism" and focusing on the psychopathology of Hitler as a means to exculpate Germany were rejected.

Enrico Busconi did not think that Germany's *Mittellage* was "threatened from the outside or seemed threatening to the neighbors."[14] But it was evident to him that the historian Michael Stürmer and colleagues pursued a revisionist course, as also many German critics have pointed out. As far as comparisons with Soviet Russia's atrocities were concerned, the Soviet Union had never pursued a policy of systematic manhunt and annihilation of its citizens and of others, including old people, women, and little children. Only under the Nazis was the industrial annihilation of human life carried out, the hair of the victims utilized for the fabrication of slippers, their clothing and other possessions turned over to the *Winterhilfe*, the gold of false teeth of the murdered person forcibly removed and turned over to the *Staatsbank*, and human ashes used as fertilizer for vegetables. The bureaucrats organized murder in the "factories" of Auschwitz, Treblinka, and other camps, all of which had no example in the history of man. The Nazi annihilation of life allegedly not worth living had nothing comparable in extent, scope, and numbers with the crimes of Stalin's rule.

Leading German Politicians and the Holocaust

German Politics and the *Historikerstreit* were inextricably linked. German parties and politicians played a major role in its development and individual political leaders took issue with some aspects of the dispute. As politics influenced the historians, so did historiography impact the opinions of the politicians. Annemarie Renger's voice was one of the stronger German voices rejecting any attempt to relativize Auschwitz, Vice-President of the German *Bundestag* and President of the German-Israeli Society of Parliamentarians, she stressed "the obligation of all Germans to make good what the Third Reich had sinned *vis-à-vis* Europe." She blamed the unleashing of racial hatred, the extermination of the Jews, and Nazi "nihilism."[15] On September 21, 1949, she had sharply denounced the government declaration of Konrad Adenauer of the preceding day, considering it rather weak. She had proclaimed the obligation of every German to offer the victims the necessary help.

Following the efforts especially of Carlo Schmid, the German *Bundestag* on September 27, 1951, had begun a more active policy, the policy of *Wiedergutmachung* (compensation). After the resumption of German diplomatic relations in May 15 with Israel, there also began official cooperation between the two states. Still, it took a quarter of a century after Germany's liberation through the Allies until the first active Chancellor Willy Brandt visited Israel in 1973. His genuflection before the memorial of the Warsaw ghetto in 1971 had impressed skeptics in Israel. In 1985 the German President Richard von Weizsäcker also voiced on occasion of his visit to Israel the historic responsibility of the Germans for the crimes committed against the Jews.[16]

According to Annemarie Renger, there have been reverse developments in German-Israeli relations as marked by the Eichmann trial, the discussion centering around the "lapse" or "limitation of national-socialist crimes," and on account of the Bitburg cemetery episode. Renger asserted that in this context must also be listed the *Historikerstreit*, marked by tendencies to minimize the crimes of the Hitler regime. In her view, there could be no more computing (*Aufrechnen*) between Gulag Archipelago and Auschwitz. In view of German obligations, including those of politicians and historians, the feud over historic theses cannot be carried on without regard to the sensitivities of the victims of National Socialism. "One cannot relativize Auschwitz just as Israel cannot be understood without the history of the Holocaust."

The causes of the failure of the Jewish emancipation in Germany cannot be sought in the atrocities of Stalinism; they are in the first place a consequence of an intolerable nationalism and, second, the result of a definite social development in Imperial Germany and in the Weimar Republic. It was convenient with the help of a senseless Nazi ideology and an insane, murderous anti-Semitism to arouse the envy of the many, including impoverished segments, against a small religious and ethnic minority and to whip up hatred against it.

Anti-Semitism was also based on ignorance regarding the important role of the Jews in German intellectual, political, and economic history. In other countries in which likewise strong anti-Semitic currents existed, resistance against excesses such as racism were due to a progressive tradition of the bourgeoisie. It was different, however, in Germany and Austria with their strong feudal and monarchist tendencies.

While, according to Renger, the overwhelming majority of German citizens had allegedly no anti-Semitic prejudices, she conceded that "thoughtless utterances of leading personalities" could arouse latent hostile sentiments. While presently there were now only a few militantly anti-Semitic groups in Germany, they should be taken seriously. They ought to be combatted juridically. Renger pointed to the growing extensive traveling of Germans to Israel as a positive development. There were also numerous meetings between parliamentarians of the German *Bundestag* and of the Israeli *Knesset* and growing relations between Germans and Israelis, political parties, *Landtage*, Christian-Jewish institutions, trade unions, *Volkshochschulen*, teachers' associations and youth and sport organizations of both countries. For many years close cooperation has also existed between the Max Plank Society and the Weizmann Institute in Rechovot. The joint foundation for scientific research and development was created in 1986. Renger concluded by expressing the wish to "overcome the darkest chapter of our history." This required a special feeling of responsibility towards Israel. "Because of the past, the present Israel is part of our history."

Like Renger, Hans-Joachim Vogel, presiding officer of the Social Democratic Party and simultaneously president of the SPD parliamentary group in the *Bundestag*, zeroed in on the *Historikerstreit* which drew fresh attention to the annihilation of the Jews ("Neues Ungemach aus dem Historikerstreit.")[17] This article was written in response to a request by the *Tribüne* for a contribution about the status of the relationship of the *Bundesrepublik* to Israel. A great majority of Germans would spontaneously reply that it was "good" and a majority of politicians in Germany would even answer "very good." Like the previous contributor Renger to the *Tribüne*, Vogel pointed to the growth of German tourist traffic to Israel in 1989. Germans had surpassed even the number of American visitors in Israel. Forty-eight German cities had established partnerships with Israeli communities, twelve additional ones were prepared. There were numerous contacts between the Histraduth and the DGB (*Deutscher Gewerkschaftsbund*) and close cooperation agreements between individual trade unions.

Yet Vogel admitted that it would be an illusion to call German-Israeli relations normal. As Willy Brandt formulated it, "an alleged normality" would in the end probably be "masked brutality." Despite the manifold persecutions of the Jewish people throughout its history, the Nazi mass killing of Jews was a singular event. This uniqueness has resulted in "embarrassment and obfuscation." One preferred to talk of the "Holocaust" rather than of the murder of millions of Jews. One should understand the "restraint, in many respects even rejection of the word 'Deutschland,' by many Israelis." It behooved Germans to make certain that an event of such inconceivable dehumanization be not forgotten. When he, Vogel, in 1964 as *Oberbürgermeister* of Munich made his first visit to Israel, he had visited Yad Vashem. He knows that for most of the visitors it is an oppressive obligation to demonstrate to the surviving Jewish relatives' sadness and sympathy. It has oppressed me and aroused me to read during the so-called *Historikerstreit* that some Germans criticized Jews as being "obsessed" with the question of guilt. In truth, what is involved is the humanity and to make certain, as Th. W. Adorno admonished, that "those murdered are not cheated of the single thing which our powerlessness can donate them, "memory." "On encountering the presence of Jewish suffering in Israel, not only young Germans should be touched to give thought to the past of Jewish life in Germany."

In view of the shadow of our relationship to the state of Israel it should not be astonishing that ever since the resumption of diplomatic relations with Israel, the relationship was often easily shaken.[18] Vogel blamed the special diplomatic "nonchalance" of German politicians *vis-à-vis* other states. Though the attitude of the citizens of the *Bundesrepublik* to the Arab-Israeli conflict was generally quite positive in regard to Israel, still the opinion turned twice in favor of the Arabs, in May 1981, when Israeli Minister President Begin had criticized Chancellor Helmut Schmid and the official German suggestions in their entirety and had rejected any meeting, and again in October 1982 when the massacres in both refugee camps Sabra and Shatila aroused repulsion and indignation. "These German reactions were regularly only of short duration." What terrified us, however, was that on such accounts the "past did not overcome" surfaced! The comments on the Lebanon war were rather unfavorable even in otherwise liberal and leftist dailies—"I make exception in regard to *Vorwärts*"—and was expressed "in a manner which perhaps may have been justified, but the form was improper." Thus came the identification of the Lebanon war with Auschwitz, and the behavior of Israeli soldiers was identified with that of the SS. One had "the impression that for many Germans these events were an occasion to lift the burden from the fathers when one said that the Israelis behaved not differently." Willy Brandt said then correctly in the *Bundestag* "that one did not escape the responsibility for Auschwitz by pointing to Beirut."[19]

Polls in Israel about the German-Israeli relationship had shown similar irritations. While in 1972, about 40 percent of Israelis believed in the rebirth of National Socialism in Germany, the number increased after Begin's utterances in 1981, to about 55 percent. He, Vogel, was personally especially affected by the cowardly murder of members of the Israeli team at the Munich Olympic games. A further deterioration followed after the agreements of the conservative government with Arabic states regarding exports of weapons, which caused deep embitterment on the Israeli side. In the *Bundestag*, Vogel himself admonished in the name of the SPD that the survivors of the national-socialist racial insanity, who had found their home in Israel, should never again feel threatened by German arms. New hardships threatened German-Israeli relations through the historians' feud, which evidently was not a scientific but a political dispute. Every attempt to revitalize Nazi crimes must "diminish our international reliability." As a result of this dispute, Germany's international reliability has not improved, but has been rather shaken. Vogel was especially aroused since some Germans during the feud claimed that the persecution of the Jews had furthered the creation of the state of Israel. As if the Jews had to be grateful to the Germans for their persecution and annihilation!

Vogel pointed to Moses Hess who had combined Socialism with Zionism and especially to Theodor Herzl. The German Social Democrats owed a very great deal to Karl Marx, Ferdinand Lasalle, Eduard Bernstein, and Rosa Luxemburg. The link-up of Socialism and Zionism had especially taken root in the person of David Ben-Gurion. Willy Brandt had recently recalled the support which the International Group of Democratic Socialists in 1944 in Stockholm had extended to the Jewish community in Palestine. In conclusion, Vogel voiced the view that a lasting solution of the Near East problem must include the rights of self-determination of the Palestinian people as well as the right of the existence and security of the state of Israel. Like his party, he made no attempt to show that the granting of full self-determination of the Palestinian people, as interpreted by an Arab spokesman, could seriously and adversely affect the survival of the Jewish state and people in the Near East by disregarding their security needs.

Among numerous critics of Israel and the Jews, the Party of the Greens was often prominent. Otto Schultz, however, a deputy of the Party in the *Bundestag* took a somewhat different view, especially regarding German guilt ("Das Blut lässt sich nicht abwaschen, Falsche Gleichungen in den Schluchten der deutschen Geschichte").[20] Referring to the harsh Israeli military rule in the occupied areas, he criticized German "self-satisfying condemnation" of Israel. He rejected the argument that the Jewish people, because of its persecution in the Nazi era, had "a special obligation toward pacifism." He questioned that the debate in the *Bundestag* would fulfill the hope of the participants to lighten "the German burden." There was a "false" but "avid identification" by many means to place the draconic Israeli military actions in the occupied region on one plane with the German Nazis' mass murder of the Jews. Schultz had only recently heard the utterances of a German who expressed his repugnance at the brutalities of the Israelis toward the Palestinians. In the same breath this individual was infuriated because the Jews still reproached Germans with "the old stories of persecution and annihilation." "His logic was: We are even [quitt]." But Schultz wrote: "Blood, however, cannot be washed off." "We must resist the temptation of acquitting." Germans could not "save themselves from the shadow of the past. 'Neither forget, nor despair!' This demands the alliance of the conscience with Israel, Israel as hope and refuge for the Jews of the entire world."

Schultz demanded the right of existence for Israel as well as the right of self-determination for the Palestinians. He rejected the points of the view of both Shamir, who insisted on a Greater Israel, including the occupied areas, and on the other side the PLO Foreign Minister Kadmir, who asked for all of Palestine (*Gesamtpalästina*), including Israel. The latter of course meant the destruction of the Jewish state. Schultz placed his hope upon the Israeli peace movement, the numerous Israeli officers and soldiers who refused to follow orders and upon the Jews in the diaspora who allegedly, in their overwhelming majority, supported conciliation with, if not appeasement, of the Arabs. Though Schultz's analysis of the problem of the Near East was apparently incomplete, he took a position, regarding the question of German guilt, sharply at variance from many of his political associates.

Klaus von Dohanyi, the first mayor of the Free City of Hamburg, strongly asserted in his article "For securing the right of the Jewish People to Exist," that the Germans had "no right to forget." "The desperate search of the Jews for refuge and a homeland against the thugs of the Third Reich, the murder of millions of human beings of the Jewish faith after nearly two thousand years of diaspora, have irrefutably demonstrated the necessity of a state-secured existence of Israel."[21]

The Jews of Hamburg had been German citizens, had possessed great influence and reputation. Yet they were not spared anti-Semitism, and the guilt of the citizens of Hamburg was not smaller than that of other Germans. A reconciliation with the Jews required not only solidarity, but was an imperative in view of German "historic responsibility" for the past.

In an editorial of the *Tribüne* the issue, as usual, had both German and Israeli contributors, and was dedicated to the fortieth anniversary of the foundation of the state of Israel. It stressed the great sympathetic German understanding for Israel and the Jewish people, a sympathy which refrained from "knowing-all [*besserwisserisch*] advice." For such advice does not behoove the least of us Germans, "especially not *vis-à-vis* Israel and the Jews."[22]

The Communist Interpretation of the Holocaust. An Evaluation

On March 12 and 13, 1987, on occasion of a dialogue in the Erich Ollenhauer-Haus in Bonn about the legacy of German history, "Prinzipielle Unterschiede," the traditional communist point of view was subjected to sharp criticism by the historian Jürgen Kocka. As he developed: "The proper categorization of the national-socialist dictatorship into German history—and through comparison—into the world historical context was a lasting problem in Germany," as also shown during the last month of the so-called *Historikerstreit* which had surfaced with vehemence in the *Bundestag*. In the DDR, according to Kocka, the interpretation of National Socialism and anti-Semitism had differed from that of West Germany. In the DDR, German fascism had been pictured almost exclusively as the product of politics of the then ruling minorities, of the monopolistic bourgeoisie of the finance capital, and of the Junkers, all of whom jointly with brown desperadoes did violence to the innocent and basically progressive people. The Nazis seduced and enslaved the Germans until they were liberated in 1945. After complete loss of power by the dominant cliques, the Germans east of the Elbe, became, according to communist mythology, the bearers of progressive policies.

According to Kocka, however, the reality was much more complicated than this East German thesis claimed. National Socialism had actually gained a solid base in the population. It was rooted in the people despite the resistance existing among various social strata. The history of the German people and the history of German fascism were to this day closely intertwined. It drew attention to a bad symbiosis between Germans and Jews.

For years communists in the USSR and in the Germanies have kept silent about the Jews being the special target of Nazi persecutions. It was largely Jewish authors and organizations outside the Soviet Union which established centers of documentation and publication, focusing upon Jewish persecution and annihilation in the USSR. As early as the late 1930s, the Soviets, to appease the Hitlerites, suppressed news of Jewish discrimination in Germany and later in occupied Poland, while pursuing themselves, especially since the purges of the late 1930s, an increasingly anti-Semitic course. It was for domestic as well as foreign policy considerations that the Soviets tended to repress the Nazi atrocities against the Jews during the war and thereafter.[23]

During World War II, masses of Jews died in the deportation transport, in the concentration camps, and in the ghettos. The mass killings by the SS were accomplished by mass shootings and in gas wagons. The mass murder was due also to deliberate maltreatment, to epidemics, to planned undernourishment, and exhaustion. In addition, the mobile *Einsatz*—SS soldiers—"liquidated" Jews both in the USSR and in Eastern Europe. At least three million people were assassinated in Chełm, Belzec, Bobibor, Treblinka, Majdanek, and Auschwitz. The Nazis made great efforts to remove all vestiges of the mass murders by providing mass graves and cremation installations. Though the Soviets knew first-hand of the special Nazi hatred of Jews, they kept silent about it. They may have feared the rise of anti-Semitism on Russian soil, since it was also directed against Bolshevism, which they claimed to have been the instrument of the Jews.

Persistence of Populist Anti-Semitism in East and West Germany

Since the unification of the two German states, anti-Semitism never uprooted in the DDR and never vanished from the *Bundesrepublik* has, despite the circumstances that only few Jews in Germany had survived, flared up again especially in the East. Much earlier, at the time of the Slansky trial in neighboring communist Czechoslovakia and at the show trials of that period, the anti-Zionist and pro-Palestinian attitude of the leadership of the SED, of both Party and State, made the Jews a steady and open target in East Germany as in the rest of Eastern Europe. The Polish "anti-Semitism without Jews"[24] found a replica in the neighboring DDR which vied with Russia and East European Jew-hatred fostered by the Communists. Following the years and decades after the Nazi Holocaust, East Germans had never aimed at extirpating Jew-hatred. German communists and former Nazis have marched next to each other on the same high road of anti-Semitism. The East German communists used the few prominent Jews or those only partly descended from Jews like the "Viertel-jude" Gysi and a few others such as Kurt Hagen, Herman Axen, Ibrahim Böhm, ard Wolfgang Schur to fan a new anti-Semitic campaign in East Germany to gain political advantage. The German *Tribüne* pointed to scrawling anti-Semitic slogans including the painting of swastikas and writing slogans such as "Juda verrecke" [Jews perish], to the defilement of graves in several cities of the DDR, and the sending of anonymous threatening letters to the effect that the "hearth of Buchenwald" was waiting for Jews. Letters asserting that "Hitler lives" reached the *Centrum Judaicum* in Ostberlin.[25] Even before the unification of Germany, anti-Jewish hatred was riding high.

In West Germany too, anti-Semitism, though often repressed after 1945, has never vanished from the scene. According to the Allenbach polls in the early years of the *Bundesrepublik*, almost two-thirds of the German population found in National Socialism "a good idea" which was only "badly executed." Two-thirds of the population favored "drawing a final balance" under the past! Numerous special investigations about anti-Semitic attitudes in the Federal Republic revealed the existence of considerable religious and racial prejudices. Considering the negligible number of Jews in West Germany—about 30,000—this clearly revealed the anomaly and absurdity of the persistent anti-Semitic propaganda.

A general xenophobia directed against all aliens, Turks, blacks, and others has contributed to the rejection also of the Jews. Party affiliation of the Germans was not a factor in influencing decisively the attitude toward the Jews. Forty-seven percent of the CDU, 55 percent of the SPD, 60 percent of the FAP and 63 percent if the "Greens" thought that Israeli policy toward the Palestinians was comparable to Nazi policy toward the Jews. Hostility thus to Zionists and Jews was not much affected by the political leanings of the Germans.

In the autumn of 1987 the *Antisemitismusforschung der TV* in Berlin have accepted the assignment of the Anti-Defamation League of B'nai Brith in New York to assess the depth and the extent of Jew-hatred in Germany. While disclosing that 88 percent of the West Germans and of West Berlin did not know Jews "more closely" they pointed to a new strain of Jew-hatred, the resentment of many Germans of being held responsible for the deeds of their forefathers and their own desire to draw a "Schlusstrich"[26] under the past, being convinced that Jews carried "Mitschuld" (were "co-responsible") for the hatred that led to their persecution. Since the past was not "ended," many Germans reacted with anger and hatred to the accusation of the accusers! They also again resented their bad reputation in Europe and the world, a legacy of the atrocities which had been committed by their ancestors.

In the DDR Marxist-Leninist historians have faced great difficulties giving a rational, economic explanation to the annihilation of the Jews on the basis of the profit interests of the dominant monopoly capital and finance capital. They seemed unable to explain national-racist hatred, being handicapped by their own dogmatic materialist conception of history and even by restrictions imposed upon objective analysis by political prejudices and alleged Soviet national interests. Their abstruse attempts at "scientific," economic explanation of racial mass murder contradicted Nazi policy that "economic considerations are principally not to be considered in the solution of the Jewish question." Despite all evidence to the contrary, the communists have insisted that ultimately "socialism" would completely solve the Jewish question.[27] They have of course buried in silence that the Soviet non-aggression treaty with Germany in late August 1939 unleashed the war which made possible the Nazi annihilation of the Jews.

West German historians have found it difficult coming theoretically to grips with the causes of the mass murder of the Jews. In the first years after the war a few German scholars have considered their annihilation a regrettable "Betriebsunfall" [industrial accident] of German history and have attributed it to Hitler's "demonic character." Foreign authors have traced it back to "disastrous traditions of German intellectual history," to its "tortuous path." Léon Poliakov, a specialist in the history of anti-Semitism, has elaborated the theory that the annihilation of the Jews had served to draw the German people in a gigantic collective crime in order to tie it indissolubly to Hitler and National Socialism, establish the complicity of the Germans, and thus make German surrender less likely.

What Should Be Done? Jewish History in German Schools

Did German historians, focusing on the atrocities of National Socialism and the Holocaust in particular, come up with concrete suggestions to avoid a repetition of German "misdeeds"? They pointed to the prevention of the development of another totalitarian state, the need for the political and moral reeducation of the people with special focus on democratic thought and practice, the protection of minorities and civil rights, and the shedding of racial, national, and religious prejudices. Some authors, focusing on the remaining tiny Jewish minority in Germany, have stressed the necessity of revising the curriculum to remove centuries old anti-Semitic prejudices from the German cultural scene. They have pointed to the introduction of courses at German universities on the history of Jews and Judaism and that of anti-Semitism throughout the ages and the urgent need to acquaint teenagers with the essence and teachings of Judaism and the religious, cultural, and economic role of the Jews from antiquity to the modern age, and the need to impress upon them tolerance and the shedding of nationalist and racial biases so prevalent in the Hitler era and unacceptable since in the world at large.

Next to abolishing all traces of nationalist and racist discrimination in German politics, economy, and law, major efforts in education were required to erase all vestiges of anti-Semitism in German life. The *Lehrerzeitung*, 1987[28] published an article for the treatment of Jewish history in West German textbooks. One should avoid painting the Jews exclusively as victims and objects of history. Next to a brief presentation of the significance of Judaism for the history of religions, the textbook writers should make clear that Jews since 1500 lived relatively secure and by no means always in subordinate positions in Christian society. The students should gain a perception on the Jews' remarkable economic, scientific, and artistic achievements since the beginnings of the Enlightenment. The Zionist movement should not be treated exclusively as a reaction to anti-Semitism but also as an expression of Jewish striving for identity in modern society. The central role of anti-Semitism in national-socialist ideology and its importance for the politics of the Third Reich and its worldwide propaganda should be emphasized. Its anti-Jewish policy in

Germany since 1933 until the mass murder should not be treated in a casual manner.

The deprivation of Jewish rights and the social isolation started openly long before the beginning of the Holocaust. During this period only a few Germans protested against it and offered help for the Jews. The genocide should be accurately described and the question of the Jewish persecution and the murder of peoples should be honestly posed and not avoided. The same held true of dealing with an uncritical terminology of anti-Semitism.

Other scholars and publicists have stressed the importance of focusing on teaching in particular about the role of German Jews in the German cultural realm, of stressing the achievements and contributions of Jews to German *Kultur* to remove the web of lies and distortions spun by centuries of German and foreign Jew-hatred from the historic record, and present objectively the history of German-Israeli relations since the birth of the state of Israel in 1948, not excluding the occasional flare-up of anti-Semitism after the relentless hostile propaganda of National Socialism. It grew out of the general xenophobia of the extreme Right prior and after the impact of the recent German re-unification and its inflamed aftermath. Partly, however, if was also the result of distinctly anti-Jewish communist propaganda in the USSR and in the satellite countries and the DDR and of generally ignoring the destructive power of anti-Semitism in the world at large.

EPILOGUE

From the Fall of the Berlin Wall to the Reunification of Germany

After the fall of the Berlin wall there occurred a tremendous upsurge of German nationalism which aroused contradictory sentiments throughout the world. It caused anxiety in Israel as well as among many European neighbors of Germany, and also in the U.S. While the world greeted the end of Soviet domination in the DDR, neither the Jews nor the peoples of Europe had forgotten the preceding era of Nazi hegemony in Europe and the German intoxication with strident nationalism and arrogant dominance, and feared its possible recurrence.

In Germany the national intoxication seized almost all parties. Though Willy Brandt had for many years rejected reunion of the two Germanies, he welcomed that "now grows together what belongs together." The editor of the *Die Spiegel*, Rudolf Augstein, emphasized the unifying bond of German national consciousness. He concluded that apparently the German people asked for something different from what some German writers and philosophers wanted. Hans Joachim Vogel, presiding officer of West German Social Democrats, voiced the thought that November 9, 1989, when the Berlin wall began to crumble, was a "memorable" day, "tied up with German fate," stressing its national significance rather than the resumption and continuation of the German Revolution of 1918 with its strong democratic and socialist overtones.

It was not surprising that, after the crumbling of the Berlin wall, Bonn and Jerusalem disagreed concerning the creation of a unified Germany, though Israel was by no means the only state which expressed misgivings about its potential threat to Jewish and European security. In France, Great Britain, Russia, and most other European states the first reactions to the impending unification of Germany were ambivalent, though spokesmen for these countries and others changed their views when faced with the inevitability of this union. Even German voices had been previously raised against the unification. Yizchak Shamir, Minister-President of Israel, said in an interview with PBS, perhaps in a little diplomatic manner, that the great majority of the German people had during the Nazi regime decided to murder millions of the Jewish people. "Everyone among us can think that [the Germans] should they once again have the opportunity, will try again [to kill Jews]." Chancellor Helmut Kohl took this impassioned, though not incomprehensible utterance as occasion to send a personal letter to Shamir to express his great displeasure that the chief of the Israeli government had voiced the fear that the Germans would again resort "to the past crimes" against the Jews. "Like you, Mr. Prime Minister," wrote Kohl, "I am of the opinion that the misdeeds committed in the German name must not be suppressed. The memory of it must remain a steady admonition for us and coming generations. On the other hand, however, I am of the conviction that you, as head of the government of the state of Israel which entertains friendly relations with us, are with your judgment not doing justice to contemporary Germany, indeed denying them justice."[1]

In his reply Shamir retreated only slightly:

> Nobody could prophesy to which result the current wave of enthusiasm and nationalism will ultimately lead to—the least the Jewish people. But our historic experience with Germany in the thirties and forties of this century has burnt itself indelibly into our memory. We cannot forget the images of the cheering masses in the 1930s and what happened thereafter. We preserve the memory of the Jews who were then murdered in the 1940s. As Minister President I have the duty to express our doubts and anxieties.

The Israeli Foreign Minister Moshe Arens on February 15, 1990, on occasion of a visit to Bonn, distanced himself from the Israeli Premier. Israel, he stressed, must not only look to the past but also to the future and expressed confidence in the democratic institutions which existed now for forty years in the *Bundesrepublik.*[2]

News from Germany since then have been discouraging. The raging hostility by neo-Nazis and Rightists, the frequently weak responses of the German government in spite of mass demonstrations against violent xenophobia and anti-Semitic utterances and excesses have raised fears never quite repressed. Extreme nationalism and have shown strong revival and have underlined Günther Grass' earlier warnings: "He who at present gives thought to Germany and seeks replies to the German question, must also think of Auschwitz."[3]

Though only a very small number of Jews still live in Germany, the past continues to haunt its inhabitants. Jew-hatred has survived. The heavy hand of the past has not been lifted and German authorities have often failed to combat newly threatening intolerance and outrages consistently and vigorously. Some aspects of the *Historikerstreit* which has raised false and often ludicrous issues about German-Jewish history may have been dismissed by a majority of German scholars, but a vociferous German minority continues to cling to false dogmas and has not ceased to propagandize them, claiming support in the writings of some German scholars. These claims have often been exaggerated. Yet the circumstance that they could be made raises serious questions about the sensitivity and true objectivity of some German historians even after the tragedy of the Holocaust.

On the other hand, many German historians have perceived the obligation to take an unambiguous stand on matters relating to anti-Semitism in general and Jewish survival in Israel in particular. While after the Gulf War the Helmut Kohl government kept to the sidelines of the conflict—which proved irritating to Germany's allies[4]—130 prominent historians who were aroused by the lack of official Germany to Mid-Eastern developments, called publicly for solidarity with Israel and the Israeli population, threatened as it was by "poison gas." Disregarding the political and tactical differences which the *Historikerstreit* had brought to light; they called upon Germans "to deepen the conscience of a special responsibility and to encourage their Israeli colleagues." "As German historians who professionally are involved in the history of the Third Reich and the annihilation of European Jewry of the Second World War and the international order of the post-World War II period," these professors,

> specializing in the teaching of German and German-Jewish history of recent times appealed to the German people to recall the past and their nation's involvement. The Germany of our fathers has attempted to annihilate the Jews of Europe through gas. This ethnic murder has not been prevented by us Germans, but only through the readiness of Americans, English, Russians and other peoples to put an end to it.

They reminded the German peace activists, many of whom during the Arab-Israeli clashes and disputes had adopted a pro-Arab and anti-Israeli point of view, that since Auschwitz everyone must know that "worse than war is possible." During the last years German profit-makers have, knowingly or unknowingly, supported the Iraqi dictator and the murder of the Jewish people.

> The German government did not know how to prevent this. . . . In this hour when Israel is again exposed to the threat by gas, we know, irrespective of the necessary willingness of Jews and Arabs to negotiate, where we have to stand. The Jewish people needs more than German gas masks, German defensive weapons, and German millions! It needs the solidarity of all Germans![5]

Among the signers were distinguished historians such as Karl Dietrich Bracher, Fritz Fischer, Dietrich Geyer, Eberhard Jäckel, Werner Jochmann, Wolfgang Michalka, Hans Mommsen, Julius H. Schoeps, Ernst Schulin, Hans-Ulrich Wehler, Heinrich-August Winkler, and many others.

Clearly, historians are not permitted to bury the past, but are professionally and morally obligated to uncover and illuminate it, including all of its aspects. As the historian Theodor Heuss, who became President of the German Federal Republic expressed it:

> We must not forget, are not allowed to forget, matters which human beings would like to forget because [forgetting] is so pleasant. We must not forget the Nuremberg laws, the Jewish star, the burning of the synagogues, the transportation of Jewish people into the unknown, into the misfortune, into death. No one, whatever his or her national origin, should try to trivialize and minimize these facts.[6]

The *Historikerstreit* of 1986–87 has both a prologue and an epilogue. The latter is evidenced by the continuation of the polemics in the late 1980s as well as in the early 1990s. Some of the major participants have continued their polemics in books and articles during the last years while others have made a new entrance into the arena. Among the first-named were the philosopher Jürgen Habermas, whom revisionists have accused of having commenced the dispute in the summer of 1986, with the *Nachfolgenda Revolution*, 1990, and his younger disciple, the historian Hans-Ulrich Wehler, the author of *Entsoraung der deutschen Vergangenheit. Ein polemischer*

Essay zu dem Historikerstreit, 1991. Both men also wrote several shorter articles about this subject, as did W. J. Mommsen, *Die Nation und Geschichte über die Deutschen und die deutsche Frage*, 1990, and Jürgen Kocka and L. E. Hill authored smaller publications in 1990 and 1991 about the *Historikerstreit*. Immanuel Geiss, who had taken a moderate position in the early period of the dispute, wrote in 1992 the diatribe *Der Hysterikerstreit [!] Ein unpolemischer Essay*, against the main opponents of the revisionists, apparently influenced by a Hungarian political thinker, István Bibó, who had accused German historians at "the Left" of the "German hysteria." Geiss's polemics show the radicalization and deterioration of the argumentation of some German neo-Conservative historians. Ullrich Volker aimed his criticism against Geiss already in 1991 denouncing him as a "provocateur." In France too the echo to the *Historikerstreit* had not abated. The historian Alfred Grosser wrote about *Genocide in the Memory of Peoples*, which was published in Munich in 1990.[8] German impatience and resentment of the continuing accusations leveled against them raised in 1990 questions by Klaus Michael Groll, *Wie lange haften wir für Hitler?* The persistent dispute did not unearth any new sources or offer startling novel interpretations, but repeated earlier accusations, disclosing the tenacity of emotions stirred up ever since 1986.

These sentiments are not likely to be completely muted and to disappear into thin air in the foreseeable future. This is also demonstrated by German reactions to the opening of the Holocaust Memorial Museum in Washington, D.C. The German government's press spokesman, while denying a *Washington Post* story that the German government had wanted an exhibit in the Memorial on post-war Germany and its decades of democracy and had offered "millions of dollars" in exchange, admitted that it would have welcomed if the museum had included information on "German Resistance to National Socialism."[9] A Munich historian, an informal advisor to Chancellor Helmut Kohl, observed that Germany has changed since 1945. A writer in the *Frankfurter Allgemeine Zeitung* went further, claiming that the Museum's emphasis on gas chambers and death camps "had less to do with the German past than with the American present," and the Washington correspondent of *FAZ* complained that a visitor to the Museum would leave with "the lasting impression that these are the Germans and this is Germany." Clearly, Germans are resentful of the lasting memory of the Holocaust and of reminding Germans of past history and crimes which came close to wiping out not only German Jews out also much of the rest of European Jewry. What is overlooked is that the Museum, while focussing on the Jewish catastrophe, contains a world-wide warning.

NOTES

Notes to Chapter 1

1. H. V. Treitschke, *Deutsche Geschichte des neunzehnten Jahrhunderts*; see also A. D. Low, "Treitschke," in Buse, ed., *Encyclopedia of Recent German History*, 1994.

2. H. V. Treitschke, "Ein Wort über unser Judentum," *Preussische Jahrbücher*, November 1879 and January 1980.

3. H. Bresslau, see A. D. Low, *Jews in the Eyes of the Germans* (1979), 372.

5. Theodor Mommsen, *Auch ein Wort über unser Judentum* (1880), also Low, *op. cit.*, 375–376.

6. J. Sydney Jones, *Hitler in Vienna, 1907–1913*, 1983, Briarcliff, N.Y. and Fleming, G., *Hitler and the Final Solution* (1982, 1984), ch. 1.

7. General Erich von Ludendorff, *Lebenserinnerungen, 1941–1951.*

8. Prince Hubertus Loewenstein, *Tragedy of a Nation: Germany 1914–1934*, 1934.

9. H. Rauschning, *The Revolution of Nihilism. Warning to the West* (1939), 91.

10. H. Rauschning, *The Conservative Revolution* (1941), 67, 94–95, 97, 218–219, and 225.

11. Friedrich Meinecke, *German Catastrophe. Reflections and Recollections*, 1950 (in German, 1946), S. B. Fay, ed., Introduction, 1946, 9–11, 15–16, and 75..

12. Lucy Dawidowicz, *The Holocaust and the Historians*, 1981, 58–59.

13. Gerhard, Ritter, *German Resistance. Carl Goerdeler's Struggle Against Tyranny.*

14. *Ibid.*, 619; also Low, "Treitschke," see 1.

15. Ritter, see 13. and Low,, in Duse ed., *Encyclopedia of Recent German History*, 1994, "Walter Frank."

16. Treitschke *Preuss. Jahrbücher*, see also Boehlich, ed. *Der Berliner Antisemitismusstreit*, 1965. See 3., Low, *op. cit.*, p. 3.

17. Houston Stewart Chamberlain, *Foundations of the Nineteenth Century* (1912), I, 353.

18. A. Hitler, *Mein Kampf*, S. B. Fay, ed., (New York, 1939) 253 and 335.

19. J. Nadler, *Literaturgeschichte der deutschen Stämme und Landschaften*, 1932, 7.

20. For this quote and the following ones, see Low, *Jews in the Eyes of the German*, 1979, 84.

21. Hans Rothfels, *The German Opposition to Hitler. An Assessment* (1961), 31–33.

22. G. Ritter, *Carl Goerdeler und die deutsche Widerstandsbewegung*, 1951, chap. 11.

23. *Ibid.* 178.

24. A. D. Low, "Carl Goerdeler," in Buse, ed., *Encyclopedia...*, 1994.

25. G. Ritter, *op.cit.*, 301–302.

26. *Ibid.*, 441–442.

27. *Trials of the War Criminals before the Nuremberg Military Tribunal, November 14, 1945-46*, Vol. 1, 74, 186–8, 203, 214–215, 225–226, 234, Washington, 1949–1953 (14 vols.).

28-29. J. von Ribbentrop, *Memoirs*, (Introduction by A. Bullock).

30. Alfred Rosenberg, *Mythos des Zwanzigsten Jahrhunderts*, and *Letzte Aufzeichnungen. Ideale und idole der national-sozialistischen Revolution*, 1955, 314–315, 343, and 347.

31. Albert Speer, *Inside the Third Reich*, trans. by Richard and Clara Winston, 49–50.

31b. Dr. Frank, Hans, *Im Angesicht des Galgens*, 1953.

31c. Baldur von Schirach, *Ich glaubte au Hitler*, 1967.

31d. See 27., Schirach at Nuremberg, May 24, 1946.

32. Hans Grimm, *Die Erzbischofsschrift. Answer of a German. An Open Letter to the Archbishop of Canterbury*, (trans. by L. Hudson, 1957), 1–3, 7, 11–12, 18, 25–26, 32, 34, 45, 49, 59, 69–70, 73, and 78.

33. *Ibid.*, 89.

34. *Ibid.*

35. Heinrich Hauser, *The German Talks Back* (H. Morgenthau), Introduction).

36. Alexander Abusch, *Der Irrweg einer Nation*, 1945, 228–229, 235, and 238.

37. Karl Jaspers, *Die Schuldfrage*, 1946.

38. Gerd Tellenbach, *Die deutsche Sckuld als Not und Schicsal*, 1947.

39. Walther Hofer, *National-Sozialismus und die deutsche Geschichte*, 1957.

40. Erich Kordt, *Wahn und Wirklichkeit*, 1948, 13, 15, 343 and 347.

41. Ian Kershaw, "Antisemitismus und Volksmeinung," in M. Broszat and Elke Frohlich, eds., Vol. II of *Bayern in der N. S. Zeit*, 347.

Notes to Chapter 2

1. Ostarü, *Deutsche Konservative Partei-Deutsche Aufbaupartei* (DKP-DAP); Kurt Tauber, *Beyond Eagle and Swastika*, I, 63 and 449.

2. K. Tauber, *op. cit.*, chap. 4.

3. Kurt Schumacher, *Reden, Schriften, Korrespondenzen 1945–1952*, 699–700; 3c. *Ibid.*, 699–700 and 508ff.

4. Meeting of Adenauer and Israelis, Paris, April 1951.

5. Adenauer, *Bundestag*, September 27, 1951.

6. Ratification by German Parliament of Wiedergutmachung agreement, March 4, 1953, and Adenauer, *Memoirs, 1953–55.*

7. K. Tauber, *Beyond Eagle and Swastika*, 1967, Vol. I, 66. also 83ff. See also Manfred Jenke, *Verschwörung von Rechts* Berlin, chap. 2, *Rom Rechtsdadikalismus Nazismus*, 46ff, and H.-H. Knütter, *Ideologien des Rechtsradikalismus im Nachkriegesdeutschland* Bonn, 1961.

8. Tauber, 171–172.

9. *Ibid.*, 109.

10. *Ibid.*, 208ff, 229ff.

11. *Ibid.*, I, 210.

12. *Ibid.*, 229–239.

13. *Ibid.*, 243–253, Sir Oswald Mosley, especially 244.

14. *Ibid.*, 270 and 273.

15. *Ibid.*, I, Chap IX, about Stahlhelm and Waffen-SS, also M. Jenke, *op. cit.*

16. *Ibid.*, I, 885ff.

17. *Ibid.*, Chap. X.
18. *Ibid.*
19. *Ibid.*, I, 367.
20. *Ibid.*, Chap. XII, 475–481.
21. *Ibid.*
22. *Ibid.*
23. *Ibid.*, 505ff.
24. *Ibid.*, 510–514.
25. Tauber, *op. cit.*, I, 753 and 759.
26. Alfred Rosenberg, *Letzte Aufzeichnungen.*
27. *Ibid.*, *Deutsche Gemeinschaft*; Tauber, *op. cit.*, 768–765; also Jenke, *Verschwörung von Rechts*, 261ff.
28-30. *Deutsche Gemeinschaft*, Tauber, *op. cit.*, I, 774–775.
31. *Ibid.*, 678.
32. Mathilde Ludendorff, Tauber, *op. cit.*, 671–675.
33. Barnard Willms, *Die deutsche Nation*, 52.
34. Maurice Bardèche. *Nuremberg òu la terre promise.*

Notes to Chapter 3

1. Nationaldemokratische Partei (NDP), H. H. Knütter, *Ideologien des Rechtsradikalismus im Nachkriegsdeutschland*, 1961.
2. J. Fest, *Hitler* (New York: Vintage, 1974–75), 50.
3. Richard Kühnl, *Nationalismus. Die nationale Frage.* (Cologne, 1986).
4-5. Joseph Frank, *Frankfurter Rundschau*, January 14, 1987.
6. *Bayern-Kurier*, February 2 and March 30,1985.
7. Richard von Weizsäcker, May 8, 1985, *Verhandlungen des Bundestages.*
8-9. Alfred Dregger, *Die Zeit*, 12 November 1986.
10. Mau H. and J. Krausnick, *German History, 1933-45. An Assessment of German Historians*, (London, 1964).
11. E. Jäckel, "Der Weg zum Mord an den Juden," *Hitler's Herrschaft, Vollzug einer Weltanschauung*; also E. Jäckel and J. Rohwer, eds., *Der Mord an den Juden im Zweiten Weltkrieg*, 1985.
12. *Ibid.*, Hitler to Admiral Horthy, April 17, 1943; see also R. Hilberg, *Perpetrators, Victims . . .* , 1933, 18.
13. E. Jäckel, "Hitler orders the Holocaust," in *Hitler in History* (1984), 44–45.
14. *Ibid.*, 47.

15. *Ibid.*, 57–58 and 65.

16. G. Ritter, *The German Problem* (1965), chap. 6, 195–207 and 221–223.

17. *Ibid.*, 196.

18. *Ibid.*, 61-62.

19. J. C. Fest, see (2), 50.

20. J. C. Fest, *The Faces of the Third Reich*, 1990, 420–421.

21. *Ibid.*, 422–424.

22. Quoted by Fleming, *Hitler and the Final Solution*, 1984, 23.

23a. *Ibid.*; 23b. Fleming, *op. cit.*, 42.

24. *Ibid.*, 42 and 52–54; quoted from HR, 19, Bundesarchiv Koblenz.

25. Fleming, see 22., 56–57 and 59; also from Eichmann Trial, Jerusalem, session 107, July 24, 1961, F 1/RH.

26. J. Streicher, *Der Stürmer*, December 25, 1941; Fleming, *op. cit.*, 69.

27. Fleming, *op. cit.*, December 28, 1941; also from *Eichmann Trial*, Jerusalem, session 107, July 24, 1961, F1/RH.

28. S. Friedländer, Introduction to Fleming's study, XXIV–VI.

29. *Ibid.*, XXX–XXXI.

30. J. Thiess, *Architekt der Weltherrschaft. Die Enziele Hitler's* (1975), 4.

31. *Ibid.*, 43 and 86.

32. *Ibid.*, 45.

33. Uwe Adams, *Judenpolitik im Dritten Reich* (1979), 304ff.

34. *Ibid.*, 341 and 358.

35. Julius Schoeps, letter to M. Dizengoff, 1933, *Tribüne*, 1990.

36. D. Peukert, "Alltag und Barbarei," *Gewerkschaftliche Monatshefte*, No, 3, 1987.

37. Correspondenz M. Broszat mit S. Friedländer, *Tribüne*, 1989.

38. See Nr. 36.

39. H. Grimm, *Die Erzbischofsschrift.*

40. Tauber, *op. cit.*, chap. XIII, also I, 206.

41. *Ibid.*, 252–253.

42. *Ibid.*, I, chap. XI.

43. Uebersch—"ar, *Tribüne*, 1989, 164.

44. Alfred Rommel, *ibid.*, 8.

45. E. Jäckel, "Der Weg zum Mord an den Juden," in *Hitler's Herrschaft . . .*

46. H. Mommsen, "Nationalsozialismus, als vorgetäuschte Modernisierung," in H. H. Pehle, *Der Historische Ort des Nationalsozialismus*, 1990.

47. R. Hillberg, *The Destruction of European Jews* (1961, first ed.).

48. Christopher Browning, *The German Foreign Office and the Final Solution* (1978), 289.

49. M. Marrus, *The Holocaust in History*, 50.

50. Ribhegge, *Tribüne*, Nr. 2, 1987; see also "Stellenweise Glatteies," *Die Zeit*, 2 June 1987.

Notes to Chapter 4

1. Nolte, "Die Vergangenheit,die nicht vergehen will," *Frankfurter Allgemeine Zeitung* (*FAZ*) 6 June 1986.

2. A. Hillgruber, in Piper, ed., *Historikerstreit, Die Dokumentation der Kontroverse. . . um die Judenvernichtung*, 1987.

3. Raul Hillberg, "Tendenzen in der Holocaust-Forschung," in W. H. Pehle, ed., *Der historische Ort des Nationalsozialismus* (Frankfurt am Main, 1990), 71–80.

4. R. Reagan, quoted in G. H. Hartmann, *Bitburg in Moral and Political Perspective*, chap 2.

5. *Ibid.*

6. Friedländer, see 4., 81–9

7. Golo Mann, *Der Antisemitismus*, and R. von Weizsäcker, *Die Zeit*, 8 July 1945.

8. R. Augstein, see footnote 10.

9. *Bundestag*, 13 January 1985.

10. J. Habermas, in Piper, *op. cit.*

11. A. Hillgrüber, "Zweierlei Untergang . . ." in Piper, ed., *Historikerstreit . . .*

12. A. Hillgruber, "Zwischen Mythos und Revisionismus," *ibid.*, 69.

13. *Ibid.*, 71.

14. Nolte, see footnote 1.

15. Habermas, see footnote 10.

16. *Ibid.*

17. Nolte, *Three Faces of Fascism*, 1966 (also in German).

18. *Ibid.*, 4O9–410.

19. *Ibid.*, 293.

20. *Ibid.*, 293–294.

21. *Ibid.*, 358.

22. *Ibid.*, 400–401.

23. A. Nolte, *Deutschland und der kalte Krieg* (1974).

24. *Ibid.*, 136–137, 332–333, and 336.

25-26. F. Gilbert, *American Historical Review*, 81 (1976) 6180ff; also 82 (1977), 235–236.

27. M. Broszat and the twin brothers Hans and Wolfgang Mommsen are prominent functionalist historians who opposed the view of the racist ideologues and "intentionalists" and tended to deny that the primary motivation of National Socialism from the start to the finish had been the annihilation of the Jews. The functionalists emphasized the importance of the "machinery of destruction" inherent in the Nazi system of government and the alleged "weak" dictatorship of Hitler who permitted his satraps to fight for turf and for "Polykratie." German historical writing embraced both intentionalists and functionalists and historians who chose an intermediate course. In dealing with the elimination of the Jews, German historians have exhibited either sentiments and concepts of humanity and empathy and denounced Nazi crimes as well as German passivity and unquestioning subordination of the German people to authority and its commands. Other German historians have shown tendencies of minimizing populist writers, even denying Nazi crimes, and blaming Jewish victims for alleged character weaknesses and errors. Among the sharpest German critics of the Holocaust were both intentionalist and functionalist historians. An intentionalist who placed all or most of the blame primarily on Hitler tended thereby to acquit the German people. Some functionalists, on the other hand, had no intention to hold the German people blameless for the mass murder and the atrocities.

See also the article by Paul Passauer in the *Tribüne*, 1990, "Verhöhnung der Opfer. Vom Historikerstreit zum Historikerskandal." The author considered Nolte's remarks about the "European Civil War" an "attack upon Zeitgeschichte." His language bristled with "inhumanity and lacking phantasy." As Nolte wrote, "The deported Jews could nowhere find a place in the terribly overcrowded ghettos or especially in the concentration camps." Nolte also asserted that the killing of hundreds of thousands Jews in the camps was a "surprising" [*auffallend*) development.

28-29. K. Hillebrand, review of Hillgruber's book in *Histor.*

Zeitschrift (H.Z.), 1987 in Piper, *Historikerstreig*, 1987; also *ibid.*, J. Fest, *Nolte, Germany and the Cold War* (1974).

30. E. Nolte, *Germany and the Cold War*, (1974).

31. E. Nolte, *Marzismus und Industrielle Revolution*; about a few remarks relating to Jews and anti-Semitism, see 86ff. and 479f.; also Nolte, *FAZ*, November 5, 1978.

32. H.-U. Wehler, in Piper, *op. cit.*

33. Nolte, *Fascism*, 358.

34-35. Nolte, *Germany and the Cold War*, 7.

36. Nolte, "Die Verganganeheit . . .," *FAZ*, June 6, 1986

37. *Ibid.*

38. Fest, see footnote 9.

39. Nolte, "Antwort an meine Kritiker . . .," 1987.

40. Piper, ed., *op. cit.*, 46; Nolte, *Der Europäische Bürgerkreig 1917–1945 . . .* (1987), 504, 512–513.

41. A. Hillgruber, *Germany and the Two World Wars* (1967), 2nd ed., 1981, preface.

42-46. *Ibid.*, chaps 5 and 9.

47. Himmler, *Meldungen an den Führer über die Bandenbekämpfung.*

48. Keitel, *Trials of the War Criminals before Nuremberg . . . 1945–46*, I.

49. See footnote 41.

50. A. Hillgruber, "Zweierlei Untergang . . ."

51. Hillgruber, "Habermas . . ." in *Geschichte in Wissenschaft und Unterricht*, 12 December 1986.

52. Fritz Haug, *Das Argument*, May 1987.

53. Thomas Nipperday, in Piper, ed., *Historikerstreit*; also *Die Zeit*, 10 July 1985 and 17 October 1986.

54. W. Mommsen, "Die Vergengenheit . . ." in *Nation und Geschichte. . .*, 107–118.

55. *Der Spiegel* (1986), 36 and 66ff.

56. Augstein, *ibid.*

57. O. Köhler, "Kohl befiehlt, wir folgen," *Konkret* 10 (1986), 36ff.

58. Hillgruber interviews Kohl, "Vergangenheit, die Zukunft werden soll," *Das Argument*, May 1987.

59-60. *Ibid.*

61. M. Broszat, *Die Zeit*, 3 October 1986.

62. K. Hillgruber, *The Foreign Policies of the Third Reich* (1973).

63. Hildebrand, *FAZ*, July 31, 1986.

64. H. Z. Hildebrand, 1987, listed also in Piper ser. *Historikerstreit*, 1987.

65. Joachim Hoffman; see also G. Gillesen, *FAZ*, 2 February 1986, about Stalin's alleged aggressive plans.

66. Uwe Adam, *Die Judenpolitik in Dritten Reich*, 451.

67-68. See footnote 65.

69. M. Broszat, " Hitler and the Genesis of the Endlösung," *Vierteljahrshefte. . .* 25 (1977), 739ff.

70. See footnote 65.

71. M. Stürmer, in Piper ser., *Historikerstreit.*

72. Christian Meier, at Trier, October 1986

73. Christian Meier, *FAZ*, November 1986.

74. Historical Convention, Berlin, 2–3 October 1986, Chr. Meier.

75. Chr. Meier, "At the Turning Point of German Historical Memory," *FAZ*, 28 June 1986.

76. *Ibid.*; also *Süddeutsche Zeitung*, 24 July 1987.

77. H. Mommsen, in Piper ser., *Historikcrstreit.*

78. A. Dregger, *Die Zeit*, 12 November 1986; Arno Klönne, "Bundestagswahl, Historikerdebattte . . ."

79. P. Stadler, "Rückblick auf einen Historikerstreit . . ." *H.Z.* (1986), Vol. 247, 15–26.

Notes to Chapter 5

1. Th. Heuss quoted in *Tribüne*, 1985, Heft 10, 92ff.

2. Hans-Ulrich Wehler, *Entsoraung der deutschen Vergangenheit. Ein polemischer Essay zum Historikerstreit*, 1988.

3. *Ibid.*, 164.

4. *Ibid.*, 171.

5. *Ibid.*, 173.

6. *Ibid.*, 176.

7-9. *Ibid.*

10. J. Kocka, J., *Frankfurter Rundschau*, 10 April 1977.

11. *Ibid.*

12. H. A. Winkler, in Piper, ed., *Historiksrstreit*, Munich, 1987, 152.

13. E. Jäckel, *Nuremberger Zeitung* 20 September 1986.

14. J. Fest, in Piper, *op. cit.*,

15. Himmler, declaration, 8 October 1943.

16. "Wem gehört die deutsche Geschichte?", M. Broszat: Broszat developed the theory of the inevitability of the annihilation of the Jews, actually conceived earlier by Jewish historians such as Gerald Reitlinger, L. Poliakov, Lucy Dawidowicz, and others. This was the so-called ideological school to which Georg Mosse also pointed when elaborating on the "crisis of German ideology." German historians such as A. Hillgruber and K. Hildebrand saw the key to Hitler's priorities as rooted in his foreign policy linked with ideology, (p. 3030, Schlomo Aronson, *H.Z.* or *Vierteljahrshefte . . .*) and a number of noted German historians such as H. Mommsen and others also stressed the interchange of ideology and foreign policy, but in combination with societal developments in Germany, as the key to comprehending the Nazi policy of exterminating the Jews.

17. See footnote 16, 117.

18. M. Broszat, "Plaidoyer . . . National Socialism," *Merkur* 39 (1985), 373–385.

19. M. Stürmer, *Dissonanzsn des Fortschritts*; also F. A. Stürmer, *FAZ*, 16 August 1986.

20. *Ibid.*

21. A German-Jewish Dialogue: M. Broszat and Raul Friedländer; see also Broszat.

22. *Ibid.*

23. *Ibid.*

24. M. Broszat and K. Schwabe, *Die deutschen Eliten und der Weg om dem Zeitem Weltkreig*, 1984, 28.

25. *Ibid.*, 32–34.

26. K. D. Bracher, *FAZ*, 6 September 1986; 26b. H. Mommsen, "Die Endlösung Judenfrage in Dritten Reich," *Geschichte und Gesellschaft*, 1983, 381–420; reprinted in H. Mommsen, *Nationalsozialismus und d. Deutsche Gesellschaft. Ausgew. Aufsätze*, 1991, 184–232.

27. H. Mommsen, Merkur,H., September 1986; also H. Mommsen, *Blätter für deutsche und internationale Politik*, October 1986, "Geschichtsbewusstsein und Relativierung des National-Sozialismus."

28. W. Mommsen, "Neither denying nor forgetting liberates us from the past . . .," *Franfurter Rundschau*, 1 December 1986.

29. K. H. Janssen, *Die Zeit*, 27 November 1986.

30. R. Löwenthal, *FAZ*, 29 November 1986.

31. H. Mommsen. See 27.

32. M. Broszat, considered the British publicist David Irving's writings on the Third Reich and Hitler as likely causing "confusion" among people not familiar with all details, including history teachers. Driven by an "adventurous passion," the terrible "simplifiicateur" aimed at the "Entdämonisierung" [elimination of the demonization] of Hitler. Yet in all fields, including warfare, "the monster Hitler" did not exhibit the image of normality, or of a "normal" military leader. See also the criticism of Irving by Allen Bullock, *New York Times Review*, 26 June 1977, and that by E. Jäckel, *FAZ* 25 August 1977. M. R. Marrus, "History of the Holocaust. A Survey of Recent Literature," *Journal of Modern History*, Nr. 1, March 1987, referred to Irving's "egregious misuse of documentation," 117.

33. D. Peukert, "Alltag und Barbarei," *Gewerkschaftliche Monatshefte*, Nr. 3, 1987.

34. R. Hillberg, *Perpetrators, Victims, Bystanders*, Part 1, 5.

35. E. Nolte, *The European Civil War*, 1987.

36. Immanuel Geiss, *Evangelische Kommentare*, Heft, 2 February 1987.

Notes to Chapter 6

1. F. Vranitsky, *Tribüne*, Heft 105, 1989, 50–54.

2. *Sieg*, Austria, *Döiz*, Nr. 10, October 1990.

3. George Claire, 1973, Schönberg, *Tribüne* (see 1).

4. Gerhard Botz, "Österreich und die natlonal-soziaiistische Vergangenheit. Verdrängung, Pflichterfüllung und Geschichtsklitterung," in D. Diner, *Ist der Nationalsozialismus Geschichte?*, 1987, 141–152.

5. *Ibid.*

6. Robert Knight, "The Waldheim Concept: Austria and the Nazis," *Times Literary Supplement* and *The Frankfurter Rundschau*, 9 March 1987.

7. Zeev Sternhell, *La droite révolutionnaire*, Paris, 1978.

8. Leggewie, Claus, "Collective Memory . . ." in D. Diner, *Ist der Nationalsozialismus Geschichte?*, 1987, 120–140.

9. L. R. "Quarante ans après l'effondrement du nazisme . . ." in *L'Allemagne d'aujourdhui*, 1987, 235–264.

10. *Züricher Zeitung*, F. Luchsinger, Jan. 18-19, 1987.

11. *Die Zeit*, Jan. 14, 1987.

12. *N. R. C. - Handelsblad*, Rotterdam.

13. *The Hague Courant.*

14. Rusconi, Enrico, "Italien und der deutsche Historikerstreit," in D. Diner, *Ist der Nationalsozialismus Geschichte?*.

15. Annemarie Renger, *Tribüne,* 1989, #111, 113–125.

16. *Ibid.*

17. H. -J. Vogel, *Tribüne,* 1989, 100–112.

18. *Ibid.*

19. *Ibid.*

20. Otto Schultz, "Das Blut lässt sich nicht abwaschen . . ." *Tribüne,* 1989, #111.

21. K. V. Dohanyi, see 15.

22. Editorial, *Tribüne,* 1989, #109.

23. A. D. Low, *Soviet Jewry and Soviet Policy,* 1990, 141–144.

24. Paul Lendvai, *Anti-Semitism without Jews,* N. Y., 1971.

25. H. Hermann Bracher, *Tribüne,* 1989, #110, 8–11 and 98ff.

26. *Ibid.* 1989, #110, 216ff.

27. See 23.

28. *Lehrerzeitung,* 1987, D/RS, 8-W, 7–8.

Notes to Epilogue

1. Exchange of Shamir-Kohl, quoted in full by G. Sterner, *Tribüne,* (28) 1989, #111, 14ff., also 1990, #113, 6–12.

2. *Ibid.*

3. *Ibid.*, 1991, #11, 10ff.

4. Voices in Britain grew louder asking why the English should take risks in the Middle East while Germans increasingly participated in anti-war demonstrations which, given the circnrstances, had an anti-Allied and anti-American point. The British paper *Today* accused Germany of stabbing Britain in the back. Björn Enghohn, prime minister of Schleswig-Holstein, warned that anti-Americanism was quite improper. The American journalist Henryk M. Broder accused the German "friends of peace" that at the time of the outbreak of the Gulf War they did not condemn the aggression by Saddam Hussein and his provocative and unyielding behavior.

5. German historians, *Tribüne*, 1991, #117, 10ff.

6. Th. Heuss.

7. Raul Hilberg, an American historian of Austrian and Jewish descent, author of the seminal study *The Destruction of European Jews,* (1961), published in 1992 the penetrating book *Perpetrators, Victims, Bystanders. The Jewish Catastrophe 1933–45.*

8. While critical of French "memory," Alfred Grosser tends to be too apologetic of the Germans, defending even extremists, too critical of what he calls the "oversensitivity" of Jews, and trivializing the *Historikerstreit*, not done by the Germans of either side, and the attitude of the revisionists and apologists.

9. L. Wieseltier, "After Memory," *The New Republic*, 3 May 1993, 16–26 quotes the *Washington Post* and the *Frankfurter Allgemeine Zeitung*.

SELECT BIBLIOGRAPHY

Public Documents

Akten zur Deutschen Aussenpolitik 1918-1945, Series D, X, X–XIII, Göttingen, 1951; Series E., Vols. I–II, Göttingen, 1969–1972.

Documents on German Foreign Policy 1918–1945,. Series DV, Washington, D.C., 1953.

Jüdisches Historisches Institut, Warsaw, *Faschismus-Ghetto-Massenmord. Dokumentation über Ausrottung und Widerstand der Juden in Polen während des Zwelten Weltkrieges*, Berlin, 1960.

Trials of the War Criminals before the Nuremberg Military Tribunals, 14 vols., Washington, D.C., 1949–1953, Vol. I.

Books

Abusch, Alexander. *Der Irrweg einer Nation*, 1945.

American Jewish Yearbook. Annual edition.

Antisemitenhammer, Anthologie, Schrattenholz, ed., Düsseldorf, 1994. Other editions since.

Arendt, Hannah. *Eichmann in Jerusalem*, New York, 1965.

The Origins of Totalitarianism, New York, 1951 (also 1958).

Augstein, R. *et al.*, eds. *Historikerstreit. Dokumentation der Controverse um die Einzigartigkeit der national-sozialistischen Judenvernichtung*. Munich, 1987.

Ayçoberry, Pierre, *The Nazi Question: An Essay on the Interpretation of National Socialism*, Munich, 1981.

Bardèche, Maurice, *Nuremberg oder die Falschmünzer*, Wiesbaden, 1957.

Baron, Salo, “European Jewry before and after Hitler,” *American Jewish Yearbook*, 1962.

Bartels, Adolf, *Einführung in das deutsche Schrifttum für deutsche Menschen*, Leizig, 1933.

———, *Hebbel und die Juden*, Munich, 1922.

———, *Lessing und die Juden*, Leipzig, 1934.

Bartov, Omer, *The Eastern Front 1914–18. German Troops and the Polarization of Warfare*, London, 1985.

Bauer, Yehuda, *History of the Holocaust*, New York, 1982.

Baynes, N. H., ed. *The Speeches of Adolf Hitler*, Berkeley, 1984.

Beiträge für Sozialgeschichte des Alltags unter National-Sozialismus, Wuppertal, 1982.

Ben Chorin, Shalom, *Germania Judaica*, 1982.

Ben-Elissar, Eliahu, *La diplomatie du IIIe Reich et juifs*, Paris, 1969.

Bernstein, R. J. *Habermas and Modernity*, Cambridge, 1985.

Bessels, Richard, ed., *Life in the Third Reich*, Oxford, N.Y., 1987.

Binion, Rudolf, *Hitler among the Germans*, New York, 1976.

Boehlich, W., ed., *Der Berliner Antisemitismusstreit 1879–80*, Frankfurt am Main, 1965.

Böll, Heinrich, *Auseinandersetzung mit der Vergangenheit*, Cologne, 1982.

———, *Wo warst du Adam?* Opladin, 1951.

Boeg Horst, *et. al.*, *Der Angriff auf die Sowjetunion. Das deutsche Reich und der Zweite Weltkrieg*, Vol. 4, Stuttgart and Freiburg, 1983.

Bosch, M., *Persönlichkeit und Struktur in der Geschichte*, Düsseldorf, 1977.

Bracher, Karl-Dietrich, *The German Dictatorship. Origin and the Structure and Effect of National Socialism*, Introduction P. Gay, New York, 1970.

Brehm, Bruno, *Das zwölfjährige Reich*, Graz, 1960–61.

Broszat, M. *Die deutschen Eliten und der Weg in den Zweiten Weltkrieg*, New York, 1984 (1989).

———, and Elke Fröhlich, eds., *Alltag und Widerstand. Bayern in National-Sozialismus*, Munich, 1987.

Broszat, M., Hans-Adolf Jacobsen, and H. Krausnick, *Koncentrationslager, Kommissarbefehle, und Judenverfolgung*, Freiburg, 1965.

———, "Korrespondenz mit Saul Friedländer," *Die Tribüne*, 1989.

Browning, Christopher A., *Fateful Months. Essays on the Emergence of the "Final Solution"*, New York, 1986.

———, *The Final Solution and the German Foreign Office*, London, 1978.

Bullock, Alan, *Hitler and Stalin*, Berlin, 1991.

Büsch, Otto and Peter Fürth, *Rechtsradikalismus in Nachkriegsdeutschland*, Berlin and Frankfurt am Main, 1957.

Chamberlain, H. St. *Foundations of the Nineteenth Century*, New York, 1912.
Childers, Thomas, *The Nazi Voter*, Chapel Hill, 1983.
Conquest, Robert, *The Harvest of Sorrow: Soviet Collectivization, Terror, Famine*, New York, 1986.
Craig, Gordon A., *The Germans.*

Davidowicz, L. S., *The War against the Jews*, New York, 1975, second ed. 1985.
_____, *The Holocaust and the Historians*, Harvard, 1981.
Diner, Dan, *Ist der Nationslsozialismus Geschichte? Zur Historisierung und Historikerstreit*, Frankfurt am Main, 1987.
Diwald, Helmut, *Geschichte der Deutschen*, Berlin, 1978.
Domarus, M., *Hitler, Reden und Poklamationen 1932-45*, 2 vols., Würzburg, 1962–63.
Dorpalen, Andreas, *German History in Marxist Perspective*, Detroit, 1985.

Eberan, Barbro, *Luther? Friedrich der Grosse? Wagner? Nietzsche? Wer war an Hitler schuld? Debatte um Schuldfrage 1945–49*, Munich, 1983.
Eichberg, Henning, *Nationale Identität*, Munich, 1978.
Eley, Geoff, *Reshaping the German Right. Radical Nationalism and Political Change after Bismark*, New Haven, 1980.
Engelmann, Bernt, *Germany without Jews*, Bantam.
Ettinger, Schmuel, "Fascism, Communism, and the Jewish Question in Romania," in *Europe between the Wars. An Outline.*
Evans, Richard J., *Rethinking German History: Nineteenth Century Germany and the Origins of the Third Reich*, London, 1987.

Feder, Gottfried, *Die Juden*, Munich, 1933.
Fest, Joachim, *The Third Reich*, London, Boston.
_____, *Hitler* (Vintage), trans. by R. and C. Winston, New York, 1974–75.
_____, *Hitler, eine Biographie*, 2 vols., Berlin, 1973.
_____, *The Face of the Third Reich*, London, 1979; also New York: Pantheon, 1970. trans. by M. Bullock.
Fischer, Fritz, *Griff nach der Weltmacht*, Düsseldorf, 1961, English version London, 1967.

Fischer-Galati, Stephen, "Jews and non-Jews in Eastern Europe 1918–1945," Vago Bela and G. L. Mosse, New York, 1974.

Fitzgibbons, Constantin, *Denazification*, London, 1969.

Flechtheim, Ossip, *Die deutschen Parteien seit 1945*, Berlin, 1953.

Fleming, Gerald, *Hitler and the Final Solution*, Berkeley, 1984.

Frank, Walter, *Nationalismus und Demokratie in Frankreich's Dritter Republik*, Hamburg, 1933.

Friedländer, Henry and Sybil Milton, eds., *The Holocaust: Ideology, Bureaucracy, and Genocide*, The San José Papers, Milwood, N.Y., 1980.

Friedländer, Saul. *Reflections of Nazism*, New York, 1984.

Fritsch, Theodor, *Der Antisemitenkatechismus*, 1893, and numerous later editions.

Ganzer, K. R., *Richard Wagner*, Munich, 1934.

Geiss, Immanuel, *Die Habermas-Kontroverse. Ein deutscher Streit*, Berlin, 1988.

_____, *Der Hysterikerstreit. Ein unpolemischer Essay*, Bonn, Berlin, 1992.

Gilbert, Martin, *The Holocaust. The Jewish Tragedy*, Glasgow, 1986.

_____, *Auschwitz and the Allies*, London, 1980.

Goebbels, Joseph. *Tagebuch*, H. Heiber, ed., 1961.

Graml, H. Klaus and Dietrich Denke, eds., *Nach Hitler. Der schwierige Umgang mit unserer Geschichte. Beiträge von M. Broszat*, Munich, 1986 (1987).

_____, *Die Reichskristallnacht. Antisemitismus und Judenverfolgung im Dritten Reich*, Munich, 1988.

Grau, W., *Die Judenfrage in der deutschen Geschichte*, 1937.

Greive, Hermann, *Geschichte des modernen Antisemitismus*, 1984.

Grimm, Hans, *Die Bischofsschift. Answer of a German. An open letter to the Archbishop of Canturbury*, trans. by Lynton Hudson, Dublin, 1957, also Göttingen).

_____, *Volk ohne Raum*, Lippoldsberg, 1956 (also in English).

_____, *Warum-woher-aber wohin*, Lippoldsberg, 1956.

Groll, Klaus M., *Wie lange haften wir für Hitler? Zum Selbstverständnis der Deutschen von heute*, Düsseldorf, 1990.

Grosser, Alfred, *Ermordung der Menschheit. Der Genozid im Gedächtnis der Völker*, Munich, 1990.

Grunsky, K. R., *Wagner und die Juden*, Munich, 1922.

Guderian, Heinz, *Erinnerungen eines Soldaten*, Heidelberg, 1951.

Gutman, Yisrael, *Denying the Holocaust*, Jerusalem, 1985.

Habermas, Jürgen, ed. "Stichworte zur Geistigen Situation der Zeit," Frankfurt am Main, 1979.

_____, "Nachfolgende Revolution," *Kleine Politische Schiften*, VII, Frankfurt am Main, 1990.

Haffner, G. *The Rise and Fall of Prussia*, 1980.

Haffner, Sebastian, *Anmerkungen und Hitler*, Munich, 1980.

Hartmann, Geoffrey, ed., *Bitburg in Moral and Political Perspective.*

Haslinger, Josef, *Politik der Gefühle. Ein Essay über Österreich*, Darmstadt, 1987.

Hassell, Erich von, *Vom anderen Deutschland.*

_____, *The Hassell Diaries 1938–1944*, New York and London, 1947.

Hauser, Gideon, *Justice in Jerusalem*, Jerusalem, 1961 (also 1966).

Hauser, Heinrich, *The German Talks Back*, Preface by Hans Morgenthau, 1947.

Heiber, H., *Walter Frank*, Stuttgart, 1966.

Heiden, Konrad, *Der Führer. Hitler's Rise to Power*, Boston, 1944.

Henning, Erike, *Historikerstreit. Was heisst und zu welchem Ende studiert man Faschismus?*, 1988.

Hierl, Konstantin, *Gedanken hinter Stacheldraht*, Heidelberg, 1953.

Hilberg, Raul, *The Destruction of European Jews*, Chicago, 1961; 2nd ed. 1985. German versions, Berlin 1982 and 1990.

_____, *The Holocaust Today*, Judaic Studies, Syracuse University, 1988.

_____. *Perpetrators, Victims, Bystanders*, New York, 1992.

Hildebrand, Klaus, *Das Dritte Reich*, Munich and Vienna 1979 (in English 1979 and 1984).

_____, *Das Dritte Reich in der deutschen und Europäischen Geschichte*, 108–116.

_____, *Das Dritte Reich im Urteil der Geschichtswissenschaft*, Munich, 1979. 112–116.

_____,ed., *Wem gejört die deutsche Geschichte? Deutschlands Weg vom alten Europa in die europäische Moderne*, Cologne, 1987.

_____, *Germany and Two World Wars*, trans. by D. C. Kirby, Cambridge, Mass. and London, 1981.

_____. *Deutsche Aussenpolitik 1933–1945*, Stuttgart, 1971.

_____. *Vom Reich zum Weltreich, Hitler, NSDAP und koloniale Frage, 1919–1945*, Munich, 1969.

_____, and W. Michalka, eds., *National-sozialistische Aussenpolitik*,

Darmstadt, 1978.

Hill, E. L. "Holocaust and der 'Historikerstreit'," in Donat H. and L. Wieland, *"Auschwitz erst möglich gemacht?" Überlegungen zur jüngsten konservativen Geschichtsbewältigung*, Bremen, 1991.

Hillgrüber, Andreas,*Die deutsche Grossmacht und Weltpolitik im 19. und 20. Jahrhundert*, Düsseldorf, 1977.

_____. *Hitler's Politik in Strategie und Kriegsführung, 1940–41*, Frankfurt am Main, 1965.

_____, *Zweierlei Untergant. Die Zerschlagung des Deutschen Reiches und das Ende des europäischen Judentums*, Berlin, 1986.

Hitler, Adolf, *Mein Kampf*, New York, 1939.

Hitler's Zweites Buch. Ein Document aus dem Jahre 1928, G. L. Weinberg, ed., Stuttgart, 1961.

Hitler spricht, Leipzig, 1967.

Hoggan, David L. *Der erzwungene Krieg. Die Ursachen und Urheber des Zweiten Keltkrieges*, trans. M. E. Noyes and H. Grabert, Deutsche Hochschullehrerzeitung, 1963.

Hofer, Walther, *Der Nationalsozialismus und deutsche Geschichte*, 1957 (also 1972).

_____, *Der Nationalsozialismus. Dokumente 1933–1945*, ed. with comments, Frankfurt am Main, 1957.

_____. *Die Diktatur Hitler's bis zum Beginn des Weltkrieges 1933–1939*, Constance, 1971.

Höss, Rudolf, *Commandant at Auschwitz*, New York, 1959.

Iggers, Georg, *Einige Bemerkungen zu neueren historischen Studien aus der DDR*, I, Berlin, 1987.

_____, *The Social History of Politics. Critical Perspectives in West German Historical Writing since 1948*, 1985.

Irving, David, *Hitler's War*, New York, 1987.

Jacobelli, Jader, ed., *Il fascismo e gli storici oggi*, Rome and Paris, 1988.

Jacobsen, H.-A., *National-sozialistische Aussenpolitik 1933–38*, Frankfurt am Main, 1968.

Jäckel, Eberhard and Jürgen Rohwer, "Der Mord an den Juden im Zweiten Weltkfieg," in *Hitler's Herrschaft. Vollzug einer Weltanschauung*, 1985–86.

Jäckel, E. *Hitler in History*, Hanover and London, 1984.

Jäckel, E. *Hitler's Herrschaft, Vollzug einer Weltanschauung.* Stuttgart, 1986.

Jaspers, Karl, *Die Schuldfrage*, 1946.

_____, *Wohin triebt die Bundesrepunlik?* Munich, 1966.

Jenke, Manfred, *Conspiracy on the Right* (also in German: *Verschwörung von Rechts? Bericht Rechtsradikalismus in Deutschland nach 1945*, Berlin, 1961.

. Kater, Michael, *The Nazi Party. A Special Profile of Members and Leaders 1919-45*, Oxford, 1985.

Kern (Kernmyer), Erich, *Deutschland im Abgrund*, Göttingen, 1963.

_____, *Der grosse Rausch. Russlandfeldzug 1941–45*, Weiblingen, 1950.

Kershaw, Ian, *The Hitler Myth. Image and Reality in the Third Reich*, 0xford, 1987.

"Antisemitisrmus und Volksmeinung," in *Bayern in der N. S. Zeit*, M. Broszat and E. Froehlich, eds.

Kleist, Peter, *Auch Du warst dapei*, Vowinckel, 1952.

Klemperer, Klemens von, *Germany's New Conservatives: History and Dilemma*, Princeton, 1961.

Knütter, Hans-Helmuth, *Ideologie des Rechtsradikalismus in Nachkriegsdeutschland*, Bonn, 1961.

Koch, H. W., ed. *Aspects of the Third Reich*, London, 1985.

Koch, F., *Goethe und die Juden*, (paper read on August 13, 1937).

Köhler, Otto, "The *FAZ* und der Historiksrstreit," in E. Pfeiffer, ed., *Die FAZ Nachforschungen*, Cologne, 1988.

Koehl, Robert, *Die Black Corps. The Structure and Power Struggle of the Nazi SS*, Madison, 1985.

Kogon, Eugen, *Der SS-Staat*, Stockholm, 1947.

Kordt, Erich, *Wahn und Wirklichkeit. Die Aussenpolitik des Dritten Reiches*, Stuttgart, 1948.

Kosick, Rolf, *Historikerstreit und Geschichtsrevision*, Tübingen, 1987.

Krausnick, Helmut, "The Persecution of the Jews," in *Anatomy of the SS-State*, New York, 1965.

_____, and H.-H Wilhelm, *Die Truppe des Weltanschauungskrieges*, Stuttgart, 1981.

Kwiet, Konrad, *Selbstbehauptung und Widerstand, Deutsche Juden im Kampf 1933–1945*, Hamburg, 1984.

Kühnl, Reinhard, *Streit ums Geschichtsbild in der Historikerdebatte*, 1987.

Laska, Vera, *Nazism, Resistance, and the Historians*, Cambridge, Mass., 1981.

Laval, Pierre, *The Diary of Pierre Laval*, New York, 1948.

Laqueur, Walter, *The Terrible Secret. Suppression of the Truth about*

Hitler's "Final Solution", London, 1980.

———, *Germany Today - A Personal Account*, Boston, 1985.

———, *Was niemand wissen wollte. Nachrichten über Hitler's "Endlösung."*

Lehrerzeitung, D/R/S 8-W, 8 July 1987. Emphehlungen über die Behandlung der jüdischen Geschicht in bundesdeutschen Geschichtsbüchern.

Levi, Primo, *Ist das ein Mench?* Frankfurt, 1961.

Levin, Nora, *The Holocaust. The Destruction of European Jewry 1933–1945*, New York, 1971.

Lifton, Robert Jay, *The Nazi Doctors' Medical Killing and the Psychology of Genocide*, New York, 1986.

Lipstadt, Deborah E. *Beyond Belief. The American Press and the Coming of the Holocaust 1933–1945*, New York, 1986.

———, *Twentieth Century*, Princeton, 1957.

Littell, Franklin H. and H. G. Locke, eds., *The German Church Struggle and the Holocaust.* Detroit, 1974.

Lonsbach, R. N., *Friedrich Nietzsche und die Juden*, Stockholm, 1934 (also 1968).

Low, Alfred D., *Jews in the Eyes of the Germans. From the Enlightenment to Imperial Germany*, Philadelphia, 1979.

———, *Soviet Jewry and Soviet Policy*, New York, 1990.

Loewenstein, Prince Hubertus, *The Tragedy of a Nation. Germany 1918–1934.* Introduction by Wickham Steed. 1938–1939.

Löwenthal, Richard, *Romantischer Rückfall*, Mainz, 1970.

Ludendorff, General Erich, *Vom Feldherrn und Weltrevolutionär und Wegbereiter deutscher Volksschöpfung. Meine Lebenserinnerungen von 1926 bis 1938*, 2 vols. Stuttgart, 1941–1951.

Lutz, Hermann, *"Nation of Criminals" in the Center Europe*, n.d.

Mann, Golo, *Der Antisemitismus*, Munich, 1961.

Mann, Thomas, *Sieben Manifeste zur jüdischen Frage 1936–48*, A. Berendson, ed., 1949.

Maier, Charles S., *The Unmasterable Past: History, Holocaust, and German National Identity*, Cambridge, Mass., 1988.

Marrus, Michael Robert, *The Holocaust in History*, Toronto, 1987.

Marrus, M. R. and R. A. Paxton, *Vichy France and the Jews*, New York, 1981.

Martin, Bernd, and E. A. Schulin, *Juden als Minderheit in der deutschen Geschichte*, Munich.

Massing, Paul D. *Rehearsal for Destruction: A Study of Political*

Anti-Semitism in Imperial Germany, New York, 1949.
Mau, Hermann and Helmut Krausnick, *German History 1933-45. An Assessment of German Historians*, London, 1961.
Meier, Christian, *Vierzig Jahre nach Auschwitz. Deutsche Geschichtsschreibung heute*, Munich, 1987.
Meinecke, Friedrich Wilhelm, *The German Catastrophe: Reflections and Recollections*, Harvard, 1950, in German, 1946.
Mendelssohn, Ezra, *Jews of East Central Europe between the Two World Wars*, Bloomington, Ind., 1983.
Michaelis, Meir, *Mussolini and the Jews: German-Italian Relations and the Jews in Italy 1922–45*, Oxford, 1978.
Michalka, W., *Joachim von Ribbentrop und die deutsche Englandpolitik 1933–1940*, Mannheim, 1976.
Mohlen, Arnim, *Die Konservative Revolution in Deutschland 1918–1932*, Stuttgart, 1930.
Mommsen, Hans, *Gechichtsdidaktik. Probleme, Projekte, Perspektiven*, 1986.
_____, *Der Nationalsozialismus und die deutsche Gesellschaft. Ausgewählte Aufsätze*, Reinbek, 1991.
Mommsen, Theodor, *Römische Geschichte*, III, many editions.
Mommsen, Wolfgang J. *Deutsche Parteiprogramme*, Munich, 1960.
_____, *Nation und Geschichte über die Deutschen und die deutsche Frage*, Munich, 1990.
_____, *Max Weber und die deutsche Politik, 1890–1920*, Tübingen, 1959.
Mosley, Sir Oswald, *The European Revolution.*
_____, *My Life*, London, 1968.
Mosse, Georg, *The Crisis of German Ideology*, New York, 1981.
Mühlen, Norbert, *The Survivors. Report on the Jews in Germany Today*, New York, 1962.
Nadler, Josef, *Literaturgeschichte der deutschen Stämme und Landschaften*, 4 vols., Regensburg, 1929–32.
Neumann, F. *Behemot, The Structure and Practice of National Socialism 1933–40*, Mannheim, 1976.
Noakes, Jeremy and Geoffrey Pridham, *Nazism 1919–1945. A Documentary Reader*, 4 vols., Exeter. 1983–1989.
Nolte, Ernst, *Deutschland und der Kalte Krieg*, 2. Aufl. Stuttgart, 1974.
_____, *Three Faces of Fascism: Action Française, Italian Fascism, National Socialism*, New York, 1965 (also 1963 and 1966).

———, *Faschismus in seiner Epoche*, Munich, 1966 (in English, New York, 1965, 1968).

———, *Marxismus und Industrielle Revolution*, 1983.

———, *The European Civil War*, 1987.

———, *Das Vergehen der Vergangenheit. Antwort an meine Kritiker, Historikerstreit*, 2nd ed., Munich, 1988; also Frankfurt, 1987.

———, "Die Endlösung und das deutsche Ostimperium," in *Deutsche Grossmacht und Weltpolitik im 19. und 20. Jahlhundert*, Düsseldorf, 1981.

Pätzold, Kurt, ed., *Verfolgung, Vertreibung, Vernichtung, Dokumente 1933–42*, Frankfurt am Main, 1984.

———, "Von der Vertreibung zum Genozid," *Faschismusforschung, Positionen, Probleme, Polemik*, Cologne, 1980, 181–208.

Pehler, Walter, ed., *Der Judenpogrom 1938. Von der Reichskristallnacht zum Völkermord*, Frankfurt, 1988.

———, *Der historische ort des Nationalsozialismus*, Frankfurt am Main, 1990.

Pelinka, Anton and Erik Weinzierl, eds. *Das grosse Tabu. Österreichs Umgang mit seiner Vergangenheit*, Vienna, 1987. Peukert, Detlev, "Wer gewann der Historikerstreit? Keine Bilanz," Peter Glanz, *et. al.*, eds., *Vernunft riskieren: Klaus von Dohanyi z. 60 Geburtstag*, Hamburg, 1988.

Pfeiffer, Harmanus, ed., *Die FAZ. Nachforschungen über ein Zentralorgan*, Cologne, 1988.

Piper, R., ed., *Historikerstreit. Die Dokumentation der Kontroverse um die Einzigartikeit der national-sozialistischen Judenvernichtung*, Munich, 1987.

Poliakoff, L., *Histoire de l'antisémitisme de Voltaire à Wagner*, Paris, 1968.

Pronay N. and K. Wilson, eds., *The Political Re-education of Germany and Her Allies after World War II*, London, 1985.

Pulzer, G. J., *The Rise of Political Anti-Semitism in Germany and Austria*, London and New York, 1964.

Rabinbach, A. and Jack Zipes, *German Jews since the Holocaust*, New York, 1986.

Raeder, Erich, *Mein Leben*, 2 vols., Tübingen, 1957.
Rassinier, Paul, *Die Lüge des Odysseus*, Wiesbaden, 1959.
Rauschning, Hermann, *The Conservative Revolution*, New York, 1941.
_____, *Hitler Speaks*, London and New York, 1940.
_____, *The Revolution of Nihilism. Warning to the West*, New York, 1939 (also in German).
Reitlinger, Gerald, *The Final Solution. The Attempt to Exterminate the Jews of Europe, 1939-45*, New York, 1961.
_____, *The S.S.: Alibi of a Nation 1922-1945*, New York, 1957.
Remer, Otto Ernst, *12. Juli, 1944*, Hamburg, 1941.
Reventloff, Count, *Juda's Kampf und Niederlage in Deutschland*, Berlin, 1937.
Ritter, Gerhard, *The German Problem*, Columbus, 1965, ch. 6.
Rougemont, Denis de, *La part du diable*; also *The Devil's Share*, New York, 1944.
Rückerl, A., *The Investigation of Nazi Crimes 1945-1978*, London, 1979.
Rusconi, Gian Enrico, ed., *Germania passato che non passa. I crimi nazisti et l'identicà tedesca*, Turin, 1987.

Salomon, Ernst von, *Der tragebogen*, Hamburg, 1961.
Sarge, Richard, *Faschismustheorien*, Munich, 1976.
Schechtmann, J. *Postwar Population Transfers in Europe, 1945-1955*, London, 1979.
Schieder, Th., *Hermann Rauschning's Gespräche mit Hitler als Geschichtsquelle*, Opladen, 1972.
Schirach, Henriette von, *Preis der Herrlichkeit*, Wiesbaden, 1956.
Schleunes, K. A., *The Twisted Road to Auschwitz*, Urbana, Ill., 1970.
Schmidt, Johann, A. "Those Unfortunate Years." *Nazism in the Public Debate of Postwar Germany*, Indiana University Press, 1987.
Schmidt, Manfred, *Albert Speer. Das Ende eines Mythos*, Munich, 1982.
Schmidt, Paul, *Hitler's Interpreter*, New York, 1951.
Schulze, Hagen, *Wir sine was wir geworden sind*, Munich, 1987.
Schumacher, Kurt, *Reden-Schriften-Korrespondenzen 1945-1952*, Berlin and Rome, 1985.
Schwabe, Klaus, *Deutsche Hochschullehrer und Hitler's Krieg (1936-44)*, 1988.
Seabury, Paul, *Die Wilhelmstrasse. A Study of German Diplomats under the Nazi Regime*, Berkeley, 1954.

Seidel, Gill, *The Holocaust Denial, Anti-Semitism, Racism, and the New Right*, London, 1986.

Seifert, Wolfgang, *Das ganze Deutschland*, Munich, 1986.

Snyder, Louis L., *Roots of German Nationalism*, Bloomington, Ind. and London, 1978.

Soucek, Theodor, *Wir rufen Europa. Vereinigung des Abendlandes*, n.d.

Speer, Albert, *Der Sklavenstaat*, Stuttgart, 1981.

——, *Inside the Third Reich. Memoirs.*, trans. Richard and Clara Winston, Avon Books, 1970.

Stern, Frank, *Jews in the Mind of Germans in the Postwar Period*, Bloomington, Ind., 1993.

Sternhell, *La droite révolutionnaire*, Paris, 1978.

Stiefel, Dieter, *Entnazifizierung in Österreich*, Vienna, 1981.

Strauss, G., *Deutschland und der Dritte Weltkrieg*, Staribeg.

Streit, Christian, *Keine Kameraden*, many editions.

Stürmer, Michael, *Dissonanzen des Fortschrittes. Essays über Geschichte und Politik in Deutschland*, Munich, 1986.

——, "Kein Eigentum der Deutschen. Die deutsche Frage," Werner Weidenfeld, ed., Munich.

——. *Die Identitaet der Deutschen*, Munich.

——, ed., *Die Weimarer Republik*, 1980.

Strauss, Franz Josef, *Verantwortung vor der Politik. Beiträge zur deutschen und internationalen Politik, 1980–85*, Munich, 1985.

Tal, Uriel, *Christians and Jews in Germany. Religion, Politics, Ideology in the Second Reich*, trans. N. Jacobs, Ithaca, N.Y., 1975.

Tansill, Charles. C., *Back Door to War. Roosevelt's Foreign Policy 1933-4*, Chicago, 1952.

Tauber, Kurt P., *Beyond Eagle and Swastika. German Nationalism beyond 1945*, 2 vols, Wesleyan University Press, 1967.

Tellenbach, Gerd, *Die deutsche Not als Schuld und Schicksal*, Stuttgart, 1947.

Thiess, Jochen, *Architekt der Weltherrschaft. Die 'Endsiele' Hitler's*, Düsseldorf, 1976.

Treitschke, H., *Deutsche Geschichte des neunzehnten Jahrhunderts*, 1876, 5 vols., Leipzig, 1979–1890 (also an English version, 4 vols).

——, "Ein Wort über unser Judentum," *Preussische Jahrbüch- er*, November 1879 and January 1980.

Trevor-Roper, H. R., "Hitler's Kriegsziele," in W. Michalka, *Nationalsozialistsische Ausssenpolitik*, Darmstadt, 1978.

Uwe, Dietrich Adam, *Judenpolitik im Dritten Reich*, Pädagogische Hochschule, 1979.

Veblen, Thorstein, *Imperial Germany and the Industrial Revolution*, New York, 1915.

Vogel, Hans Joachim, *Tribüne*, 1989.

Volker, Ulrich, "Der Schlichter als Provokateur-Immanual Geiss und uer Historikerstreit," in H. Donat und L. Wieland, eds., *Auschwitz ist möglich gemacht, Jungste Konservative Geschichtsbewältigung*, Bremen, 1991.

Waffen-S.S. in Bild, 2nd ed., Göttingen, 1957.

Waite, Robert G. L., *The Psychopathological God in Adolf Hitler*, New York, 1977.

Weber, Alfred, *Farewell to European History*, New Haven, 1948.

Wehler, Hans-Ulrich, *Entsorgung der deutschen Vergangenheit. Ein polemischer Essay zum Historikerstreit.* Munich, 1989 (also 1991).

_____, *Deutsche Historiker*, Frankfurt am Main, 1980.

_____. *Die moderne deutsche Geschichte in internationaler Forschung 1945–77*, Göttingen, 1978.

_____, *The German Empire 1871–1918*, Dover, 1985.

_____, "Historiography in Germany Today," in J. Habermas, ed. *Observations on the "Spiritual Situation of the Age."* Cambridge, Mass., 1984.

_____. *The German Empire 1871–1918*, trans. K. Traynor, Dover, N.H., 1985.

Weinberg, Gerhard, *Foreign Policy of Hitler's Germany. Starting World War II*, Chicago, 1980.

Wehler, H.-U., *Entsorgung der deutschen Vergangenheit? Ein polemischer Essay zum 'Historikerstreit'*, Munich, 1991.

Weizsäcker, Ernst von, *Memoirs von Ernst von Weizsäcker*, Chicago, 1951.

Weizmann, Chaim, *Letters and Papers of Ch. Weizman*, Series A: Letters, Vol. XIX, January 1935–June 1940, Jerusalem, 1977, 145.

Westenhagen, C. V., *Nietzsche, Juden und Anti-Juden*, Weimar, 1936.

Weyman, David G. *The Abandonment of the Jews: America and the Holocaust*, New York, 1984.

Wiebe, Hans-Herman, *Die Gegenwart der Vergangenheit. Historikerstreit*, Bad Segeberg, 1989.

Wieland, Christoph M., *Wieviel Welt (Geld-)Kriege müssen die Völker noch verlieren?* Hamburg, 1957.

Winkler, H. A., *Mittelstand, Demokratie und National-Socialismus*, Cologne, 1972.

———, *Das Primat der Innenpolitik*, Frankfurt am Main, 1970.

Winnig, August, *Europa-Gedanken eines Deutschen*, Berlin, 1952.

Ziesel, Kurt, *Dankt das Abendland ab?* Eckartschriften Noll, June 1963.

The following books could only be checked after completion of the manuscript and do not focus on German historiography:

Browning, Christopher R., *The Path to Genocide. Essays*, Cambridge University Press, 1992.

Knowlton J. and T. Cates, translators, *Forever in the Shadow of Hitler. Original Documents of the Historikerstreit . . .*, Cambridge University Press, New York, 1992.

Segev, Tom, *The Seventh Million. The Israelis and the Holocaust*, New York, 1992.

Articles and Reviews

Arndt Ino and Wolfgang Scheffler, "Organisierter Massenmord an Juden in nationalsozialistischer Literatur," *Vierteljahrshefte . . . für Zeitgeschichte*, 1976, 105–135.

Aronson, Schlomo, "Die dreifache Falle: Hitler's Judenpolitik, die Allierten, und die Juden," *Vierteljahrshefte . . . für Zeitgeschichte*, 1984, 28–65.

Augstein R., "Die neue Auschwitz Lüge," *Der Spiegel*, 6 October 1986; also *Geschichte in Wissenschaft und Unterricht* 37 (December 1986), 41 and 725–738, 1986.

Bartov, Omar , "Historians on the Eastern Front," *Jahrbuch des instituts für deutsche Geschichte*, 16, Tel-Aviv, 1987.

Bauer, Yehuda, "Genocide: Was it the Nazis' Original Plan?" *Annals of the American Academy of Political and Social Science*, 1984, 35–45.

Bauer, Wilhelm, "Treitschke und die Juden," *Der Weltkampf*, August 1944.

Benz, Wolfgang, "Judenvernichtung aus 'Notwehr'," *Vierteljahrshefte . . .*, 1981, 615–630.

Berghahn, V. R., 2 reviews, *The New York Times Book Review*, 18 April 1993, 3.

Botz, Gerhard, "Österreich und die national-socialiatische Vergangenheit," in D. Diner, *Ist der Nationalsozialismus Geschichte?*

Bracher, K. D., "Rechtsradikalismus und die Bundesrepublik," *Collogium*, X, 1956, Hefte 2,3,4.

_____, "Zeitgeschichtliche Erfahrungen als aktuelles Problem," *Aus Politik und Zeitgeschichte*, supplement to *Das Parlament*, B II, 1987 and 14 March 1987.

Broszat, M., "Hitler and die Genesis der Endloesung," *Vierteljahrshefte für Zeitgeschichte* 25 (1977), 739–775.

_____, "Wo sich die Geister Scheiden?" *Die Zeit*, 3 October 1986.

_____, "Plaidoyer für eine Historisierung des National-Sozialismus," *Merkur* 39 (1981).

Brumlik, Micha, "Die Wiedergeburt des machstaatlichen Zynismus," *DVZ/Die Tat*, 13 February 1987.

Burt, Richard, speech on 23 May 1986, *Merkur* 40 (1986), 864–874.

Clausen, Detlev, "Nationale Identität," *Links*, February 1987.

Corni, Gustave, "Neue deutsche Unruhe. Das Ausland und der innerdeutsche Streit . . . aus italienischer Sicht," in *Streitfall deutschen Geschichts-und Gegenwartsbewusstseins in den achziger Jahren*, Essen, 1988, 131–140.

Craig, Gordon A., "The War of the German Historians," *New York Review of Books*, 15 January 1987.

Diner, Dan, "The Historians' Controversy - Limits to the Historization of National Socialism," *Tikhun* 2 (1987).

Draper, Th., "New Conservative History," *Review of Books*, 16 January 1986.

Evans, Richard, "A Normal Guide of Genocide," *New York Times Book Reviews*, 20 January 1989.

_____, "The New Nationalism and the Old History. Perspectives in the West German Historikerstreit," *Journal of Modern History*, Vol. 59, December 1987, 761–797.

Frankfurter Rundschau, 'Vom roten Faschismus' and "Braunen Bolschewismus. Auch ein Beitrag zur aktuellen Historiker-Debatte," 20 January 1987.

Fest, J., "Die geschuldete Erinnerung," *Frankfurter Allgemeine Zeitung*, 29 August 1986.

Frankfurter Allgemeine, "Bei sich zu Hause...," 6 May 1987.

Friedländer, Saul, "West Germany and the Burden of the Past: The Ongoing Debate," *Jerusalem Quarterly* 42 (spring 1987), 3–18.

Gieselbrecht, André, "Le débat des historiens sur le nazism," *L'Allemagne d'aujourd'hui* 99 (1987), 233–264.

Geiss. Immanuel, "Auschwitz, asiatische Tat," *Der Spiegel*, 10 October 1986.

Gilbert F., Review, *A.H.R.*, 81 (1976), 6180–6120; also 82 (1977) 235–236.

Goldhagen, Erich, "Der Holocaust in der sowjetischen Propaganda und Geschichtsschreibung" *Viertel jahrshefte. . . .* 28 (1980), 502–507.

_____, "Weltanschauung und Endlösung. Zum Antisemitismus der nationalsozialistischen Führerschichte," *Vierteljahrshefte . . .*, 24 (1976), 376–405.

Grab, Walter, "Zur nationalen Apologetik Fest's, Nolte's and A. Hillgruber's, *Zeitschrift für Sozialgeschichte des 20. and 21. Jahrunderts*, February 1987.

Freeden H., "Eine Debatte unter Deutschen. Wie israelitische Geschichtsforscher auf die neue Unbegangenheit reagieren," *Frankfurter Rundschau*, 14 November 1986.

Habermas, J. "Rückwartsrevision der Geschichtsbilder?" *Neue Gesellschaft*, 1985, 366–386.

_____, *Die Zeit*, 3 October 1986.

_____, "Das Zeitalter der Tyrannen," *FAZ*, 11 August 1986.

Haug, W. F., "Vergangenheit die Zukunft werden soll, Historikerstreit," *Das Argument*, May 1987.

Heigert, H., "Die Zeit des Verdrängens," *Süddeutsche Zeitung*, 14 and 15 March 1987.

Hewig, H., "Andreas Hillgruber, *Central European History* 15 (1982) 186–198.

Hildebrand, Klaus, "Wer dem Abogrund entrinnen will. . ." *Die Zeit*, 1 November 1986.

_____, "Monokratie oder Polykratie?" in Hirschfeld and Kettenacker, eds., *Führerstaat, Mythos und Realität*,1974.

_____, *FAZ*, 31 July 1986.

_____, *Die Welt*, November 1986.

_____, *H.Z.*, 7 January 1987.

Hillgruber, Andreas, "Endlösung und das deutsche Ostimperium," *Vier- teljahrshefte . . .*, 1985.

_____, "Die ideologisch-dogmatische Grundlage der national-sozialistischen Politik der Ausrottung der Juden in den besetzten Gebieten der Sowjetunion und die Durchführung 1941-44," *German Studies Review* 2 (1979), 263–296.

_____. "J. Habermas, K. M. Janssen, und die Aufklärung, Anno 1986," *Geschichte in Wissenschaft und Unterricht*, 1 December

1986.

_____, "War in the East and the Extermination of the Jews," *Yad Vashem Studies*, 18 (198?).

Huettenberger, Peter, "National-sozialistische Polykratie," *Geschichte und Gesellschaft*, 103—132.

Jäckel, Eberhard, "Die elende Praxis der Untersteller: das Einmalige der national-sozialistischen Verbrechen lässt sich nicht leugnen," *Die Zeit*, 12 September 1986, *Nüremberger Zeitung*, 20 September 1986.

Jantgen, Karl-Heinz, "Die Qual mit der Geschichte. Streit um zwei Deutschland-Museen," *Die Zeit*, 10 January 1986.

_____, "Also ein Volk ohne Schatten?" *Die Zeit*, 27 November 1986.

Jarausch, Konrad, "Removing the Nazi Stain. The Quarrel," *German Studies Review*, 1988.

Jeismann, Karl-Ernst, "Die deutsche Geschichts als Instrument im politischen Streit," *Frankfurter Hefte*, 3, 41 (1987), Nr. 5.

Joffe, Joseph, "The Battle of the Historians, A Report from Germany," *Encounter*, 69, June 1987, 72–77.

Kadritzke, Niels, "Zweierlei Untergant in düsterer Verflechtung," Zur politischen Dimension der Historiker-Debatte, *Prokla (Probleme des Klassemkampfes)*, 17, 1987, Nr. 1.

Kershaw, Ian, "Nuova Inquietudine Tedesca," *Passato a Presente* 16 (1988) 159–164.

Knight Robert, "The Waldheim Contest, Austria and Nazism," *Times Literary Supplement*, Nov. 5, 1987.

Klönne, Arno, "Bundestagswahl, Historiker-Debatte, and Kulturrevolution von rechts," *Blätter für deutsche und internationale Politik*, Nr. 3, 1987.

Kaltenbrunner, Gerd-Klaus, "Eine Antwort an den Politologen Kurt Sontheimer," *Rheinischer Merkur*, 12 December 1986.

Kocka, Jürgen, "Hitler sollte nicht durch Stalin und Pol Pot verdrängt werden. Über Versuche deutscher Historiker die Ungeheuerlichkeit von national-sozialisti scher Verbrechen zu relativieren," *Frankfurter Rundschau*, 23 September 1986.

_____, "Vom 'roten Fawschismus' und 'brauen Bolschewismus'," Ibid., 20 January 1987.

Koehl, Robert, "Feudal Aspect of National Socialism," *American Political Science Review*, 54 (1960), 921–933.

Koelnischer Stadtanzeiger, "Verootene Fragen. Der Historiker - Streit um die N. S. - Zeit," 21 October 21, 1986.

Korman, Gerd, "The Holocaust in American Historical Writing," *Societas*, 2 (1972), 251–270.

Krausnick, Helmut, ed., Denkschrift Himmler, *Vierteljahrshefte . . .*, Vol. 2, April 1987, 194.

Kulka, Otto, D., "Die deutsche Geschichtsschreibung über den N.S. and die 'Endloesung.' Tendenzen und Entwicklungsphasen 1924–84, *H.Z.*, 1985, 599–640.

———, "Public Opinion Nazi Germany and the Jewish Question," *Jerusalem Quarterly* 25(1982), 121–124 and 26(1983), 34–45.

Kwiet, Konrad, "Historians of the German Democratic Republic on Antisemitismus and Persecution," *Leo Baeck Institute Yearbook*, 1976, 173–198.

Leggewie, Klaus, "France's collective memory and National Socialists," in D. Diner, *Ist der Nationalsozialismus Geschichte?*, 1987, 120–140.

———, "Kein Pardon. Ausländische Reaktionen auf den West-deutschen Historikerstreit und den Beitrag des Philosophen Jankélvitch," *Leviathan* 45 (1957), Nr. 1.

Die Lehrerzeitung, D/R/S, 8-W, 7–8, 1987.

Life Magazine, "Eichmann Talks about His Own Damning Story," 28 November 1960, 19–25.

Löwenthal, Richard, "Verzerrte Zeitgeschichte,," *FAZ*, 27 November 1986.

Lozek, G., "Der Streit geht weiter . . .," *Zeitschrift für Geschichtswissen*, 36 (1988), 5–12.

Lübbe, Herman, "Der National Socialismus im deutschen Nachkriegsbewusstsein," *H.Z.*, Nr. 236, (1983), 579–599.

Luchsinger, Fred, *Neue Zürcher Zeitung*, 18–19 January 1987.

Maier, Christian, "Verurteilen und Verstehen," *FAZ*, Nr. 146, 28 June 1986.

Meier, Chs. S., "Immoral Equivalence: Revising the Nazi Past for the Kohl Era," *New Republic*, 1 December 1986 .

Markham, J. W., "Election Eve Talk with H. Kohl," *New York Times*, 21 January 1987.

———, "German book sets off new Holocaust debate," *New York Times*, 6 September 1986.

Marrus, Michael R. "The History of the Holocaust. A Survey of Recent Literature," *Journal of Modern History*, 59(1987), 114–160.

Mason, T. W., . "Der Primat der Politik. Politik und Wirtschaft im

N. S.," *Das Argument*, Vol. 8, 1966, 471–494.

Mommsen, Hans, "Aufarbeitung und Verdrängung des Dritten Reiches in westdeutschen Geslichtsbewurstsein," *Gewerkschaftliche Monatshefte*, 3, 1987.

_____, "Die Realisierung des Utopischen der Judenfrage im Dritten Reich," *Geschichte und Gesellschaft* 9(1983), 381–420.

_____, "Das Ressentiment als Wissenschaft. Anmerkungen zu E. Nolte's 'Der Europaeische Bürgerkrieg, 1917–45. N. S. und Bolschewismus," *Geschichte und Gesellschaft*, 14(1988), 495–512.

_____. "Die Last der Vergangenheit," J. Habermas, ed., *Stichworte. . .*, Frankfurt, 1979.

_____, "Suche nach der verlorenen Geschichte? Bemerkungen zum historischen Selbstverständnis der Bundesrepublik," *Merkur* 10 Sep- tember 1986.

Le Monde, 22 January, 1987, "Débat historique, débat politique."

The New Republic, Review, 1 December 1986.

New York Review of Books, 20 November 1986.

The New York Times Magazine, 16 November 1986.

Neue Züricher Zeitung. Fred Luchsinger, 18–19 January 1987, and "Dürfen Deutsche keine Patrioten sein?" April 1987.

Nolte, Ernst, "Die Sache auf den Kopf gestellt. Gegen den negativen Nationalismus in der Geschichtsbetrachtung," *Die Zeit*, 31 October 1986.

_____, "Vergangenheit, die nicht vergehen will," *FAZ*, 6 June 1986.

Nipperday, Thomas, "Unter der Herrschaft des Verdachtes. Wissenschaftliche Aussagen . . .," *Die Zeit*, 17 October 1986.

Ostpreussenblatt, No. 23, Hupka, 7 June 1986.

"Pankranz, die Quellen und der neue Gesslerhut," *Die Welt*, 11 August 1986.

Das Parlament, "Vom Untergang mit der Geschichte, Eine Experten-Anhörung zum Deutschen Historischen Museum in Berlin," 31 January 1987.

Pätzold, Kurt, "Wider die neue Auschwitzlüge," *Zeitschrift für Sozialgeschichte*, 2 (1987).

_____, "Vom Verlorenen, Gewonnenen und Erstrebtem: Wohin der neue Revisionismus steurt?" *Blätter für Deutsche u. Internationale Politik*, 31 (1986), 1452–1463.

Perger, W. S., A review, *Deutsches Allgemeines Sonntagsblat*, 27 July 1986.

Peukert, Detlev J. K., "Alltag und Barbarei. Zur Normalität des

Dritten Reiches," *Gewerkschaftliche Monatshefte*, Nr. 3, 1987.

Pietrov, Bianka, "Deutschland im Juni 1941 - Opfer sowjetischer Aggression? Die Kontroverse über die Präventivkriegsthese," *Geschichte und Geselschaft* 14 (1988), 116–135.

Pietrow, Bianca, "Deutschland im Juni 1941 - ein Opfer sowjetischer Aggression," *Geschichte und Gesellschaft* 14 (1988), 116–135.

Pulzer, Peter, "Germany: Whose History?" *Times Literary Supplement* 2–8 October 1987.

Reinprecht, Christoph and Hilde Weiss, "Antisemitismus, ein Thema in deutschen Schulbüchern," *Internatiorale Schulbuchforsehung*, 12 (1990).

Reissmüller, Johann Georg, "Verschwiegene Zeitgeschichte," 16 November 1986.

Ribhegge, Wilhelm, "Stellenweises Glatteis. Über den Zustand der deutschen Gewissenschaft," *Die Zeit*, 6 February 1986.

Rusconi, Gian Enrico, "Italien und der Historikerstreit," in D. Diner, *Ist der Nationalsozialismus Geschichte?* 1987.

Sage, Richard, "Faschismustheorien," *AHR*, 84 (1979), 367–388.

Sartre, J.-P., "Portrait of an anti-Semite," *Partisan Review* 13 (1946), 163–178.

Schilly, Otto, "Das Blut lässt sich nicht abwaschen," *Tribüne*, 1 January 1978, Heft 108, 120–122.

Schirrmacher, Frank, "Das Zeitalter der Tyrannen. Eine Entgegnüng auf J. Habermas und Klaus Hildebrand," *FAZ*, 10 July, 31 July and 11 August 1986.

Schmidt, Walter, *Frankfurter Rundschau*, 4 October 1987.

Schneider, Peter, "Hitler's Shadow. On being a self-conscious German," *Harper's Magazine*, September 1987, 49–54.

Schoeps, Julius, *Der Tagesspiegel*, 10 January 1988.

Schoeps, Julius, "Treitschke Redivivus? Nolte und die Juden," *Der Tagesspiegel*, 10 January 1988.

Schorsch, Ismar, "German Anti-Semitism in the Light of Postwar Historiography," *Leo Baeck Yearbook*, Vol. 19, 1974.

Schulze, Hagen, Review, *Die Zeit*, 26 September 1986.

_____, "The Historikerstreit in Perspective," *German History*, 1988.

Sicken, Bernhard, "Zum öffentlichen Gebrauch der Geschichte. Bemerkungen zum sogenannten Historikerstreit," *Geschichte, Politik, und Didaktik*, 1988, Heft 3-4.

Sontheimer, Kurt, "Maskenbilder schmücken eine neue Identität," *Rheinischer Merkur*, 12 December 1986.

Spoerl, Gerhard, "Sinnstifter unter sich," *Die Zeit*, 16 October 1986.
Stadler, P., "Rückblick auf einen Historikerstreit. Versuch einer Beurteilung aus nichtdeutscher Sicht," *H.Z.*, 1988, 15–16.
Stern, Gregor, *Tribüne*, 1990, Heft 113, 6–12.
Stürmer, M., *Das Parlament*, Nr. 20–21, 11–14 May 1986.
_____, *FAZ*, 16 August 1986.
"Wo sich die Geister scheiden?" *Die Zeit*, 3 October 1986, and *Stadtblatt*, Nr. 2, Vol. 7, 20 February 1987.
Strauss, J. F., *Bayern-Kurier*, 9 February and 4 May 1985.
Strauss, Herbert A., "Antisemitismus und Holocaust als Epochenproblem," *Aus Politk und Zeitgeschichte*, Nr. 8, 11 (1987).
Süddeutsche Zeitung, "Geschichte ist ein rohes Ei." 24 January 1987.
Thadden, Adolf, V., "Der Russlandfeldzug-Überfall oder Präventivkrieg 1941," *Nation Europa*, Nr. 3 (1987).
Thamer, Ulrich, "Der Nationalsozialismus in der deutschen Geschichte. Anmerkungen zum Historikerstreit," *Geschichte, Politik, und ihre Didaktik*, 1986, Heft 3/4.
Trevor-Roper, H. R., "Hitler's Kriegsziele," *Vierteljahrshefte . . .*, Vol. 8, 121–133.
Ueberschär, "Historikerstreit und Präventivkriegthese . . .," *Tribüne*, 103 (1987), 108–116.
Vogel, H. J., *Tribüne*, 1990, Heft 111, 111–120.
Westfälische Nachrichten, Gerhart Cerwick, Eigenbericht, Die Geschichte nicht verharmlost. Historikerstreit bewegt nach wie vor die Gemüter. Kolloquium.
Weizsäcker, Richard, *Frankfurter Allgemeine Zeitung*, 6 May 1987.
Winkler, H. A., "Auf ewig in Hitler's Schatten? Zum Streit über das Geschichtsbild des Deutschen," *Frankfurter Rundschau*, 14 November 1986.
Die Zeit, 14 January 1987.

INDEX